richest source of metaphor for aesthetic theory and the richest in-spiration for the other arts; in Pater's terms, it becomes the biggest lender in the economy of the arts. One important reason for this is that modernism in painting was historically a crucial half-step in advance of modernism in the other arts. By 1914, Cubism had abandoned the traditional representation of space; it had broken with the traditional attitude towards materials and had incorpo-rated real objects in collages, papiers collés, and constructions; Kandinsky, Kupka, and others had painted abstract, nonrepresen-tational paintings—in short, most of the distinctive features of modernist painting were in place. Literature and music were far less advanced: the twelve-tone system was years away, as was stream-of-consciousness or the discontinuity and fragmentation of Eliot's *The Waste Land* or *The Cantos* of Ezra Pound. The period that marks the emergence of high modernism in music and litera-ture is the early 1920s, not 1908–14, as in painting.

Painting, therefore, was the art that showed the others that one could overthrow the old conventions. Painting set the example that the other arts followed; artists in every European country and in the United States felt they had much to learn from painting and set out to learn from it. The composer Arnold Schönberg, who associated with Kandinsky and his circle in Munich, for example, became a fairly respectable Expressionist painter. The poet Guil-laume Apollinaire, though he never painted, associated with painters almost to the exclusion of poets and tried in his poems to construct an equivalent to the paintings of his friends. Of mixed Polish and probably Italian descent, but living in Paris, he associated primarily with the Cubists, and Cubism seems the central moment in modernism in a way no other movement in any other art could. But Apollinaire also associated with the Italian Futurists, and even though Futurism began as a movement of poets, today it is known primarily as a movement of painters. The superior vitality of paint-ing in this period is shown once again in the way the Futurist writers, like so many others, were quick to become spokesmen for the Futurist painters. Gertrude Stein was another foreign writer resident in Paris who was oriented more towards painting than her own art, literature, and she was far from being the only American writer with that orientation. Wallace Stevens, W. C. Williams, and

Hart Crane were all deeply influenced by modern painting, and the aesthetic of modern American poetry is an aesthetic largely derived from modern painting. Unlike Stein or Stevens, Ezra Pound, the arch-modernist in American verse, did not content himself with collecting modern art, though he did that; and unlike Williams or Crane, he did not content himself with borrowing much of his aesthetic from painters, though he also did that. Joining forces with the English painter and writer Wyndham Lewis, the French sculptor Henri Gaudier-Brzeska, and others, Pound founded his own art movement, Vorticism, the subject of this book. Hence, if these instances can be taken as representative, and I think they should be, painting was the central art for modernism, the art having the greatest impact, the art seen as the most modernist. It was towards the condition of modernist painting that modernist art in general aspired.

Greenberg's characterization of modernism as a purist reaction against the romantic melding of the arts, however, should not be completely rejected. For the lending and borrowing among the arts in the modernist period are often subtle and under the table. Greenberg is perfectly correct in discerning a quest for purity in the evolution of the arts in modernism: painting rejected much that had been literary or anecdotal in its heritage; architecture rejected the decorative and became less allied with painting and the decorative arts. Moreover, the limitations of the various arts were much less something to be deplored and transcended if possible. The Wagnerian *Gesamtkunstwerk* is a premodernist ideal; the modernist sensibility is more likely to wonder why one would want to fuse the arts together. They work better on their own. Pater's formulation is again pertinent for modernism: "The arts are able, *not indeed* to supply the place of each other, but reciprocally to lend each other new forces."

However pertinent, Pater is still a little vague: how does one art lend another new forces? How do the arts influence each other while at the same time remaining themselves? Pater himself is borrowing here, consciously or unconsciously, from Baudelaire who in "L'Oeuvre et la vie de Delacroix" wrote that "les arts aspirent, sinon à se suppléer l'un l'autre, du moins à se prêter réciproquement des forces nouvelles." (The arts aspire, if not to take one own ability to cross the boundaries between the arts enables him, not to eliminate those boundaries, but to see precisely where they should be drawn. This discussion, of course, does not tell us where they should be drawn, and as we have neither the original painting nor the story as Lewis wrote it in 1908, we cannot say what Lewis in 1908 thought a painter's painting (or a writer's writing) was. However, this 1908 insight into the way the arts work best together provides the basis for the aesthetic theory of Vorticism, and it received a fuller theoretical articulation there.

Paradoxically, that articulation came not from Lewis, the only man in Vorticism who worked in more than one art, but from Pound, the poet in the movement. Pound, I suspect, was under a certain pressure to legitimate his status in what was, in numerical terms, overwhelmingly a painters' movement. His interest in this issue must also have been quickened by the phenomenon of Lewis, who personified the interaction of the arts Pound could only talk about. Pound stressed that the key to the Vorticists' position was that they "wished a designation that would be applicable to a certain basis for all of the arts" (G-B 81). That not all of the arts were included in Vorticism was above all a function of the small number of artists involved in the movement. Though no Vorticist architects or musicians were in evidence in 1914, Lewis's *The Caliph's Design* (1919) was among other things a sketch of what Vorticist architecture might be. And Pound's essay "George Antheil" (1924) begins: "The Vorticist Manifestos of 1913–1914 left a blank space for music; there was in contemporary music, at that date, nothing corresponding to the work of Wyndham Lewis, Pablo Picasso or Gaudier-Brzeska."[5] So Vorticist music was conceivable, though in the period of Vorticism none existed, and Pound in 1914 tried to place Antheil retroactively in the slot he would have had in Vorticism.

The various arts are linked in Vorticism in two ways, practically through the activity of the movement (as we shall see later), and theoretically through the aesthetic outlined particularly in Pound's writing of the Vorticist period. But Pound's Vorticist theory about linking the arts is in complete harmony with Lewis's description in "Beginnings" of how his painting and writing interacted. The most important aspect of Pound's theory is his notion of the "primary

pigment," which is essentially an application of the image of the
vortex to aesthetics. Douglas Goldring gives perhaps the best account of what the term *vortex* meant to those using it at the time:

> The meaning of the Vortex and Vorticism as propounded by Lewis
> was simplicity itself. "You think at once of a whirlpool," he ex-
> plained, "at the heart of the whirlpool is a great silent place where
> all the energy is concentrated, and there at the point of concentra-
> tion is the Vorticist."[6]

In his art, the Vorticist tries to occupy the place where all of the
energy concentrates, the still point of the vortex, and this image is
a contribution to relating the arts because it implies that each art
should do only what it can do in the most concentrated or intense
fashion. Each art, in Pound's account, has an essential element not
found in other arts, such as the image in poetry and form in painting. The best work in each art is that which relies exclusively upon
that element, the primary pigment of that art, because it creates
the most concentrated, most intense kind of art, "the picture that
means a hundred poems, the music that means a hundred pictures,
the most highly energized statement" (*Bl* #1, 153). The Vorticist,
according to Pound, is the artist who relies upon the primary pigment alone.

Admittedly, what this theory might mean in practice is not entirely clear: what kind of music means a hundred pictures and how
does it mean that? But six months after *Blast* #1 was published,
Pound in an article entitled "Affirmations II Vorticism" restated
the theory somewhat more clearly:

> Vorticism is the use of, or the belief in the use of, THE PRIMARY
> PIGMENT, straight though all of the arts.
>   If you are a cubist or an expressionist, or an imagist, you may
> believe in one thing for painting and a very different thing for poetry.
> You may talk about volumes, or about colour that "moves in," or
> about a certain form of verse, without having a correlated aesthetic
> which carries through all of the arts.[7]

Clearly, Pound thought that in Vorticism he had found a "correlated aesthetic" that carried across the arts, and from the vantage

point offered by Vorticism he considered these other movements as incomplete because they were only concerned with a single art.

Thus, just as in Lewis's essay, the arts are linked in Vorticism primarily in a negative fashion. Each art does certain things best and the artist should stick to those things and not try to do what another art or artist can do better. In order to learn what each art does best, of course, one has to cultivate a considerable awareness of the other arts. Cultivating such an awareness is a justification for movements involving more than one art like Vorticism: they can give other painters, for example, the kind of understanding of how to make their paintings painters' paintings, as Lewis developed by working in more than one art. In short, a "correlated aesthetic" such as Vorticism's stimulates the interaction of the arts with the aim of making the arts more distinct. The practical activity and the theory of the movement should teach the artist who works only in one medium what Lewis's own experience taught him: the boundaries within which each art works best. Delineation is certainly one of the things Pound learned from his involvement with Vorticism. In this period, Pound praised modern painters such as Whistler, Kandinsky, and Picasso for making their painting less literary: "Whistler said somewhere in the *Gentle Art:* 'The picture is interesting not because it is Trotty Veg, but because it is an arrangement in colour.' . . . Whistler and Kandinsky and some cubists were set to getting extraneous matter out of their art; they were ousting literary values" (*G-B* 85).[8] The primary influence of such painting on his work—as we shall see—was in the direction of making his poetry less painterly, in the sense of being less concerned with pictorial images.

Pound's idea of the "primary pigment" is, I think, intended to provide a principle of order for the process of informed exclusion. But the correlation of the arts in Vorticism did not lead simply to exclusion. As we can see from the *Timon* drawings of 1912 (fig. 1), the experiments in typography in Pound's poetry and in *Blast,* and in the collective effort that resulted in *Blast,* the arts of literature and painting also "lent each other new forces" in the Vorticist movement, creating new ways for painting and literature to interact fruitfully without creating a fusion of or confusion between the two. It is a testimony to the fact that correlating the arts was central to Vorticism that a magazine, not a painting or a book of poems, should have been the movement's most impressive and important artifact.

The concern with correlating the arts conditioned the response of the Vorticists to the movements against which they were trying to define themselves, primarily Cubism and Futurism. Cubism was a strong influence on Vorticist painting, but Cubism as a movement had little to teach Vorticism as it was too exclusively a movement of painters, though the poet Guillaume Apollinaire was a close friend of the Cubists and wrote about their art extensively. The importance of Apollinaire in the promotion of Cubism does demonstrate both the utility of writers for artistic movements and the extent to which poets at this point were taking their inspiration from painting. Pound, like Apollinaire, was inspired by artists and put his talents to work to promote their work: in this respect, he is the Apollinaire of Vorticism. But he is more than that. As a poet, Apollinaire remained outside of Cubism, which offered no basis for a movement across the arts. Pound saw this limitation at the time: "Obviously you cannot have 'cubist' poetry or 'imagist' painting" (*G-B* 81). Though recognizing the superior vitality of painting in this period, Pound insists upon Vorticism's linking the arts, if only to give him a place in the movement.

Futurism, in contrast to Cubism, was far more concerned with bringing poets and painters and other artists together. Futurism was therefore an important forerunner of and influence on Vorticism's interest in linking the arts, an influence both to be absorbed and reacted against. Futurism was launched in Paris in 1909 when the poet F. T. Marinetti published the first Futurist manifesto in *Le Figaro*. Those who signed this first manifesto were exclusively poets, but from 1910 on it was joined first by a "Manifesto of the Futurist Painters," and then by manifestoes of musicians, sculptors, architects, and by manifestoes on every subject from a "Futurist Manifesto of Lust" (1913) to the "Futurist Reconstruction of the Universe" (1915). Futurism, thus, unlike Cubism, saw itself as a movement across the arts, though like Cubism it quickly became known primarily as a movement in painting.

The fact that the Futurists would devote separate manifestoes to each art shows that they recognized the differences among the

to whip a Europe long accustomed to peace into the suicidal war fever of 1914. Moreover, the Futurists did not merely talk about such things. In 1912, when the Italian critic and painter Ardengo Soffici criticized a Futurist exhibition in an article in *La Voce,* the Futurists took the train from Milan to Florence and attacked Soffici and the other *vociani* in a café. Accounts vary as to who got the best of it, but the astonishing sequel to the fight is that the three *vociani,* Soffici, Giovanni Papini, and Giuseppi Prezzolini, took the train back to Milan with the Futurists, becoming friends and allies as a result of the fight. The next year Papini and Soffici began to publish *Lacerba,* which became the leading Futurist journal.[14]

Not only did the Futurists incarnate aggressiveness, they seemed to communicate it throughout European artistic circles. Marinetti went on a lecture tour of Russia in 1914 and encountered a great deal of hostility there. In Moscow, the Rayonist painter Mikhail Larionov "invited his fellow Russians to hurl rotten eggs at Marinetti"; in Saint Petersburg, the Russian Futurist poet Khlebnikov printed a leaflet hostile to Marinetti and tried to distribute it before Marinetti's lecture there.[15] But Khlebnikov and Larionov were paying Marinetti the compliment of imitation: they borrowed his methods as they attacked him.

Guillaume Apollinaire, friendly with the Futurists as well as the Cubists and author of a Futurist manifesto, "L'Antitradition futuriste," made the mistake in an article on the 1914 Salon des Indépendents of saying that the painter Robert Delaunay (a personal friend of his up to this point) was essentially a Futurist and that he had been an excellent influence on a certain Henry Ottmann. Both Delaunay and Ottmann responded with letters of protest, Ottmann's so offensive that Apollinaire charged Fernand Léger and Andre Billy to demand an apology. Delaunay in turn was one of Ottmann's seconds, though the quarrel was resolved short of a duel.[16] Once again, hostility to Futurism took the form of imitating Futurism's aggressiveness.

Marinetti also came to England in 1914. In England, he published a manifesto on the subject of "Vital English Art," in which he praised as great Futurist painters the artists who were just about to join together as the Vorticists. They responded to this praise by becoming as irate as Ottmann. They disrupted a public lecture of Marinetti's at the Doré Galleries, repudiated Marinetti's manifesto in a letter they sent to a number of newspapers (including *The Times*), and then published manifestoes attacking Futurism in *Blast*.[17] Ironically, Marinetti's description of these artists as Futurists was at least partially responsible for their joining together as the Vorticists and led them to define and assert the real difference that existed between their art and that of Futurism. Yet, in a double irony, the kinship of the two movements was never demonstrated so strongly as in the way the Vorticists tried to distance themselves from Futurism. The mode of their attack on Futurism reveals the extent to which, like Larionov and Ottmann, they had imbibed Marinetti's notions of publicity, organization, and aggressiveness.

In the interest of making an impact on his English audience, Lewis borrowed virtually the entire arsenal of techniques developed by Futurism: the manifestoes, the typography, the aggressiveness, and the cultivation of antagonists. But for Futurism the movement became an end in itself, its own *raison d'être,* whereas for Lewis, I think, Vorticism was always only a means. Lewis implicitly registered the influence of Futurism on Vorticism in 1939 when he wrote:

> As to these methods of the mob-orator, they really had to be used: 1914 was not 1939—if you were a "movement" you were expected to shout. One was surrounded—one was hemmed-in—by mob-orators. To lift his voice, in 1914, was as essential to a *chef de bande,* as it was in 1915 to a drill-sergeant. (*WLOA* 58)

Lewis knew as well as Marinetti that he had to shout to be heard—and it was Marinetti who taught him how to shout—but the difference between them is that Lewis genuinely wanted to be heard, whereas Marinetti, one suspects, simply enjoyed shouting.

Vorticism remained a grouping of individual artists, partisan and aggressive, but not sectarian in spirit in the manner of Futurism. No Vorticist wanted the effect on society desired by Futurism; *Blast* #1 openly ridicules Futurism in this regard:

We want to leave Nature and Men alone.

We do not want to make people wear Futurist Patches, or fuss men to take to pink and sky-blue trousers.

We are not their wives or tailors.   (*WLOA* 25)[18]

Blast, the central artifact of Vorticism and in W. C. Wees's opinion, "perhaps the most successful of all Vorticist works of art," is the best place to see how Vorticism borrows from Futurism yet differs considerably from it in spirit.[19] The title alone suffices to reveal the presence of the Futurist spirit of aggressiveness. The idea of blasting and blessing various things was borrowed directly from Apollinaire's "L'Antitradition futuriste" manifesto which first attacks a list of people and things under the heading "MER . . DE . . aux" and then praises a list of people under the heading "ROSE aux."[20] It is entirely fitting that both in Apollinaire's manifesto and in *Blast* the attacks come first. Entirely consonant with the primacy of blasting in *Blast* are the discussions of other artists and movements in the various manifestoes and in Lewis's "Vortices and Notes" which are uniformly critical and highly polemical in tone. In *Blast,* Vorticism seems to present itself as a movement in the Futurist spirit, sectarian, partisan, and aggressive.

But a closer look begins to dispel this sense. The blasts and blessings are different from Apollinaire's straightforward lists: they are detailed, paradoxical, and humorous. The first thing to be blasted, England, is also the first to be blessed. France is also both blasted and blessed, as is humor. Apollinaire had blasted mostly monuments (Oxford, Shakespeare, museums) and those who maintain them (professors and reactionaries) while blessing only artists and critics with avant-garde associations. In contrast, *Blast* blasted and blessed a bewildering variety of things from Rabindranath Tagore to prizefighters, from tea shops to the Post Office. W. C. Wees has provided us with information about everything blasted and blessed and has made informed guesses as to why they would be blasted or blessed, but I suspect that he has given the matter rather more consideration than it deserves or than the blasters and blessers gave it at the time.[21] They probably genuinely preferred ABC Tea Shops to Lyons Tea Shops, but they could not have been blasting Lyons Tea Shops "without exception" with quite the spirit of solemnity typical of such movements and manifestoes. Some of that English humor which is both blasted and blessed comes into play here. These men did not take their likes and dislikes as seriously as Marinetti took his, and therefore generate a sense of openness in Vorticism not to be found in Futurism.

This openness is expressed in other ways. *Blast* #1 contained a courteous obituary of Frederick Spencer Gore, accompanied by two reproductions of his paintings which show how little there was in common between his Camden Town style and Vorticism. Two drawings by Jacob Epstein were reproduced, though he refused to affiliate formally with Vorticism, and in *Blast* #2 a painting by C. R. W. Nevinson was reproduced, though Nevinson was the chief English representative of the Futurism attacked elsewhere in *Blast* at great length. Poems by T. S. Eliot, a short story by Rebecca West, and a poem and part of a novel (*The Good Soldier*) by Ford Madox Ford (then Hueffer) appeared in *Blast,* though none of these artists should be considered Vorticists.

Hence, whereas the Vorticists borrowed the methods of the Futurists, their aims remained distinct. They did not want to make the world Vorticist; they wanted to make Vorticist art. Vorticist art in 1914 meant above all the art of painting, as Vorticism was numerically overwhelmingly a movement of painters.[22] Despite the talk about linking the arts, painting dominated. The domination of painting is yet another link between Vorticism and Futurism, which began as a movement of poets but quickly became known as a movement of painters.

That Vorticism was primarily a movement of painters does not necessarily contradict my earlier claim that the correlation of the arts was central to Vorticism. The theory of Vorticism was that the arts have a great deal to learn from each other. The fact that Vorticism in practice was mostly an affair of painters and sculptors merely defines the direction of influence, which was from painting to literature. Pound knew perfectly well in 1914 that literature had a great deal to learn from the visual arts. That is why Vorticism interested him.

I have already argued that painting was the central art of modernism, in 1914 by far the most vital of the arts. Hence it was only natural that, though Vorticism from the beginning was conceived

of as a movement across the arts and though it developed a rudi-
mentary theory linking the arts, the center of Vorticist activity
was painting. This centrality of painting did not exclude Vorticist
literature, however, but instead allowed it to come into being. The
existence of a movement across the arts created an important
channel of influence across the arts, and a literature came into
being heavily influenced by the developments in painting and
sculpture. This influence naturally took some time, and so the
literature I intend to call Vorticist largely dates from after the
formal demise of the Vorticist movement, though it draws its
inspiration from the aesthetic developed in and by Vorticist art.

It is important that the Vorticist aesthetic, as it was worked out
in painting and sculpture, was much less involved in technical
concerns necessarily specific to one art than either Imagism or
Cubism. It was therefore comparatively easy to translate the
aesthetic theory of Vorticism, as expressed in *Blast* and elsewhere,
from one art to another. For this reason, though developed more
with reference to painting and sculpture than to literature, the
aesthetic of Vorticism found an enduring expression in the writings
of Lewis, Pound, and others, in a modernist variant of *ut pictura
poesis*.

In creating a movement in painting that greatly influenced literature as well, the Vorticists also form part of a long English tradition. For the sister arts of literature and painting have long had
exceptionally friendly relations in England, as is shown by the close
relationship of Hogarth and Fielding, by Blake's unique contribution to the two arts and attempt to unite them, and by the Pre-
Raphaelite movement in painting, poetry, and design. Vorticism is
of course quite different from these earlier movements or links
across the arts, and I see no direct influence from them on Vorticism, though Lewis always wrote quite favorably about all of these
artists and though Ford Madox Ford, the Pre-Raphaelite painter
Ford Madox Brown's nephew, represented a personal link between
the Pre-Raphaelites and the Vorticists. The Vorticists in fact were
not particularly English: of the important Vorticists, only David
Bomberg and Edward Wadsworth were born in England; Gaudier-
Brzeska was born in France, and Jacob Epstein, Ezra Pound, and
Wyndham Lewis were all born in North America. So it is perhaps

inaccurate to place the international cast of Vorticism in any English tradition at all; however, part of what led them to create a
movement across the arts in London in 1914 may have been the
fact that England has traditionally been a hospitable environment
for the kind of thing they were trying to do, to link all of the arts,
particularly literature and the visual arts, in a "correlated aesthetic."

Therefore, though literature is part of Vorticism from its inception, I intend first to discuss Vorticist painting and sculpture. Only
after I have elaborated the aesthetic conceptions of that art shall
I discuss the works that carry these conceptions across to literature. My premise, however, is less that the literature is an imitation
of the art than that both are attempts to embody a common program. Lewis himself called Vorticism "a program, rather than an
accomplished fact" (*WLOA* 339). The programmatic and deliberate
nature of this art is not something I enthusiastically endorse, and
indeed the programmatic literary Vorticism of Lewis's *Enemy of
the Stars* or Pound's "The Game of Chess" is only one of two kinds
of literary Vorticism I intend to trace. Far more interesting but
also more elusive is the unconscious or implicit literary Vorticism:
so much of twentieth-century literature seems Vorticist without
quite realizing it, and notions first adumbrated in the Great London
Vortex of 1914 permeate the masterpieces of Anglo-American
modernism. I have restricted my discussion of the more unconscious and belated Vorticism to the works of Lewis and Pound.
Even so, some may wish to deny me this admittedly broad use of
the term. However, I am not claiming that *The Cantos* of Ezra
Pound, for example, are Vorticist in toto. What I am claiming is
that one road to understanding *The Cantos* (and not merely *The
Cantos*) takes us through Vorticist art. We need to take that road
before returning to my claim.

2   The Aesthetic of Vorticism

I have argued up to this point that the fundamental originality of Vorticism is that it theorized about—not simply stumbled into—the interaction of the arts. The painting and the sculpture are, frankly, less original. Its style, though strikingly new in English art, owes a great deal to the Continental avant-garde of the immediate prewar. For this reason, the discussion that follows, in order to specify the particular features of the Vorticist style and aesthetic, often returns to the European background for elucidation. It also frequently refers to the polemics in *Blast* written by Wyndham Lewis, to an extent that may make it seem as if Lewis were the only Vorticist. It would be more accurate to say that Lewis was the only articulate Vorticist painter, and therefore the burden of articulating the position of the movement fell upon him. But what he articulated is embodied in the work of a number of artists, not just his own work. Vorticism did have a group style, though it had one dominant voice.

However, these polemics are in two respects more important for my purposes than the paintings themselves. First, Vorticism, like quite a few other twentieth-century art movements, often looked better on paper than it did in paint. Its theory was in many cases more interesting, more original, and more intelligent than its practice. As André Malraux has remarked, "Artists build their theories round what they would like to do, but they do what they can."[1] Second, the theory is of greater relevance to my theme because it is easier to translate aesthetic theory into literature than it is to translate methods of painting. The fact that Vorticist aesthetic theory was richer and more suggestive in its implications than Vorticist painting was in practice is part of what made that aesthetic theory so stimulating for writers.

The impact of Vorticist painting on literature has not been understood partially because the aesthetics of Vorticism has not really been treated. The history of the movement has been exhaustively treated by W. C. Wees in his *Vorticism and the English Avant-Garde* (1972) and by Richard Cork in his two-volume study *Vorticism and Abstract Art in the First Machine Age* (1976), and Cork has discussed the works produced by the movement in great detail. My account of the movement's history is indebted to the studies of both men, and my discussions of individual works of art are indebted to Cork throughout. But I am attempting to discuss the aesthetic theory of Vorticism in a much more rigorous manner than their historical / documentary approaches allowed. Paintings and sculptures serve as illustrations; it is the ideas behind Vorticism, the ideas that make their way across the arts to literature, that I seek to explain. As the ideas find their embodiment first in the painting, we need first of all to treat the style of Vorticist painting.

Dynamic Form: The Style of Vorticism

The critiques of other art movements found in *Blast* are directed primarily at Cubism and Futurism.[2] The critiques of Vorticism, it must be confessed, are often most intense when they seek to conceal an indebtedness. In accordance with this logic, the style of Vorticist art is most deeply indebted to Cubism and Futurism. (By Cubism I mean, in the following discussion, exclusively Analytical Cubism; collage and other innovations of Synthetic Cubism had no demonstrable influence on the style of Vorticism, though Lewis's subsequent critique of those innovations will concern us later.)[3] Vorticism accepted Futurism's critique of Cubism, but in turn formulated a critique of Futurism from a standpoint indebted to Cubism. Following these two vectors one arrives at the style of Vorticist art.[4]

The Futurist painters on the occasion of their first Paris exhibition in February 1912 declared themselves to be "absolutely opposed" to Cubist painting. According to the catalogue of this exhibition (which also went to London), the Cubists

> are furiously determined to depict the immobility, the frozenness, and all the static aspects of nature; they worship the traditionalism

of Poussin, of Ingres, of Corot, ageing and petrifying their art with a passéist obstinance that remains, for us, absolutely incomprehensible.[5]

In opposition to this "static art," the Futurists painted objects in motion. Among their favorite subjects were trains, automobiles, and people engaged in physical activity or in demonstrations or riots. Futurism was almost named Dynamism instead, and the rejected name would have been at least as appropriate. Umberto Boccioni, the most articulate Futurist painter, declared that it was his aim in his art to "dare lo stile del movimento" (to render the style of movement),[6] and the style of Futurism was predominately a style of movement. In their paintings, the Futurists tried to render movement by showing the object painted in the sequence of positions it would occupy while in motion.

Behind the Futurists' concern with making their paintings dynamic lies a general valorization of motion and change, as Boccioni demonstrates in this passage: "Noi vogliamo sostituire alle vecchie emozioni statiche e nostalgiche le violente emozioni del moto e della velocità e l'ebbrezza dell'azione, perchè esse solo possono ispirare idee plastiche nuove." (We wish to substitute for the old static and nostalgic emotions the violent emotions of speed and change and the rapture of action, because these alone can inspire new plastic ideas.)[7] The Futurists' exaltation of the new is linked to exaltation of motion, because what was modern in their view—the automobile, the airplane, the factory, the modern city and its masses—was dynamic. The Futurists also sought a renovation of subject matter to accompany their renovation of style. They painted the city and industrial subjects, not only because these lent themselves to the dynamic and forceful treatment the Futurists advocated, but also because they insisted that art had a responsibility to respond to and incorporate these new forces which were transforming society. Moreover, only through such a response could art avoid an academic preoccupation with stylistic matters. The first "Manifesto of the Futurist Painters" declared: "È vitale soltanto quell'arte che trova i propri elementi nell'ambiente che la circonda." (Only that art is vital which finds its material in the environment which surrounds it.)[8] By i propri elementi they meant the constitutive elements and events of society; the preferred subjects of Futurist art are such elements—work, recreation, transport, politics, and war.

Hence, both their orientation towards subject matter and their simplistic view that dynamism equals modernity impel the Futurists' attack on Cubism and their charge that the Cubists worshiped the past. The fact that the Cubist revolution in pictorial means confined itself to those means is for the Futurists an indication of the purist and hence academic and conservative nature of that revolution. Moreover, to work in the traditional genres of portraiture, landscape, and still life, as the Cubists did, no matter how innovative one's treatment of those genres might be, was, as far as the Futurists were concerned, to be fatally academic. Finally, if the dynamic is modern, the static is part of the past, and Cubism, in rejecting the dynamism of Futurism, once more reveals its passéist orientation.

It is easy to see the limitations of this perspective on Cubism. The Futurists were overly adroit at finding a passéist under every bush and blind to the way in which the Cubist transformation of the means of representation involves far more than "academic" concerns. But the essential point for our purposes is that Lewis's critique of Cubism in *Blast* reflects the Futurist critique as I have outlined it to this point, though he expresses himself with more wit and less denunciatory thunder. For Lewis Cubist art is heavy and static whereas the Vorticist ideal in art is to be energetic and electric. Lewis discusses Cubism almost exclusively in terms of its still lifes, *nature mortes* in French, and Lewis uses the French phrase with great relish as it epitomizes Cubism for him. He calls these *nature mortes* "too inactive and uninventive for our northern climates" (*WLOA* 65–66). They are tasteful but lack energy and dynamism, and their subject matter is embarrassingly trivial: "HOWEVER MUSICAL OR VEGETARIAN A MAN MAY BE, HIS LIFE IS NOT SPENT EXCLUSIVELY AMONGST APPLES AND MANDOLINES. Therefore there is something to be explained when he foregathers, in his paintings, exclusively with these two objects" (*WLOA* 65). All of this is essentially a lively reiteration of the Futurist position. But Lewis goes beyond that position in one respect. He considers what he finds lacking in Picasso's Cubist paintings to be a product of Picasso's inherent sentimentality. As he puts it in *Blast* #2:

> The whole of the modern movement, then, is, we maintain, under a cloud.
>
> That cloud is the exquisite and accomplished, but discouraged, sentimental and inactive, personality of Picasso.
>
> We must disinculpate ourselves of Picasso at once.   (*WLOA* 66)

The Futurists would have agreed with the last point but they would have been bewildered by the reason, for by that criterion they, too, were sentimental. In keeping with this, the opening piece of *Blast* #1 calls the Futurist "a sensational and sentimental mixture of the aesthete of 1890 and the realist of 1870" (*WLOA* 26).

Futurism in fact attacked Cubism for being too analytical, for dissecting objects instead of identifying with them. Lewis endorses the analytical nature of Cubism, or rather faults it for being insufficiently analytic. Here we can see Lewis rejecting Futurism in turn from a standpoint close to Cubism, though on this point Vorticism is *plus cubiste que les cubistes*. This critique was not indebted explicitly to Cubism as the Cubists never responded to the Futurists' attack on them. We know that the Cubists were aware of Futurism as Picasso incorporated fragments of the Futurist magazine *Lacerba* in two papiers collés in 1914; the two groups also had some personal contact through Apollinaire and Gino Severini, the one Futurist painter resident in Paris. But there was no articulate Cubist response to Futurism beyond one article by Apollinaire criticizing its excessive attachment to the subject at the time of the first Futurist exhibition in Paris.[9] Lewis's critiques of Futurism, however, are implicitly in debt to Cubism, as he sought to guard against the faults he saw in Futurism in his own art through borrowings from Cubism.

What in Lewis's view is missing in Futurist painting, to put it as simply as possible, is a sense of form. In trying to be dynamic, the Futurists succeeded merely in being fluid and imprecise; their art was too formless and blurred. What caused this formlessness was their wish to be faithful to the sensations they received in the presence of the subject; the Futurists in fact explicitly declared that "*painting* and *sensation* are two inseparable words."[10] For Lewis those two words must be separate. A concern with sensation alone obscures any sense of an objective world out there to be painted, and prevents the formation of a properly analytical attitude toward that world.

This aim of Futurism, as Lewis notes, harks back to the aesthetic of Impressionism. Boccioni, moreover, conceded "la mia preoccupazione di continuare l'impressionismo" (my preoccupation with continuing Impressionism).[11] Well before the period we are concerned with, Cézanne had already reacted against the unstable, fluid aspect of Impressionism, proposing "de faire de l'impressionisme an art aussi durable que celui des musées" (to make of Impressionism an art as durable as that of the museums).[12] One way of putting the Vorticist position is that it wished to make of *Futurism* something as durable as the art of the museums. It wished to continue what it saw as the geometricizing tendency of Cézanne and Cubism but with the chaotic art of Futurism as its starting point.

The Vorticist perception of the importance of Cézanne is indebted to the criticism of Roger Fry and Clive Bell, whose view of Cézanne may be summed up in two words, design and form. Bell went so far as to claim that "Cézanne is the Christopher Columbus of a new continent of form."[13] Cézanne was of pivotal importance in the history of art, according to Bell and Fry, because he reasserted the primacy of form or design for the painter.[14] He made the composition, the formal arrangement of the shapes on the canvas, the central concern of the painter, not whatever that composition was intended to represent. The Vorticists take over from the work of Fry and Bell the sense that the work of Cézanne and that of the Cubists after him epitomize form or design. They endorse the celebration of form against the fluidity or formlessness of Impressionism and Futurism. However, Fry and Bell make their appreciation of Cézanne the basis for a number of claims that the Vorticists do not accept. Fry insists that form is all that really matters in painting: "all the essential aesthetic quality has to do with pure form."[15] Clive Bell, in his enormously influential book *Art* (published in 1913), replaced Fry's adjective "pure" with "significant" and argued that "significant form" was the basis of all great art from Egyptian art to Cézanne. By adding the qualifier *pure* or *significant* to the term *form*, Fry and Bell detach form from that which it is the form of, and therefore from any sense of representational content.

In contrast, both Lewis and the Cubists wanted to retain representational content so that their forms were *forms of* something. The example of Cézanne taught them that a highly geometrical or formal style of painting could nonetheless hold on to representation, for Cézanne's painting to the end of his life remained faithful to the appearance of the objects he painted despite the degree to which he would manipulate those objects compositionally. Cubism both simplified and manipulated the objects it painted to a much greater degree than Cézanne, inspired by African art as well as Cézanne, but it did not abandon representation.[16]

Cubism not only did not abandon representation; for leading Cubist painters it offered a more truthful and profound mode of representation. Braque subsequently reflected that "when the fragmentation of objects first appeared in my painting around 1910, it was a technique for getting closer to the object."[17] Juan Gris also emphasized this realist intention:

> Today I am clearly aware that, at the start, Cubism was simply a new way of representing the world.
> By way of natural reaction against the fugitive elements employed by the Impressionists, painters felt the need to discover less unstable elements in the objects to be represented.[18]

Apollinaire remarked that "a Picasso studies an object the way a surgeon dissects a corpse."[19]

Common to all three of these formulations is the notion that modern painters can no longer stay with the appearance of objects as the Impressionists did. One must delve deeper, beyond appearances, to arrive at the truth or reality of an object. This imperative unites the increasing geometricization and simplification in the treatment of objects broadly characteristic of painting after Cézanne and the fragmentation of objects especially characteristic of Cubism. Each can be and was seen, in other words, not as a turning away from representation towards a world of pure form, but as a deepened mode of representation *through* form.

This way of talking about Cubism implicitly involves a critique of the "superficiality" of Impressionism and its heir Futurism; latent in Cubism's style of dissection and fragmentation is a claim that such a style is a more profound mode of realism. (Vorticism adopts or rather articulates this critique and seeks in its painting the same formal delving beyond appearances in the spirit—though not entirely in the style—of Cubism.) This critique is not necessarily the richest or most profound interpretation of the work of the Cubists, let alone of the work of Cézanne. But such a distinction between "reality" and "appearance" is obviously convenient for anyone seeking to defend and explain a style of painting that so blatantly fails to reproduce appearances as Cubism. It is also, as I hardly need to point out, an old distinction in Western metaphysics.

Certain critics who supported Cubism at the time revealed their awareness of the philosophical issues involved in this way of talking about Cubist painting by suggesting an analogy between the paintings of the Cubists and Kantian philosophy.[20] The pertinence of Kant, briefly, is that his contrast between the phenomenal world that we see and the noumenal *Ding-an-sich* that lies behind that phenomenal world encapsulates the distinction the defenders of Cubism drew between Impressionism (and Futurism and the old "superficial" representational painting in general) and Cubism. Olivier-Houcade in an essay of 1912, "The Tendency of Contemporary Painting," which related Kantian philosophy to Cubism, makes exactly this point: "The ruling preoccupation of the [new] artists is with cutting into the essential TRUTH of the thing they wish to represent, and not merely the external and passing aspect of this truth."[21] In an essay "What Is Cubism?" of 1913, Maurice Raynal, who continuously promoted an Idealist description of Cubism, makes much the same distinction: "Therefore, [the Cubists] no longer imitate the misleading appearance of vision, but the truer ones of the mind."[22] Thus, the philosophical argument asserts that Cubism is more profound than Futurism because it is a formal penetration beyond the appearance of things. Cubism is not a style of movement, but a style of truth.

Several points should be made about the "Kantianism" of Cubism. First, the position is not really Kantian, but rather neo-Kantian. In Kant's terms, one cannot arrive at the thing-in-itself; it is

Schopenhauer who asserts that the role of art is to represent the thing-in-itself or, to be more precise, the Platonic Idea which is the objectification of the thing-in-itself.[23] Second, one cannot assume that this defense of Cubism had any effect on Cubist painting. However, to sound Kantian for a moment, I am concerned not with the noumenal reality of Cubism, but with its phenomenal appearance in 1912-14, particularly to the Vorticists. The Idealist distinction between essence and appearance is a formative influence on Vorticism, more important, perhaps, for Vorticism than for Cubism.

Hence, to recapitulate, implicit in the style of Cubism is a critique of the style of Futurism which answers in advance the explicit Futurist critique of that Cubist style. For the French painters, modernity and truth alike are properties of the means of representation and the Futurists's identification with the phenomenal merely indicates their backwardness. For the Italians, painting cannot take place in a formalist vacuum: both subject matter and style must be responsive to the contemporary environment. Cubist painting involves a detached formal investigation of the world; Futurist painting requires a dynamic identification with it.

Vorticism is the combination of (what the Vorticists see as) the strengths of both these movements.[24] It seeks to reconcile the Cubist concern with form and Futurist dynamism by speaking of and painting dynamic forms, like the vortex from which it takes its name, which is in constant motion but has a stable form and a still center.[25] The style of Vorticist art is, as I intend to call it, dynamic formism, a reconciliation of form and flux based on the perception at the still point of the vortex that the flux has form, is formed in fact by and around the still point that the observer occupies.[26]

Vorticists want to paint and respond to the modern world as Futurists do, but not in the same way. They choose instead to draw upon the formal resources of Cubism (as in fact the Futurists tended to do despite their bluster) and upon its analytical spirit. They are therefore energetic and active in a way the Cubists are not (in Lewis's perception), but activity and change are not made a fetish as in Futurism. The subject matter of Vorticism, like that of Futurism, is modern: machines, the city, men at work in industrial settings. But whereas Futurists tended to paint the unformed chaos of modern life, Vorticist painters strive, whatever the subject, for both organized form and dynamic movement. Dynamic formism is the thread that unites the various subjects of Vorticist art, both painting and sculpture, and the style in which those subjects are rendered.

Abstract dynamic forms like the vortex were more prominent in the Vorticist polemics than in Vorticist painting, but concrete equivalents, human activities that are dynamic yet formed or patterned are found everywhere in Vorticist art. Vorticist figure painting, for example, presents man in action. Portraiture as such is almost unknown. The subject of the dance, taken up by David Bomberg, William Roberts, Gaudier-Brzeska, and Lewis, in Richard Cork's words, "ran like a connecting thread through the convoluted imagery of Vorticist art."[27] The manner in which the dance is represented in these works serves equally well as an example of what dynamic formism means as a style. One must speak of the dance and not dancers because these works concentrate on the activity and not on the person engaged in it. David Bomberg's *Russian Ballet Lithographs* (1914–19), for example, are so depersonalized that one needs the title to be sure of the subject.[28] Brightly colored shapes interact, yielding a general impression of forms in movement, but nothing much more definite than that. Gaudier-Brzeska's sculpture *Red Stone Dancer* (fig. 2; 1913) is more concrete and demonstrably human: it is clear at least that the dancer is female. But her head is a triangle and one of her breasts has an enormous rectangular nipple. The sculptor is obviously concerned with rendering sense of motion, which he does superbly, not in conveying much sense of a person. Lewis's *The Dancers* (1912) and William Roberts's *The Toe Dancer* (1914) give us more information about the figures, though the surviving studies for Roberts's *Two-Step* (1915) are as abstract as Bomberg's lithographs. But in no case is the artist's concern the dancer. The dancers are depersonalized in order to focus attention on the rhythm of the forms in a representation of the activity of dancing.

David Bomberg's two major works of the Vorticist period, the enormous paintings *In the Hold* (fig. 3; 1913–14) and *The Mud Bath* (fig. 4; 1914), both portray men in rhythmic motion, though again in neither case is the human element emphasized. What strikes the beholder first about *In the Hold* is that the entire canvas is a grid of bright and violently contrasting colors, and only gradually can one perceive the figures in the hold presumably breaking out and carrying cargo. *The Mud Bath* dispenses with such a grid, but a leap of interpretive faith (or a look at the preliminary sketches) is required to read the curved geometric shapes as men in a bath. In both cases any human interest is firmly subordinated to the formal play of shapes on the canvas. Owing to their curving lines and contrasting colors these shapes generate a strong sense of rhythm and motion despite their abstractness. This formal but dynamic play works well as a representation of the subject of the painting, as long as that subject is understood to be the activity portrayed and not the people engaged in it.

These paintings, like the studies of dancing, set form to motion or form motion in a style that is indebted to both Cubism and Futurism but is distinct from both. Line is an important element; it is used to avoid the blur characteristic of the Futurist rendition of motion. Both the predominance of line and the violent color contrasts ensure that the various shapes remain distinct, but those same contrasts and the thrusting diagonal direction of the lines prevent the forms from settling down in any static pattern.

The works we have discussed so far abstract the human figure in order to shift our focus from the person depicted to the activity that person is engaged in and to the pattern or form of that activity. In an analogous mode of dehumanization, the human figure is also often depicted in Vorticist art as a kind of machine. The most striking example is Jacob Epstein's *Rock Drill* (fig. 5; 1913–15) which in its original state portrayed a huge robot-like figure wielding a real rock drill. Most of Lewis's drawings of the period are of human figures in motion, usually engaged in physical labor or, in several instances, in combat.[29] Like Epstein's driller, these are drawn in a way that stylizes them and makes them resemble robots or machines. The rounded contours of the human figure have been replaced by crisp, diagonal lines that represent their motion in a rigid geometric manner. Obviously, this mechanization of the human figure involves more than questions of style; as we shall see later, Lewis and Epstein are portraying the dehumanization they see in the modern world around them. But my complementary point here is that this response to the modern world is articulated through the style of dynamic formism. Mechanization is a mode of stylizing motion that makes it more rigid and therefore more patterned. Hence, the human figure as treated in Vorticism is at motion, at work, often in a milieu that is characteristically modern. But that motion is controlled either through the nature of the depicted activity or through the nature of the depiction. In either case, energy or dynamism is organized and disciplined in a cold, even somewhat unpleasant, way. Severini also painted a number of canvases of dancers in this period, but one would much rather dance with one of Severini's dancers than one of Lewis's. This observation points up a crucial difference which will concern us later.

If the Vorticist is always concerned with forming his inherently dynamic subjects, he is equally concerned with making any inherently static subjects properly dynamic. Probably the central Vorticist subject, and certainly the central subject of Lewis and Edward Wadsworth in this period, is the city. Vorticist cityscapes inject a sense of dynamism into the austere modern structures they portray, while stopping short of the celebration of chaos typical of Futurist paintings of urban subjects.

Lewis's *The Crowd* (fig. 6; 1914–15), at an early stage called *Revolution* and the only work of Lewis on a major scale that survives from this period, demonstrates more clearly than any other work the transformation of a Futurist subject in Vorticist hands. Formally, the painting is dominated by a number of large and simple shapes thrusting up perpendicularly from the bottom of the canvas. These form a network that, by means of right angles (or angles close to that), divides the entire canvas. Some of these shapes are punctured by a regular series of square or rectangular shapes suggesting windows, which enable us to read the larger shapes as tall buildings. At the lower left are some figures who seem curiously detached from the rest of the painting. They are looking either at the beholder or above and to their left as if at the rest of the painting. Near them is part of a word which Lewis uses in imitation of a Cubist device. Picasso and Braque often include only part of a word, forcing the beholder to guess the rest.

Here we can read "encl" and what looks like the first half of an *o*: the obvious guess is that the word is enclosed or enclosure, and these figures certainly seem enclosed by the larger forms that surround them.

So far, then, we have a cold, static painting that is of a demonstrably modern city, and despite the choice of subject we can assume that the painter feels no great enthusiasm for this modernity. But Lewis, having set up a formal structure, puts his painting in motion. Beginning in the lower left and extending to the upper right is a network of tiny red lines. At the bottom left they look like miniature replicas of the larger shapes, small dwellings perhaps in and around the skyscrapers. But as our eyes move up and to the right these shapes are transformed into sticklike figures, who carry red flags and are swaying forward and straining to move farther up and to the right. Only some of these figures are demonstrably human, and all remain rigidly geometric: presumably they are "the crowd" of the title, engaged in some kind of revolution and not, in Lewis's vision, to be credited with a great deal of personality.

Once we grasp the subject, we can perceive a good fit between the style of this painting and its theme. Stylistically, *The Crowd* frames or encloses a dynamic Futurist cityscape in cold, imprisoning forms; and the painting depicts just such an enclosure. The figures in red represent the spirit of revolutionary dynamism, but one cannot give them much of a chance, enclosed and imprisoned as they are by the forms around them. This painting, therefore, does not really harmonize motion and form. Instead it represents them in political terms as chaos or revolution and order and sets them in opposition.

No other Lewis cityscape with figures survives from this period. But in works like the ink and watercolor *New York* (fig. 7; 1914) and the painting *Workshop* (fig. 8; 1914–15), we can see Lewis trying to inject a sense of motion in other ways.[30] The absence of figures makes these works much harder to read representationally, an issue we will be concerned with below. When the figures that inject dynamism into *The Crowd* are missing, that dynamism is recuperated in other ways. The shapes in these two works are far less regular. The rectangular grid of *The Crowd* is replaced by thrusting diagonal lines, far more characteristic of Vorticism, and in place of the relatively muted colors of *The Crowd* brilliant colors are used and placed in close proximity to one another. These changes do not make these works more human or legible representationally, as the modern city looks far more like the ordered geometry of *The Crowd* than these vortices of energy. But these dynamic forms serve to depict the energy and geometry of the modern city.

To summarize, then, no matter what the subject, even in the absence of recognizable subject matter, Vorticist painting is marked by its geometric bias. Lines demarcate angular shapes, which are manipulated for compositional reasons, not out of any fidelity to optical perceptions. However, these forms are not static, but are highly dynamic, as a sense of motion is produced by the diagonal lines and color contrasts. In some paintings, like *Workshop,* the forms seem to swirl around a center in a manner that may be deliberately modeled on the vortex. The movement's central stylistic aim is to harmonize dynamism and form, as the vortex does. Consequently the style is best characterized by the term *dynamic formism.* Moreover, the central subjects of Vorticist painting are also characterized by their dynamic formism. A close correspondence between subject and style enables a special mode of representing those subjects.

Finally, this style was arrived at by combining what the Vorticists saw as the strengths of Cubism and Futurism. Lewis developed the style before he formulated his critiques of these movements, as his *Timon* drawings (fig. 1; exhibited October 1912) already manifest a Vorticist, dynamically formal style. Rather, he criticized these movements in his art before he did in his criticism. That critique, put simply, is that the Futurists had the right idea about subject matter and the dynamism of that subject matter, but the wrong idea about how to paint it. The Vorticists wanted to employ the element of design or form which they saw as Cubism's central contribution and utilize it in the depiction of the Futurists' subject matter.

Vorticism was not alone in the immediate prewar period in registering the impact of both Cubism and Futurism. Some of the work of Kasimir Malevich in Russia, Franz Marc in Germany, and Marcel Duchamp in France manifest a similar concern with dynamic forms. But these painters restrict themselves to paintings of individual figures or animals; therefore they avoid both the all-over design of Futurism and the depersonalizing effects of that design. Even Duchamp's rendering of the nude as a kind of machine in his famous *Nude Descending a Staircase* (1912), possibly inspired by Futurist polemics against painting nudes, grants her, by virtue of her prominence and isolation, an importance that in Futurism and Vorticism the individual never possesses. In these works the person is never the subject, only the activity in which he or she is engaged.

Only one other painter, Francis Picabia, attains the degree of depersonalization found in Futurist and Vorticist art, in his 1912–13 paintings of dancers such as *Udnie (jeune fille americaine)* or *Culture physique* (both 1913).[31] We know only by their titles what these paintings are about, for in place of recognizable dancers we are given a web of interacting curvilinear forms. These paintings are dynamically formal, both in subject and in style. They demonstrate, however, that this style does not suffice on its own as a way to describe Vorticist art, for these paintings would never be mistaken for Vorticist paintings.

The essential difference is that Picabia's dancers are abstract and depersonalized but are not mechanical: the forms are curvilinear and relaxed, not angular and tense. This difference suggests that the distinctiveness of Vorticism comes from its emphasis on machine imagery, as Richard Cork suggests.[32] But Vorticism shares much of that machine imagery with Futurism. Vorticism's originality, I conclude, comes from its *attitude towards* its subject matter. A commitment to the modern does not dictate a style, but the kind of commitment does. I have touched on Vorticism's attitude here and there, but a systematic exploration is now in order. How important is it that one would rather dance with one of Severini's dancers than with one of Lewis's?

Detachment: Vorticism and the Still Point of the Modern World

The best way to define the difference in attitude towards subject matter is to continue to develop the Vorticist critique of Futurism. The *Blast* manifestoes attack Futurism for its fluidity and superficiality but most of all for the sentimental fuss it makes about machines and the modern world. While accepting the modern subject matter of Futurism for their art, Vorticists do not want to treat it in the manner of Futurism. The second manifesto of *Blast* puts it as clearly as possible: "The Latins are at present, for instance, in their 'discovery' of sport, their Futuristic gush over machines, aeroplanes, etc., the most romantic and sentimental 'moderns' to be found" (*WLOA* 31).[33] The Futurists gush about machines, according to Lewis, only because mechanization is new to Italy.[34] Familiarity with mechanization breeds detachment if not contempt and, as the modern world has by and large been created by Anglo-Saxons, it ought to be easy for them to adopt the cold and unromantic attitude appropriate to an art of the machine age. The same manifesto claims that Englishmen "are the inventors of this bareness and hardness [of industrialism], and should be the great enemies of Romance" (*WLOA* 30). Thus, because of England's historical position as the home of the Industrial Revolution, England is the natural place for great modern art to spring up (Vorticism being, of course, at least the harbinger of that art). The art should be stimulated by "the new possibilities of expression in present life" (*WLOA* 30), but opposed to Futurism's romantic attitude towards that life.

Lewis's geographic argument does not quite hold, because the machines that particularly excited Marinetti, automobiles and airplanes, were new to the Anglo-Saxon world as well. The Industrial Revolution may have taken place in England but it was virtually as removed from the sight of the average Londoner as from the average Milanese. It was only at the end of the nineteenth century that machines invaded the home and the city streets. The lateness of this invasion has been forcefully pointed out by Rayner Banham in his *Theory and Design in the First Machine Age,* and he goes on to explain why the automobile took on such significance for Futurism. Not only did the artist come into direct contact with an advanced machine through the automobile, but he could control it himself: "with the advent of the motor-car the poet, the painter, intellectual, was no longer a passive recipient of technological experience, but could create it for himself."[35] Therefore, though one grants the difference in attitude towards the machine (which can stand synecdochically for the modern world) that Lewis takes pains to establish, his explanation of that difference by means of the historical position of England and Italy is clearly inadequate. Automobiles were as new to Lewis as they were to Marinetti. The real logic behind his argument, I suspect, is Lewis's view of the national character of these countries: Italians get excited about things whereas Englishmen remain unruffled. However, the international background of the Vorticists in turn invalidates this explanation, even if one were disposed to accept it.

If one wishes to get at the distinctive attitude of Vorticism and pin down the difference between Futurism and Vorticism, one must move beyond Lewis's polemical simplifications and separate the two elements that together constitute the Futurist attitude: the modern, and the empathic identification with the modern. Marinetti proudly called this identification "modernolatry," the worship of the modern.[36] The worship of or ecstatic identification with the modern generated the inanities of Futurist propaganda—the manifesto urging the destruction of Venice, the claim that a speeding automobile is more beautiful than the *Victory* of Samothrace, Carlo Carrà's reference to the art of the past as a great joke.[37] The excesses of this propaganda are not a function of their subject matter, of their modernity, but of their attitude towards that subject matter, their modernolatry. Vorticism shares with Futurism only its insistence on modern subject matter; it does not identify with that subject matter in the manner of Futurism. Nowhere in Vorticism can one find the excesses of Futurist propaganda. The Vorticists did not paint the world of machines because they found it better or more beautiful than the past; they painted it because it was the world they lived in and they thought that art ought to treat the world the artist lived in.

The Vorticists' attitude towards their world is a crucial element of Vorticism's originality and importance and even today has not been fully recognized. Cork stresses the importance of machine forms in Vorticist art, but never really decides what attitude Vorticism takes towards the machine. On the one hand, he firmly distinguishes Vorticism from Futurism's fuss about the machine and once speaks of Lewis's dispassionate standpoint towards the machine.[38] But on the other he also puts especial stress on the inspiration the Vorticists drew from the machine and this stress leads him to consider what he correctly sees as Epstein's "tragic doubt" about mechanization as an erosion of the tenets of Vorticism.[39] Timothy Materer, who regards the modernism of Vorticism as programmatic and rigid, cannot assimilate Gaudier-Brzeska's dynamically formal investigations of human and animal forms into this conception and so he denies the label *Vorticist* to some of Gaudier-Brzeska's most characteristic works and argues that "the term *Vorticist* is particularly difficult to apply to Gaudier."[40] Finally, the latest and otherwise able study of T. E. Hulme, by Miriam Hansen, refers to Hulme's, Lewis's, and Pound's "uncritical reception of technology."[41] These three critics all make the same mistake: they fail to grasp the distinctive Vorticist attitude towards the machine.

The prominence of T. E. Hulme's writings may have partly caused this misapprehension. Even though Hulme did claim in his January 1914 lecture on "Modern Art and Its Philosophy": "In this association with machinery will probably be found the specific differentiating quality of the new art,"[42] not only would he never call a speeding automobile more beautiful than the *Victory* of Samothrace, he argues that beauty has nothing whatsoever to do with the matter: artists will use machine forms in art simply to exploit the formal possibilities inherent in machinery. He goes on to say that Roger Fry's recent remarks about "machinery being as beautiful as a rose" shows "that he has no conception whatsoever of this new art and is in fact a mere verbose sentimentalist."[43] Lewis makes the same point somewhat later in *The Caliph's Design*. Criticizing the Futurist's "paeans to machinery," he argues that the machine simply "should be regarded as a new pictorial resource . . . of exactly the same importance, and in exactly the same category, as a wave upon a screen by Korin, an Odalisque of Ingres, the beetle of a sculptor of the XVIII Dynasty" (*WLOA* 150).

But in "The Exploitation of Vulgarity," "The Improvement of Life," and elsewhere in *Blast*, Lewis goes one step beyond this formalist position. It is precisely the ugliness, vulgarity, stupidity, and insanity of the modern industrial world that offer a great opportunity to artists today, who can and should enjoy the spectacle as long as, and only as long as, they remain disgusted by it. "This pessimism is the triumphant note in modern art" (*WLOA* 50), Lewis claims, and is the reason he expects great things from English art. For Lewis adversity creates profundity. England is "the Siberia of the mind" (*WLOA* 51), and, just as the drastic winters of Russia are, according to Lewis, the reason for the profundity of the Russian mind, the mediocrity and mindlessness of England mean that it "should be the most likely place for great Art to spring up" (*WLOA* 51).

One does not have to take Lewis entirely seriously here to see that there is nothing programmatic about his adherence to modernity, and Lewis's position, the Vorticist position, provides the sharpest possible contrast to Futurism. Nothing shows this contrast more clearly than Jacob Epstein's *Rock Drill,* perhaps the central Vorticist work of art (and the source for the title of a major section of *The Cantos*). In accordance with the Futurist ideal, this work takes its elements from the society around it. However, even in its first version (fig. 5), the difference in attitude towards the machine between Epstein and, say, Boccioni is marked. But Epstein must have thought that this version celebrated the machine too much because he later cut off the stilts, got rid of the drill, and cast only the torso to produce the work known today as *Torso in Metal from the "Rock Drill"* (fig. 9; 1913–16), a study of mechanized man as a sinister but mutilated figure.[44]

Lewis is not depressed by the spectacle of mechanization in the way Epstein is; rather he uses it as a mode of satiric presentation of the modern. His drawings of the Vorticist period often depict man as a kind of machine. No empathic identification with the figures in these drawings is invited or allowed: both artist and beholder stand off and engage in detached observation. Lewis is not judging these figures as much as reflecting upon what it means to be modern, to live in a mechanized environment, and to be controlled by that mechanization.

The painter who most obviously portrayed what it meant to be, in effect, a human machine was David Bomberg. *In the Hold* (fig. 3) is as enormous, brilliant, and modern in its subject matter as the major paintings of Futurism but is far more somber in its calculations of the cost of the industrial process. One can slowly discern a leg here, a hand there, in this study of men at work in a cargo

hold, but Bomberg's focus is the work process itself and the depersonalization involved in the system he is portraying.

The degree of approximation to demonstrably human features in
any given figure in Vorticist painting, therefore, is a function of
that figure's approximation to human status in the situation depicted by the painting.[45] In other words, the Vorticist painters use
an abstract or dehumanized style in the interest of making a comment about the dehumanization of the modern world. This interest
should serve to show how far away they are from Futurism's celebration of and identification with the machine world.

The Vorticists' rejection of the modernolatry of Futurism is
significant in a number of ways. First, we should note and praise
their insight. Six weeks after the publication of *Blast* #1 in July
1914, the world was at war, and the Vorticists' more balanced
attitude towards the modern world seems in retrospect far more
sensible and more prophetic than the modernolatry of the Futurists. Second, Futurism's modernolatry is only the most extreme
example of something endemic in avant-garde art, programmatic
modernism, or the program of being modern.[46] Vorticism's rejection of that programmatic modernism before the war was a rejection of the values of the avant-garde, but, paradoxically, that
position placed it in another avant-garde. The horrors of World
War I brought about a wide revaluation of modernity, and in the
1920s a widespread rejection of programmatic modernism was led
by artists such as Picasso, Stravinsky, and Eliot. The mature
achievement of the major modernists between the two world wars
comes out of a middle way between modernolatry and classicism,
a commitment to the modern combined with a respect for and use
of the past; Vorticism was already exploring that middle way before the First World War.

Vorticist painting did not, however, get across the message implicit in its analytical treatment of the machine. What distinguished
Vorticism from Futurism was not grasped at the time, nor has it
yet been grasped.[47] The contemporary misunderstanding is easy
to comprehend: the Vorticist style was too new and too close to
abstraction to be readily legible. It is our failure which is troubling:
we still assume that because Vorticism painted the modern world,
it meant to endorse it. On the contrary, the Vorticist desires to

adopt a balanced attitude towards the modern world, not to identify with its flux and chaos but to observe and analyze it from a position of detachment. This detachment is well represented by the image of the vortex: the Vorticist occupies a still center and looks out at the flux surrounding him. The artist holds on to the still point of the modern world and looks out with detachment at that world.

I hope that by now I have succeeded in separating two things that are often confused: the election of modern subject matter and the attitude one takes towards that subject matter. Of these two components which I have been trying to separate, the latter is far more important for the Vorticists. Only the attitude of modern-olatry makes the choice of the subject all important; a more detached attitude makes that very detachment the center of attention. The Futurists' lack of detachment is a hostility towards detachment, revealed in their telling hostility to the analytical bias of Cubism. Boccioni defines the gap between his painting and Picasso's in his *Pittura Scultura Futuriste* in a way that should recall Apollinaire's description of Picasso's painting and that establishes precisely the distinction that seems to me to be crucial: "Però l'analisi dell'oggetto si fa sempre a spese dell'oggetto stesso: cioè uccidendolo. Di conseguenza se ne estragono elementi morti coi quali non si riuscirà mai a *comporre una cosa viva.*" (Therefore, the analysis of the object is always made at the cost of the object itself, that is, by killing it. Consequently, they [the Cubists] extract from it dead elements with which it is impossible to *compose a living thing.*)[48] His own practice he sees as the opposite: "Noi non vogliamo osservare, disseccare e trasportare in immagini; noi ci identifichiamo nella cosa, il che è profondamente diverso." (We [Futurists] do not wish to observe, dissect and transpose in images; we identify ourselves with the thing which is profoundly different.)[49]

The way in which the Futurists feel compelled to take the side of the modern, to identify with it as a cause, is related to the broader and complex process of identification and empathy operative in Futurist painting as a whole. The Futurists seek first of all to break down any distinction in their paintings between the object and its milieu.[50] Foreground and background, figure and ground, object and context—all are blurred together in the Futurist canvases. This formal property of their work serves a larger purpose, as they wish to break down the barrier between the painting and the object painted and, even more ambitiously, the barrier between the beholder and the painting. They wish, in their words, to blend "the painted canvas with the soul of the spectator."[51] The Futurist ideal is, therefore, that the painting effect a process of total identification. Nothing should block this process by mediating between the beholder and the environment being painted.

The Futurists were quick to claim a philosophical basis for this aesthetic idea in Bergsonianism. Boccioni vehemently attacked a French critic who saw an affinity between Bergson's ideas and "the static realizations of the Cubists."[52] Only the dynamism of Futurism was the true expression of Bergson's creative evolution. Boccioni also claimed Bergson as a source for the Futurist elimination of the space between objects,[53] but these parallels are less striking than the parallel between the Futurist attack on mediation and analysis and Bergson's.

Bergson begins *An Introduction to Metaphysics* by contrasting two kinds of metaphysics, one relative and the other absolute. His dichotomy should seem familiar: "The first implies that we move round the object; the second that we enter into it."[54] Relative metaphysics employs analysis or—and these are all his terms— representation, whereas intuition and intuition alone allows one to attain the absolute, which Bergson defines as an identification with the object. In a reversal of virtually all Western metaphysics, Bergson identifies the absolute and duration with mobility and "relative" analysis with immobility. This identification provides the basis for a sweeping attack on analysis which he condemns for only being able to come up with dead static diagrams.[55] I quote his most succinct attack:

> A representation taken from a certain point of view, a translation made with certain symbols, will always remain imperfect in comparison with the object of which a view has been taken, or which the symbols seek to express. But the absolute, which is the object and not its representation, the original and not its translation, is perfect, by being perfectly what it is.[56]

The Futurist attack on Cubism is a carbon copy of this attack on mediation. Both stem, ultimately, from a vitalist ideology: life is the source of value and what is wrong with analysis is its lack of vitality, its distance from life.

Bergsonianism was a strong intellectual current before World War I, and the Vorticists knew of Bergson's ideas through a number of channels other than Futurism. Lewis, later to attack Bergsonianism at length in *Time and Western Man* (1927), had attended Bergson's lectures at the College de France,[57] and T. E. Hulme translated *An Introduction to Metaphysics*. Pound later said that it was the fact that Hulme filled his social evenings with "crap like Bergson" that forced intelligent people (i.e., Pound and Lewis) to form their own social circle elsewhere.[58] So, though Hulme's enthusiasms were not always so objectionable to the Vorticists, it should occasion no surprise that Bergson was blasted in *Blast*. More importantly, though only once linking Futurism to Bergson, the *Blast* manifestoes and Lewis's individual "Vortices and Notes" criticized the Bergsonianism of Futurism again and again.[59] "Everywhere Life is said instead of Art," *Blast* complains, and the Vorticists felt that to uphold the values of art, it was necessary to reject the vitalism of Futurism. We have already touched upon one aspect of this, the Vorticist attack on Futurism for desiring to have an effect on life. Lewis raises this issue, perhaps the master theme of *Blast* (and of Lewis's entire *oeuvre*), in a number of other humorous but acute ways. Attacking Boccioni's desire to incorporate life and motion into his sculpture, Lewis points out: "The Futurist statue will move: then it will live a little: but any idiot can do better than that with his good wife, round the corner. Nature is definitely ahead of us in contrivances of that sort" (*WLOA* 38). Any attempt to make art live is impossible, as the art work is dead. Lewis considers that mimetic art in general is fundamentally such an attempt, and is similarly doomed to failure: "The Artist, like Narcissus, gets his nose nearer and nearer the surface of Life. He will get it nipped off if he is not careful" (*WLOA* 38). Lewis insists upon maintaining the autonomy and objectivity of art against the imitative and vitalist fallacies of Futurism (and other movements): art is not better as it resembles life more and more closely. If life is your concern, produce children, not paintings, because art must kill the objects it treats. It must, by its very nature, stand off and engage in the critical analysis Bergson attacks.

Lewis's most extended meditation on the relationship between art and life is in his first published novel, *Tarr,* which though probably begun before 1910 was not finished until 1916 and therefore is expressive of Lewis's thinking about art in the Vorticist period. *Tarr* is the story of two painters: the Englishman, Frederick Tarr, and the German, Otto Kreisler. With the polemics in *Blast* in mind, it is easy to read these two artists as figures for the two different aesthetic attitudes we have been outlining: Tarr as the detached Vorticist, Kreisler as a particularly demented Futurist.[60] Tarr explicitly claims the detached role of the observer and what he observes is, above all, the phenomenon of Kreisler, a penniless artist who rapes a model, kills a man in a bungled duel, and then commits suicide. In Tarr's retrospective analysis of Kreisler's actions, Kreisler, realizing his contemptible failure as an artist, was trying to get back into life from art. He did this by way of sex, which, according to Tarr, is as close to art as the average man can get.[61] Tarr is trying to get from life to art, and this effort accounts both for his fascination with Kreisler and his lengthy conversations about the proper regulation of sex.[62]

An attack on sex pervades Lewis's *oeuvre,* and is customarily explained by charging Lewis with misogyny. But this alleged misogyny is simply a pessimism about the liberating possibilities of sex. Michel Foucault has recently written, "We must not think that by saying yes to sex, one says no to power."[63] Foucault's position is an elegant codification of half of Lewis's position. The other half is that by saying yes to sex, one says no to art. Sex in the most fundamental way endorses and perpetuates the way things are. It is a vote of confidence in life and in our social and political arrangements. Lewis wants to interrogate all those values and sees art as the proper mode of this interrogation.

Tarr, towards the end of the novel, tries to define art for his mistress, Anastasya Vasek, in a way that reveals his aesthetic confusion, but also relates *Tarr* to Lewis's polemics against Futurism. When she asks what art is, he answers: "*Life* is anything that could live and die. *Art* is peculiar; it is anything that lives and that yet you cannot imagine as dying."[64] Anastasya makes the obvious

a lack of such confidence. The latter is "an urge to seek deliverance from the fortuitousness of humanity as a whole, from the seeming arbitrariness of organic existence in general."[70] The fear of life itself creates the desire to abstract the object in an attempt "to redeem the individual object of the outer world."[71] In art, at least, the disorder of life can be ordered; the flux of time can be escaped. In this way one can find "a point of tranquility and a refuge from appearances,"[72] the still point of the turning world.

Worringer calls this art transcendental, and it certainly has transcendental aspirations, but its focus of attention is more on the struggle against this world than access to any other. Worringer seems indifferent to—though he insists upon—the religious basis of the urge to abstraction. Of course, it must be remembered that this art was a product of the distant past for Worringer, the expression of dead cultures and exploded beliefs. There is no hint of a return to such art in his study. Nevertheless, he clearly sympathizes with the urge to transcendence, and if there is a source for his sympathy it is probably Kantian and neo-Kantian philosophy. He quotes Schopenhauer to show how philosophically, if not artistically, Western man is returning to the attitude that produces the urge to abstraction. Moreover, in what he calls an audacious comparison, he describes primitive man's desire to take the object out of its milieu as proof of his strong "instinct for the thing-in-itself";[73] Kant's noumenal world, therefore, is to be equated with the refuge from appearances, the resting point beyond the flux, which is the object of that art that obeys the urge to abstraction.

If we do what Worringer himself did not do, which is to apply his ideas to contemporary developments in art, some striking parallels obtain. Futurism and Bergsonianism are the latest examples of the urge to empathy, whereas the opposed geometric tradition descending from Cézanne is "de-organicizing" the object as it geometricizes it. However, it is Vorticism, not the works of Cézanne or the Cubists, that seems to be the most complete embodiment of Worringer's urge to abstraction, as the image of the still point of the vortex is a close parallel to Worringer's resting point beyond the flux. Moreover, the Vorticist aesthetic of detachment is, I should like to argue, an attempt to escape "the unending flux of being," originating from premises about the world and creating an art analogous to that produced by the urge to abstraction.

One might be tempted to go one stage further and argue that the Vorticist aesthetic derives from Worringer, for T. E. Hulme in London in 1914 was already applying Worringer's ideas to contemporary art. Hulme was a personal friend (or perhaps it would be more accurate to say personal enemy) of the Vorticists and his ideas had currency among them.[74] He was a vocal journalistic defender of the new English art in his articles in *The New Age*[75] and, though the article that sets out his Worringer-based perspective on modern art most clearly, "Modern Art and Its Philosophy," was published only posthumously in *Speculations* (in 1924), it was delivered as a public lecture in January 1914. Pound, at least, heard the lecture, as he wrote a review of it for *The Egoist*.[76] Hulme, looking at the widespread "primitivism" in early twentieth-century art, argued that it was a harbinger of a return to geometric anti-vitalist art which would obey the urge to abstraction. However, he argued that the phase of "primitivism" itself would be short lived. Artists seeking for formal models for their geometric art were finding them in the primitive, but Hulme asserted that in the future artists were going to base their art on the forms associated with machinery. Modern art was going to be a new geometric art in which mechanization would be the mode of stylization and de-organicization.[77]

But the art Hulme wanted was not Vorticism, and I do not think that Worringer can be assigned a formative role in the development of the Vorticist aesthetic. Hulme in fact simplified Worringer's ideas as he extended them to modern art; in W. C. Wees's words, "Hulme put Worringer's method to narrower and more polemic uses."[78] Paradoxically, the aesthetic of Vorticism is closer to Worringer's ideas than anyone could realize from Hulme's account of Worringer. Hulme insisted first of all that the new art would be religious. He borrows this point from Worringer, of course, but there is a considerable gap between Worringer's mention of a transcendental basis and Hulme's assertions of a religious revival.[79] Vorticism could be considered transcendental only in the perspective offered by neo-Kantianism, but Hulme suppresses this aspect

of Worringer's thought altogether. I have argued for viewing Vorticism's formalist rejection of appearances as a sign of an opposition to the vital and temporal, in accord with the urge to abstraction,
but Hulme's programmatic religiosity is totally foreign to its spirit.
At least partially for this reason Hulme preferred the work of Jacob
Epstein, who had extensive contacts with "official Vorticism" but
refused any formal affiliation with it, to that of the movement
itself. [80] Hulme modified Worringer's views in one other important
respect. Hulme talked less about Worringer's "urges" than the kinds
of art produced by them, which he characterized respectively as
vital and geometric. Worringer's model is subtler than Hulme's
because Worringer allows for the geometricization of the vital,
whereas Hulme, polarizing Worringer's dialectic, sees a rigid opposition between the two. For this reason he preferred the more
geometric art of David Bomberg to the overtly dynamic—if also
geometric—art of Vorticism. [81] Here, too, Hulme is antagonistic
towards the Vorticists precisely where they unknowingly are closer
to Worringer's aesthetic than Hulme. [82]

    Hulme's broadcasting of Worringer's ideas, therefore, cannot be
assigned any real influence on Vorticism's aesthetic of detachment.
However, Worringer's ideas do offer a fascinating parallel to those
of Vorticism, and Hulme's discussion of Worringer demonstrates
the extent to which artistic style is perceived around 1914 in terms
of philosophical values. Hulme anticipated Lewis, for only considerably later will Lewis present Vorticism in terms of the neo-
Kantianism which Worringer, Raynal, and others use before him. [83]
The parallel between the aesthetic of Vorticism and the ideas of
Worringer above all enable us to see that the Vorticist position has
certain philosophical implications not spelled out in *Blast.* To
adopt a detached attitude towards the modern world means to
be open to criticizing that world; to adopt an attitude of detachment in general involves an opposition to vitalism as a philosophy
of life as well as a philosophy of art. But this notion of detachment raises a number of new questions in turn: What form does
this antivitalism take? If one is detached from the world, what does
one do in it? What effect does detachment have, either on one's
life or on one's art?

    There is no *one* answer to these questions, as the concept of detachment contains within itself the possibility of a variety of stances, a variety of roles. In this context, it may be useful to recall that the first fully achieved Vorticist art was Lewis's 1912 portfolio based on Shakespeare's play *Timon of Athens* (fig. 1). Shakespeare's play is about the possibility and cost of detachment, and a brief examination of it from a Vorticist standpoint can both explain Lewis's fascination with the play and help us put names to the various roles subsumed under the concept of detachment. Moreover, *Timon* interested Lewis for a long time, as his 1927 book on Shakespeare, *The Lion and the Fox,* discusses the play at some length. His interest in the concept of detachment lasted even longer, running throughout his career. For this reason examples from Lewis's later writing as well as from *Timon of Athens* help to specify precisely what Lewis meant by the concept of detachment.

Apemantus, the railer in *Timon of Athens,* is clearly a figure who stays in the world in order to combat it. Obviously disgusted by and alienated from the environment in which he finds himself, he nonetheless does not flee that world but stays only to try to prevent any change for the worse. He refuses any favors from Timon, as he puts it, because "if I should be bribed too, there would be none left to rail upon thee, and then thou wouldst sin the faster."[84] Antisocial behavior is defended here by giving it a social function: by vexing man the unpleasant observations of the disinterested Apemantus help to keep man from getting any worse. In the play Apemantus is called a philosopher, but his kind of negative but acute observation of man is precisely what art ought to offer. Art does not do so in the world of the play, as the only artists so labeled in *Timon of Athens* are the Poet and the Painter, flatterers as corrupt as any of Timon's friends. Significantly, their work is described as being "livelier than life,"[85] and their vitalist art—by failing to oppose the world in the manner of Apemantus—is a corruption of the true function of art. It is easy to see that, in contrast, Shakespeare's play upholds that function, offering a portrait of man as negative as that offered by the detached observer Apemantus.

To call Apemantus detached may cause misunderstanding. Clearly he is filled with disgust, and one can easily imagine less acerbic, more tolerant, forms of detachment. But the term is more appropriate than it seems: Apemantus is really controlled and equable.

He rails at all of the Athenians, not because he cannot help it, but because he thinks it is good for them.

Timon, on the other hand, as Apemantus points out in Act IV, swings from one extreme to another, from total identification with the world around him to a total disgust with it. At first, he recognizes no boundaries between himself and his friends. Then, when they forcibly define those boundaries, he withdraws from the world. His role model in misanthropy is Apemantus, but as the scene between them in Act IV demonstrates, their attitudes are in fact very different. Timon hates and flees the world because it treated him so badly. But the conditional nature of this hatred indicates that he is still tied to what he hates in a way Apemantus is not. Timon eats roots, now, as Apemantus does, but Apemantus ate those roots when he could have eaten meat. His actions are the result of calculation; Timon's are a response to events.

Apemantus, as Lewis pointed out in *The Lion and the Fox,* has the best of the argument.[86] Apemantus's defense of his railing is an important source for Lewis's aesthetic. In his Vorticist art (and afterward), Lewis often portrays man as a kind of machine, a kind of robot, and this clearly is not a pro-robot activity. Like Apemantus, Lewis offers man an unflattering looking glass. And like Apemantus, Lewis offers it in the hope of being proven wrong. His theory of art is not mimetic as much as emetic: it is designed not to please, but to affront, and then to transform.

Lewis may have wanted to be Apemantus (what a choice!), but in his restlessness and rage he was far more like Timon. Timon is the greater figure, moreover, because, though antagonistic towards the world, he is nevertheless of it. Apemantus's cold objectivity is inhuman and in a sense self-defeating as Timon's fall induces more interrogation of the world's values than Apemantus ever will. It is easy to be Apemantus, if one has never felt the temptation to be Alcibiades, to act out one's savage indignation and adopt a combative and partisan stance. Timon felt that temptation, which makes his self-control and relative detachment the more profound.

Lewis, like Timon, was attracted by what he nonetheless hated and opposed, and he sought for the still point of detachment far more than he actually found it. But his quest for detachment is not irrelevant to an understanding of his *oeuvre.* Lewis alternates throughout his work between detachment and a more active antagonism. His theories of humor are essentially theories of detachment, his theories of satire theories of antagonism.[87] He alternates between a detached commitment to modernism and fierce attacks on it. Certain of his personae, Ker-Orr in *The Wild Body* for instance, are largely content to observe the world and this urge lies behind the reportage that runs through his work from *The Wild Body* to *Rotting Hill* (1951). Others are combative and truculent, like Percy Hardcaster in *The Revenge For Love* (1937), engaged in enemy action, as Lewis in his endless polemic campaigns was the Enemy. But one rarely finds either state in pure form: Percy Hardcaster's cynicism about his campaigns shocks the naive Communist Gillian Phipps into apostasy, and even Ker-Orr engages in a campaign in "A Soldier of Humour." Lewis, like Timon, could play both the roles of Alcibiades and that of Apemantus, and the central figures in his novels, like Tarr, Pierpoint, and Pullman, do the same. They are always engaged in campaigns, but one never knows what status to grant those campaigns, as these characters detach themselves from their actions as they commit them.

All of this talk of action may make Lewis seem far from attaining any still point. But it is important to understand that detachment for the Vorticists is not a synonym for indifference: to be in the still point is still to be in the world, engaged in analytical observation of it. Timothy Materer has used the image of the vortex as a way to treat the political involvement of the major modernists, and he praises Joyce most of all for staying "in the Vortex" and never succumbing to the temptation of action.[88] But that stance instead reveals his distance from Lewis and Pound and from the Vorticist aesthetic.

Eliot in a famous passage in *Four Quartets* makes a distinction close to the one I am trying to draw here when he writes:

> There are three conditions which often look alike
> Yet differ completely, flourish in the same hedgerow:
> Attachment to self and to things and to persons, detachment
> From self and from things and from persons; and, growing between
>   them, indifference
> Which resembles the others as death resembles life.[89]

Commitment or attachment (and an unfortunate kind of commitment) won out over detachment for long stretches in Lewis's (and
Pound's) career, but Eliot is correct in aligning these two positions
against the indifference that would seem to resemble detachment.
Lewis's work would not have been more fully Vorticist, more fully
detached, had he stayed in the ivory tower—or Axel's castle—and
not come out.

Obviously, one would want to distinguish between the abrasive-
ness of Lewis and the greater tranquility achieved by Eliot in *Four
Quartets*. Though every Vorticist shared the ideal of detachment,
no one was so truculent or combative as Lewis. From Eliot's perspective, the detachment of Vorticism would perhaps fall somewhere between his attachment and his detachment, perhaps not of
the still point as much as aiming towards it. But it differs from
attachment or commitment inasmuch as it sees no one to support.
Only when they saw someone worth supporting (and they were
almost always wrong) did Lewis and Pound abandon their position
of detachment, their stance of permanent opposition.

It is no accident that political terminology has entered my argument here, for one of the things that I would like to claim for the
Vorticist aesthetic of detachment is that it enables the artist to
address social and political matters. Vorticism did not want to
embrace the social world in the manner of Futurism, but, like
Futurism, Vorticism wanted to go beyond formalism, to go beyond
what it saw as Cubism's undue preoccupation with formal and
technical issues. The aesthetic of detachment, moreover, does not
necessitate a conservative approach to social and political matters.
Trotsky attacked Russian Futurism and its desire to fuse art and
life from a position that closely resembles Vorticism: "But for art
to be able to transform as well as to reflect, there must be a great
distance between the artist and life, just as there is between the
revolutionist and political reality."[90] What Trotsky says helps to
unify the various aspects of what I have been calling the analytic
detachment of Vorticism. Vorticism is far from revolutionary in
Trotsky's sense, but like Trotsky it asserts that art must be both
distant from and analytical in its approach to life. Detachment
does not mean finding a refuge from the world, a private or

privileged space, as no such space exists, at least in the twentieth century. It means opposing and interrogating the world and its values, because the only still center of the vortex is one that you create yourself.

Abstraction: A Means to Representation

In the preceding discussion of the Vorticist attitude towards its subject matter I hope that I have not made Vorticism seem perverse, holding onto subject matter though opposing that subject matter, attacking the machine world while insisting upon treating that world. Virtually everyone who has written about Vorticism would charge me, instead, with making it unrecognizable, as the generally accepted view is that Vorticist painting was abstract or nonrepresentational, and therefore without subject matter in any conventional sense. This view sees the elements of representation I have discussed as merely vestigial, and situates Vorticism in the movement towards total abstraction that swept across Europe just before World War I. I disagree profoundly with this broadly accepted view and hope to show in what follows that Vorticism had its own theory of representation, a theory of considerable interest.

Richard Cork, whose orientation is evident in the title of his study, *Vorticism and Abstract Art in the First Machine Age,* recognizes the presence of representational elements in Vorticist art, but assesses them rather differently from me:

> This larger context [which shaped Vorticism], as the subtitle of the book implies, embraces the formulation of an indigenously English form of abstraction. The Vorticists may have drawn much of their inspiration from mechanical imagery, and stopped short of believing that a totally non-representational language was either possible or desirable, but their fundamental aim lay in disengaging art from outworn representational conventions.[91]

The divergence between my position and that of others who have written on Vorticism is still larger. W. C. Wees refers to "the basically abstractionist intentions of the Vorticists" and considers what

I have focused on as exceptions to Vorticism.[92] Timothy Materer, who, as we have already seen, drives a wedge between Gaudier-Brzeska and Vorticism, asserts about what is left that "the movement's truly distinctive feature was in its use of total abstraction."[93] Anthony d'Offay, writing about the same group of artists discussed here, refuses to use the term *Vorticism* because it pushes "the extraordinary achievement of Bomberg, Epstein and Roberts"[94] to one side. But he calls abstraction the "common aim which reconciles the work of painters as different as Wyndham Lewis and Bomberg."[95]

There is rather an odd unanimity here. All of these writers recognize a gap between the degree of abstraction of Vorticism and that of, say, Suprematism or Neo-Plasticism. But that does not check their collective desire to place Vorticism in the movement towards abstraction. Hence they claim that Vorticism was "fundamentally" or "basically" abstract, or they remove Gaudier-Brzeska here, or add David Bomberg there, in order to call everything that is left abstract. Each of these maneuvers shows, despite the reluctance on the part of these writers to admit it, that Vorticism was not totally abstract: a cup that is half full is, after all, also half empty.

Anthony d'Offay makes a claim that helps alert us to the logic of this unanimity. He remarks: "Certainly our interest in the movement today must be centered on the degree of abstraction it achieved."[96] Why *must* it? Why is the degree of abstraction achieved by Vorticism necessarily more interesting than the degree of representation? I can think of only two reasons for thinking this. First, one might simply consider abstract art more interesting than representational art; in that case, however, one is unlikely to be very interested in a movement like Vorticism, given how many totally nonrepresentational painters there are to study. Second, one could be interested in the degree of abstraction achieved by Vorticism in order to assign it a place in the genesis of abstract painting. This, I think, is the position of Cork, d'Offay, and others. The stress they place on the abstractness of Vorticism falls into place as part of an attempt to increase the visibility of the movement. For if Vorticism can be seen as an early pioneer of abstraction, then it can be rescued from near-oblivion. Otherwise, from the perspective of the history of art why should we be interested in Vorticism? Whom did it influence? What did it lead to? Lewis put out only two issues of *Blast*. The Vorticists had one group show in London, at the Doré Galleries in 1915, and one in New York at the Penguin Club early in 1917. Gaudier-Brzeska and Hulme died in the war. After Vorticism, Epstein returned to a traditional style of portraiture; Bomberg, Roberts, and the others were forgotten. Lewis is known today as a writer who painted. Vorticism would seem, therefore, not to be a vortex, but a cul-de-sac.

I have my own historicist answer to these questions. Vorticism is not the isolated movement it might seem to be to an art historian because its impact was primarily on literature, not on the visual arts. But I also think that to stress the abstractness of Vorticism, as Cork, Wees, and others have done, is to distort the movement and to deny it what originality it did possess. Emphasizing Vorticism's approximation to abstraction also has the curious effect of making Vorticism a total aberration in the careers of those involved in it. Every important Vorticist who survived the war, except Edward Wadsworth, developed comparatively straightforward representational styles after the war. From Cork's perspective and from any programmatically avant-garde or modernist perspective, this development has to be judged harshly as a retreat, a failure of nerve, and Cork's final chapter makes no attempt to disguise his disappointment:

> This sudden descent from the summit of abstraction was continued in Lewis's first one-man show at the Goupil Gallery in February 1919.[97]
>
> As for the other allies, they all followed Lewis's example and controverted their earlier ideals in a faint-hearted attempt to return to representational frames of reference.[98]

I am willing to accept this assessment of the evolution of Epstein, who develops a pallid naturalism which for me holds no interest.[99] But it does not ring true in the case of William Roberts. I personally do not admire the style he developed after the war and worked in for the rest of his life, but there was nothing fainthearted about the tenacity with which he stuck to his own idiosyncratic style.[100] Moreover, the development of the painting of Lewis and of David

Bomberg makes Cork's explanation palpably inadequate.[101] Both painters descended from "the summit of abstraction" if they had ever climbed it, but they continued to paint in fresh and inventive ways. Cork's choice between "outworn representational conventions" and abstraction is artificial and Manichaean: there are simply other possibilities for the contemporary painter, possibilities explored by many modern painters other than Bomberg and Lewis. Moreover, Lewis's and Bomberg's post-Vorticist representational work has had much more influence than their Vorticist work. Lewis's series of masterful portraits in the 1920s and 1930s and Bomberg's lesser but interesting portraits helped to perpetuate a tradition of English figure painting that blossomed after 1945 in the work of such London-based artists as Michael Ayrton, Francis Bacon, David Hockney, R. B. Kitaj, and Frank Auerbach. These painters have no group style to be traced back to the Vorticists; however, Lewis's work clearly influenced Ayrton, whereas Bomberg's clearly has influenced Auerbach, and Lewis welcomed what he saw of the work of Ayrton and Bacon.[102] Not even Richard Cork, I expect, would call the work of this London School a faint-hearted retreat.

The surprisingly consistent evolution of those involved in Vorticism is or should be a problem for those who wish to see Vorticism as fundamentally abstract. Cork dispenses with the problem by reifying the avant-garde premises with which he began and dismissing the Vorticists' move away from abstraction as a retreat. No one else has even considered that the post-Vorticist painting of th artists involved in Vorticism has any pertinence at all. My sense of the relationship between these artists' Vorticist work and their subsequent work is diametrically opposed to Cork's. I see a great deal of continuity where he sees only rupture. There was no retreat from "the summit of abstraction" because Vorticism never occupied that summit. What Cork sees as vestigial I see as central: Vorticism obeyed Worringer's urge to abstraction but its painting was representational. It held onto subject matter, and, as I will show, developed its own theory of representation.

Not wishing to replace one simplification with another, I will grant that Vorticism did arrive at abstraction, but it never committed itself programmatically to abstraction. To set out a paradox which will become clearer later, it used abstraction as a mode of representation. Anthony d'Offay's exhibition, "Abstract Art in England, 1913-1915," made the best possible case for seeing Vorticism as an abstract movement, but, significantly, the works he found to exhibit were almost all drawings, preparatory sketches, and watercolors.[103] The Vorticists all did abstract drawings in the process of doing research into form, but in their major works they returned to a subject. They did so, I think, because they agreed with the Futurists that art must respond to the society surrounding it. They willingly retained subject matter in their art because only with a subject could their art have the kind of meaning they wanted.

Cork's maneuver which was destined to raise Vorticism from the dead actually helps to ensure its burial. Vorticism played no great role in the emergence of abstraction: painters in Germany, France, Italy, and Russia were ahead of the English group, and the various Continental explorations of abstract form were more long-lasting, disciplined, and influential than that of Vorticism. The originality and importance of Vorticism lie in the fact that, among the movements that arrived at total abstraction, as it did in certain works, it was the first movement to stop short, to abandon painting's new evolutionary path, and retaining subject matter, to attempt a fusion of the new abstract style with the old task of representation. What for the others was an uncomfortable middle ground between representation and abstraction, to be passed over as quickly as possible, was for these artists the place where modern art ought to situate itself.

If Vorticism puts abstraction at the service of representation, then it obviously needs to be read against the background of the emergence of styles of abstraction. That background is a rather complex set of developments across nearly one hundred years; I shall attempt to summarize it schematically in terms of three steps.

The first step in the move towards abstract or nonrepresentational painting is the retreat from the Subject broadly characteristic of nineteenth-century painting. Painters began to stop painting subjects with historical, mythological, or religious significance such as Belisarius, the Rape of Leda, or the Annunciation. Instead, the formerly less prestigious genres—landscape and still life—became the genres of importance. This shift might at first seem to have little to do with a move away from representation, as these paintings continued to be representational, but freeing painting from its domination by the Subject was an important—if unconscious—first step towards abstraction.

The next unconscious but significant step towards abstraction, a logical extension of the earlier retreat from the Subject, is the emergence of an attitude of explicit indifference to subject matter, which we could call aesthetic formalism. Formalism in this context means that what is significant in a painting is its formal elements, its shapes and colors, and that what these might represent is unimportant aesthetically. This position was central to nineteenth-century French thinking about art long before the coming of abstraction.[104] We have already seen that, in the years immediately preceding Vorticism, two English critics, Roger Fry and Clive Bell, gave this view a more systematic formulation. What established the quality of a painting was neither its subject nor its method of handling that subject, but its pure (or significant) form.

Meyer Schapiro has pointed out that in the context of this formalism "abstract art had . . . the value of a practical demonstration."[105] One way of testing the theories of formalism would be to paint abstract paintings; if a painting's value is a matter of form and color alone, then why not restrict painting simply to those things? Those painters who took the third and final step towards abstraction for the most part presented that step in such formalist terms: as representing a subject did not contribute to the aesthetic value of a painting, why do it? Art should rid itself, so they argued, of the excess baggage of representation and restrict itself to its formal means. Kandinsky realized one day that the presence of the represented object "harmed" his paintings.[106] Mondrian considered that "for pure art, then, the subject can never be an additional value."[107] Apollinaire advocated a pure painting that would be to current "impure" painting as music was to literature.[108] These painters or critics defended abstraction in terms indebted to aesthetic formalism.

Thus, as a schematic picture of a highly complex development, the movement towards abstraction can roughly be broken down into three steps: the abandonment of the Subject, the abandonment of interest in representation, and the abandonment of representation itself. The third step was taken almost simultaneously by a number of painters between 1910 and 1914. The chronology of this is both complex and confused, but Kandinsky in Munich seems to have been the first, in 1910 or 1911, to paint nonrepresentational works. He was followed immediately by a Czech painter working in Paris, František Kupka; in 1912 by the Orphist Delaunay, the Russian Rayonist Larionov, and the Futurist Balla; and in 1913 by Léger, Malevich, and Severini. But probably every statement in the preceding two sentences could be challenged. The dating of certain key works, particularly Kandinsky's and Malevich's first abstract works, is controversial, and the abstract status of the studies of light by Larionov, Balla, and Severini is problematic. Furthermore what is meant in any case by abstract is open to question.

The word *abstract* can be used to describe two different kinds of painting, depending roughly on whether it is a noun or an adjective. To call a painting an abstract indicates that the painting contains no representational elements. But to refer to a painting as abstract could mean that it is representational, though abstractly or incompletely. These two uses have not always been distinguished, and the distinction according to parts of speech is tenuous, as we often use the adjective to refer to nonrepresentational art. The efforts by critics to straighten out this semantic bog have concentrated on making the distinction between adjective and noun firm and permanent. Alfred Barr suggested that the art that still represented objects but was moving towards abstraction be called near-abstraction, and nonrepresentational painting be called pure abstraction.[109] Hilla Rebay and later Jerome Ashmore wanted to reserve the term *abstract* for Barr's near-abstraction and, following Kandinsky, to call nonrepresentational painting nonobjective, by which they meant an absence of objects, not of objectivity.[110] Finally (and recently), Harold Osborne wanted to distinguish between "semantic abstraction," which he defined as "an incomplete presentation of natural appearances," and "non-iconic abstraction," which is totally unconcerned with natural appearances.[111]

These efforts have been laudable and Osborne, in particular, is a model of clarity, but unfortunately the distinction they wish to make does not hold. Kandinsky and Mondrian moved, in Osborne's terms, from semantic to non-iconic abstraction, but the moment of changeover cannot be specified. Both painters only very slowly eliminated reference to objects in their painting. Kandinsky seemed to have eliminated such reference more quickly than he actually had. The majority of his paintings of the 1910–14 period have abstract titles like Improvisation or Composition. The titles impeded the legibility of these paintings at the time but many of the works that once seemed non-iconic no longer do.[112] Mondrian, on the other hand, as early as 1915 painted works (*Composition No. 10: Pier and Ocean,* for example) that untitled would have been considered non-iconic, but that titled make sense as a representation of appearances. Though highly abstract, Malevich's *Football Match,* also of 1915, is similarly legible representationally, but not, I think, without the title.

This distinction between semantic and non-iconic abstraction continues to be problematic long after the inception of abstract painting. Consider Mondrian's last work, *Broadway Boogie-Woogie:* does this highly abstract design represent New York through a visual resemblance or in some other way or is the title irrelevant? To move closer to the present, is one of Frank Stella's black paintings which is named after an apartment building in Brooklyn non-iconic in Osborne's sense?

There are no easy answers to any of these questions and I shall not try to answer them here. The confusion surrounding the issue of abstraction shows that one cannot really draw a firm boundary between representational and abstract painting. We can read paintings such as Malevich's *Football Match* and Mondrian's *Composition No. 10: Pier and Ocean* equally well both ways, as representations or as abstract compositions.[113] The paintings I have mentioned are far from being the only borderline abstractions, paintings that are not easily defined as abstract or representational.

The Vorticist theory of representation is an exploration of the borderline position. After blasting Cubism's indifference to subject matter and Futurism's indifference to formal matters, Vorticism blasts abstract art in turn for its indifference to the possibility of using abstraction to interpret the world. Lewis calls in his polemics on behalf of Vorticism for a synthesis of abstraction and representation, which will move beyond abstraction's formalism to a new dynamic conception of art's relation to the world.

Lewis drew a clear distinction between abstraction and the aesthetic of Vorticism. His "A Review of Contemporary Art" in *Blast* #2 discusses three groups of artists in detail, Cubism and Futurism (in ways already discussed) and Expressionism, by which he says he means the work of Kandinsky. His discussion of Kandinsky focuses on the issue of representation and abstraction, and in typically Vorticist fashion he arrives at his own doctrine about representation by attacking Kandinsky's. Lewis himself calls attention to this discussion: "In dealing with Kandinsky's doctrine, and tabulating differences [between it and Vorticism], you come to the most important feature of this new synthesis I propose" (*WLOA* 68). Lewis focused on Kandinsky because he considered him "the only PURELY abstract painter in Europe" (*WLOA* 63). By 1914, he was acquainted both with Kandinsky's theories and his art. *Blast* #1 contained excerpts from and comments by Edward Wadsworth on Kandinsky's *Über das Geistige in der Kunst.*[114] Moreover, Kandinsky had exhibited in London at the Allied Artists' Association in 1908, 1909, 1913, and 1914. Lewis, Gaudier-Brzeska, Epstein, and other Vorticists also exhibited there in 1913 and 1914, and it was at the 1913 A.A.A. that Gaudier-Brzeska and Pound originally met.[115] The works Kandinsky showed in 1913 and 1914 included some of his most advanced paintings (*Improvisations #29* and *#30*), so Lewis's critique was based on firsthand knowledge of Kandinsky's "abstract" work.[116] But if Lewis's reference to Kandinsky as a purely abstract painter is based on these works this supposition unobtrusively points up the problems with the term *abstract*. For these paintings no longer seem abstract; *Improvisation #30,* in particular, is well known for containing two cannons on the lower right which, according to Kandinsky, made their way into the painting unconsciously.[117]

Though Lewis discusses Kandinsky's work as if it were abstract, the presence of such veiled or unconscious imagery in these paintings actually supports his thesis which is that representation is unavoidable. To "attempt to avoid all representative element is an . . . absurdity" (*WLOA* 75) because "if you do not use shapes and colours characteristic of your environment, you will only use some others characteristic more or less of somebody else's environment, and certainly no better" (*WLOA* 74). Lewis does not believe that the artist can create his own forms. He must abstract them from something, and they will inevitably betray their origin (as they do in Lewis's paintings). So pure form for Lewis is an impossibility. Art cannot cut its ties to the material world: "everything is representation, in one sense, even in the most abstract paintings" (*WLOA* 73). In trying to avoid such representation, Kandinsky is forced into avoiding "almost all powerful and definite forms" and ends up being "wandering and slack." Lewis argues: "You cannot avoid the conclusion that he would have done better to ACKNOWLEDGE that he had (by accident) reproduced a form in Nature, and have taken more trouble with it FOR ITS OWN SAKE AS A FRANKLY REPRESENTATIVE ITEM" (*WLOA* 64). T. E. Hulme had already attacked Kandinsky's slack forms and criticized him for not basing his forms *on* something.[118] Lewis echoes Hulme here, even though Hulme considered Lewis to be on Kandinsky's side and attacked Lewis in the same article along the same lines. Both Hulme and Lewis thus accept the formalist view that art is above all an affair of forms, but argue that to be dogmatic about severing the link between those forms and the material world must lead to an impoverishment of art, for it is that world which suggests to the artist the shapes and forms he paints. Good art is about much more than significant form; no form is significant in itself.

However, Lewis is not simply advocating representational painting. He calls imitative realism "an absurd and gloomy waste of time" (*WLOA* 73), one more example of art trying to merge with life. His position is that "the finest Art is not pure Abstraction, nor is it unorganized life" (*WLOA* 37). He advocates a creative interplay between the two, as imitation can only render the appearance of things, not their essence or significance: "We must constantly strive to ENRICH abstraction till it is almost plain life, or rather to get deeply enough immersed in material life to experience the shaping power amongst its vibrations, and to accentuate and perpetuate these" (*WLOA* 62). This shaping power is the essence of art. Even if pure form were possible it would be less interesting than Lewis's enriched abstraction because nothing would be shaped or formed.

To see how this theory works in practice, let us consider one of Lewis's most abstract canvases, *Workshop* (fig. 8, 1914–15). To a beholder in 1914, it must have seemed completely abstract, without reference to the external world. But the forms Lewis used are abstracted, not abstract, and they betray their place of origin, the modern city. The shapes on the canvas ineluctably suggest modern buildings and the formal organization of these shapes, as we have already seen, reflects the activity or dynamism of the city. It is not a view of the city, nor is it a painting of any particular location. It is an abstract of the city, a representation of "cityness."

Lewis is characteristically Vorticist here in the way he uses the style of abstraction, not to avoid a subject, but to render what he conceives of as its essence, stripped of the clutter of detail. How the Vorticist concern with essence translates itself into formal terms is best shown by quoting an early letter of Gaudier-Brzeska, in which he comments on Baudelaire:

> I like him just because he has sacrificed the fugitive to that which endures. He encloses his idea in a severe form, the sonnet, and puts nothing but the essential, that which will remain for ever. When the principal features are expressed the secondary ones are easily imagined; if only the secondary are given, the principal ones are lost. If both are given, then they lose in intensity and one can no longer distinguish.[119]

This passage expresses the principal features of the Vorticist aesthetic: render the essence, the most intense aspect of a subject in or through a severe form, and omit the fugitive and superficial qualities. This essence will then endure and the beholder or reader can, indeed must, fill in the rest.

It is also a perfect description of Gaudier-Brzeska's own mature work. The justly celebrated *Hieratic Head of Ezra Pound* (figs. 10 and 11; 1914) encloses Pound's features in a simplified severe form. Only the principal features of Pound's head are given, and those in fact are the features that endured: the *Hieratic Head* looks far more like the aged Ezra Pound than the comparatively youthful man who sat for Gaudier in 1914.

If the extraction or abstraction of the essence of a subject is the essence of Vorticism, then works of art involving varying degrees of abstraction can be equally Vorticist. There is no need to consider Gaudier-Brzeska's *Hieratic Head* as less (or more) Vorticist than Lewis's *Workshop* because it is less abstract; both exemplify Vorticism's shaping power and concern for the essential. Many supposed exceptions to Vorticism are thus only exceptions to the critics' misconception of Vorticism: Vorticism is considerably more coherent than Materer and Wees have supposed, and that coherence does not depend on Vorticism's degree of abstraction. Abstraction is a means, not an end, to an essentialist mode of representation.

Pound in his essay of September 1914, "Vorticism," developed the most complex version of the Vorticist theory of representation. The center of his discussion is an elaborate analogy borrowed from mathematics.[120] After stating that Vorticism is an "intensive art," he says that mathematical expression can be ranked according to intensity. (I do not answer for Pound's mathematics.) Arithmetic contents itself with statements of fact such as $3^2 + 4^2 = 5^2$. It is true about itself, but it does not say anything about any other numbers: it is comparable to a mimetic painting of any given location.

A more intense statement is $a^2 + b^2 = c^2$: it can apply to a lot of facts, to many situations. It is made yet more intense when one sees that it governs the ratios of the length of the sides of a right-angle triangle. Pound compares this level of intensiveness to art criticism as it involves criticism of form, but not its creation (*G-B* 91). The next and highest level of intensity is analytical geometry. A statement that the equation $(x-a)^2 + (y-b)^2 = r^2$ governs the circle is not a statement about a particular circle, but "any circle and all circles." It is an analytic statement which is the form or essence of the circle. Pound then claims, "The difference between art and analytical geometry is the difference of subject-matter only" (*G-B* 91). Great works of art similarly "cause form to come into being" (*G-B* 92). They do not reproduce the accidental appearance of their subject, but they express its analytic form.

This discussion conveniently codifies the Vorticist theory of representation. In response to Bergson's claim that representation only produces diagrams, Vorticism replies, "exactly, art provides a schematic representation of things, like an equation or a diagram, which can never be confused with what it represents." John Berger has remarked: "The metaphorical model of Cubism is the *diagram:* the diagram being a visible, symbolic representation of invisible processes, forces, structures."[121] I am not at all convinced that the diagram is the "metaphorical model" of Cubism, but I would emphatically argue that it is a most appropriate model for Vorticism. Vorticism, not Cubism, is concerned with representing and forming process; Cubism's diagrams are static. Moreover, only a synthesis of the representationalism of Cubism and the abstraction of Kandinsky produces art sufficiently analytic to be diagrammatic. Cubism expresses too many "secondary features." Finally, Vorticism, unlike Cubism, is aware of its own diagrammatic orientation. Through its name, it diagrams itself, and in *Blast* the symbol ♣ even diagrams its name.

What Vorticism seeks to represent in diagrams, what Berger refers to as "invisible processes, forces, structures," are dynamic forms, like the vortex. Hugh Kenner in *The Pound Era* has called these forms "patterned energies" and has definitively established Pound's early and abiding interest in patterned energies and a wider context in which this interest has import.[122] Such patterned energies can be represented only through Vorticism's schematic mode of representation, which, though reducing a four-dimensional process to a two-dimensional diagram, as in the image of the vortex ♣, nevertheless gives the beholder enough information to visualize the process which is the object of representation. Vorticist painting tended to restrict itself to the palpable dynamic forms such as the dance, but the movement's name alone can serve as an index of the presence of more abstract forms.

The way diagrams can represent more complex processes schematically is itself a concise diagram of the way Vorticism resolves the question of the relation of its art to the world. Vorticism as I have presented it has oscillated between attacking the Futurist mimesis of life and attacking Roger Fry's formalist insistence on the autonomy of art which would seem to be the only alternative to mimesis. It attacks both because it wants an autonomous formal art that would nonetheless involve a loop back, a return to life. This "diagrammatic art" differs from "pure painting" or art concerned with significant form because diagrams, though abstractions, are abstractions *of* something and can be tested for their correspondence. A map is not the territory it maps, but it should be able to direct the man using it around that territory. Lewis refuses to sever art's tie to the material world because his art is such a map, intended to direct the beholder's perception of the world.

Beholders thus are meant to complete the "loop" between art and the world. It is up to them to relate the art work to the world. They not only have to see the world in the work of art, but they should also see the art work in the world. The Vorticist ideal is that the beholder should re-see the world in the art's image. This aesthetic stance—though rooted in formalism—is nonetheless an attempt to go beyond it. I would like to call this stance "affective formalism," as the form of painting is something to be valued for its effect upon the beholder.

As a Russian correspondent said to Pound after Pound had expounded his aesthetic, "I see, you wish to give people new eyes, not to make them see some new particular thing" (G-B 85). Pound got his "new eyes" from Vorticist art, and, as he is the only Vorticist to give an account of the effect that art had on him, his testimony is especially valuable. Near the end of *Gaudier-Brzeska*, Pound asks himself, "What have they done for me these Vorticist artists?" and answers:

> These new men have made me see form, have made me more conscious of the appearance of the sky where it juts down between houses, of the bright pattern of sunlight which the bath water throws up on the ceiling, of the great "V's" of light that dart through the chinks over the curtain rings, all these are new chords, new keys of design. . . .
>
> If vorticism has done this for me, I think it can do it for others. Others?
>
> Of course the rest of the world may not want a new sense of forms, or a new sense of anything. (G-B 126–27)

What these artists did for Pound, we can safely say, they did for very few of those others. But perhaps Pound was enough, as he in turn tried to transmit Vorticism's new sense of form in his art. To give people new eyes is a more complicated operation than merely to stick something new in front of their faces. It takes time, time that Vorticism as a movement did not have.

Vorticism's position on representation, not a middle way between representation and abstraction as much as a use of one as a means to the other, should be placed in relation to the other new modern strategies of representation developed in this period. From the tone of Lewis's account of other art movements in *Blast,* however, one would never guess that anything existed at all comparable to Lewis's call for a synthesis of abstraction and representation. Though it is crucial to present Vorticism's view of itself and other art movements in order to elucidate its aesthetic program, one runs the risk of accepting Vorticism's valuation of itself and other art movements. If one looks at Vorticism from the standpoint of Cubism or that of Kandinsky, one is far more likely to say that Vorticism simply missed the point of the movements it sought to criticize. Unquestionably, the achievement of Kandinsky or Picasso or Boccioni in this period is incomparably greater than that of Lewis or Wadsworth. Moreover, it must be admitted that Lewis, obstinately bent on defining Vorticism against the other *isms,* could be extremely reductive in his presentation of other movements (though some of this reductiveness was caused by Lewis's acceptance of a generally assumed perspective: Cézanne meant form, Kandinsky meant abstraction, and so on).

His discussion of Picasso's constructions, collages, and papiers collés in "Relativism and Picasso's Latest Work" in *Blast* #1 is an excellent case in point.[123] These works were exploring an area of profound interest for Lewis and Vorticism, the possibilities of nonillusionistic representation. After the "hermetic," nearly abstract final phase of Analytic Cubism, Cubism turned away from abstraction towards new modes of representation. Clement Greenberg writes that Picasso and Braque had to "choose *between* illusion and representation."[124] Their choice, their repudiation of illusion in Synthetic Cubism, is precisely the choice that Lewis wants painting to make.

But Lewis refuses to see that he shares any common ground with Picasso. He blasts Picasso's latest work for abandoning the distance between art and life: "He no longer so much interprets, as definitely MAKES, nature (and 'DEAD' nature at that)" (*WLOA* 44). Picasso is now making works of art wholly or partly out of mundane, non-artistic materials, and Lewis places this under the same anti-art rubric as Futurism: "Picasso has come out of the canvas and has commenced to build up his shadows against reality. Reality is the Waterloo, Will ,o' the wisp, or siren of artistic genius" (*WLOA* 43). Picasso is trying, in other words, to annihilate the separation between art and life (or reality) which Lewis was so quick to insist upon.

One must credit Lewis with a certain prophetic insight here. Picasso's incorporation of real objects in his works of art decisively influenced what Harold Osborne has recently called the "repudiation of artifice" in modern art.[125] The artists who figure in this are, preeminently, Marcel Duchamp, the Russian Constructivists, and contemporary American artists such as Robert Rauschenberg, and their concern is precisely to annihilate the distance between art and life. Lewis's critique of Picasso's seminal innovation is, I think, a penetrating critique (in advance) of this line of development. In contrast, Vorticism refuses to "come out of the canvas." The unreality and two-dimensionality of art is crucial to its diagrammatic, analytic stance. Vorticism wishes to interpret nature, not to make it. Its works are in traditional media. The Vorticists painted, sculpted, and drew. They sought to preserve the distinction between art and non-art; they did not paste things together or put urinals in exhibitions, activities that seemed to break down this distinction.

However, Picasso's collages and constructions cannot really be said to break down this distinction. Mundane objects are incorporated in the art work, but they in turn signify other objects, not simply themselves. One exception comes to mind: Picasso's sculpture, *Le Verre d'absinthe,* uses a real absinthe spoon, placed where it should be if it were on top of a real absinthe glass. However, this use highlights the artifice of the rest, I think, and hence emphasizes the artistic nature of the whole. The Cubists in their own work, therefore, preserve the distinction between image and object that their innovation would help to lead others to destroy.

Failing to recognize this, Lewis fails to recognize that collage is not at all at odds with Vorticism's interest in an analytic representationalism. Lewis, in short, utterly rejects Picasso's collages and constructions, whereas someone with the same aesthetic stance but a greater interest in finding allies could have easily found things to praise in these ground-breaking works.

Lewis was never comfortable sharing any common ground with anyone, fearful of compromising his integrity, not only in the period of Vorticism, but throughout his career. This attitude helps to specify the driving force behind the originality of Vorticism. So, time and again he would attack his friends as well as his enemies— T. S. Eliot and Ezra Pound as well as Virginia Woolf and D. H. Lawrence—and these attacks must have seemed perverse and maddening to those friends. This is, one may observe, a curious frame of mind for a leader of a movement, for movements after all are based on establishing a group identity. They cannot be totally atomistic.

Lewis was the most important Vorticist and following his critiques of the other "isms," as I have done, is essential to an understanding of the position of Vorticism. Nonetheless, there was a current of identification and sympathy foreign to him running through Vorticism, and the portrait of Vorticism needs to be revised to include that current. Some Vorticists did find things to praise in the work of other artists. Wadsworth translated extracts from Kandinsky for *Blast* #1. Pound always stressed the continuity in the movement of the avant-garde more than Lewis, and in "Vortex Pound" he referred to "Picasso, Kandinski, father and mother, classicism and romanticism of the movement" (*Bl* #1, 154). Gaudier-Brzeska in his "Vortex" included Brancusi, Archipenko, Dunkowski, and Modigliani along with himself and Epstein in a short list of the approved moderns in sculpture.

But beyond these details, the way this current finds its most significant expression is in the Vorticist attitude towards the use of the past, the final and most obvious way in which Vorticism shows itself not to be programmatically modernist. But Lewis is only peripherally involved in this aspect of Vorticism; Gaudier-Brzeska and Jacob Epstein are the figures commanding our attention henceforth.

Using the Past: The Ideogrammatic Loop

In stark contrast to the Futurist contempt for the past, Vorticism managed to combine an insistence on the new in art with a respect for the past and the art of the past. Lewis's *Timon of Athens* portfolio (fig. 1) is merely the most conspicuous example of this combination. Ezra Pound makes the point in his essay "Vorticism": "We are all futurists to the extent of believing with Guillaume Appollonaire [*sic*] that 'On ne peut pas porter *partout* avec soi le cadavre de son père' " (*G-B* 82). But he goes on later in the essay to specify the limits to his Futurism:

> The vorticist has not this curious tic for destroying past glories. I have no doubt that Italy needed Mr. Marinetti, but he did not set on the egg that hatched me, and as I am wholly opposed to his aesthetic principles I see no reason why I, and various men who agree with me, should be expected to call ourselves futurists. We do not desire to evade comparison with the past. We prefer that the comparison be made by some intelligent person whose idea of "the tradition" is not limited by the conventional taste of four or five centuries and one continent. (*G-B* 90)

Pound makes a typically modernist gesture here in shunting aside the "traditional tradition" of European art since the Renaissance, calling it in polemical exaggeration merely a conventional taste. But he combines this disdain with a respect for "tradition." What tradition? There are really two. First is the tradition of the new, of the avant-garde, running back to Gautier and Baudelaire, Courbet and Manet, Stendhal and Flaubert. One shows respect for this tradition by continuing its process of innovation and transformation: as Lewis says in *Blast* #2, "If we are to show ourselves worthy of the lead given us by two or three great painters of the last fifteen years, we must not abate in our interrogation" (*WLOA* 62). One honors this tradition by extending it.

The other tradition cannot be defined so easily, only as Pound does, by excluding exclusions. It is Malraux's "museum without walls," Eliot's tradition extending back to cave painting—the extravagant twentieth-century notion that the plenitude of man's cultural achievement can somehow be brought to bear on the

present. Calling this "the tradition" entails a radical redefinition of
what is meant by tradition, transforming it from a set of informing
and enriching constraints to a much broader set of possibilities.
Making virtually all of the art of the past available to the artist
creates both a great opportunity and a great burden. How is one
to make creative use of this tradition and not be overwhelmed
by it?

Precisely by making creative use of it. The Vorticist is rather
highhanded in his attitude towards the past and only selects from
the past that which in his view has some relevance to the present.
In *Blast* #1, for example, we find a rather improbable article on
Chinese geomancy by Lewis, "Feng Shui and Contemporary Form."
Lewis obviously wrote it not out of any intrinsic or scholarly interest in this aspect of Chinese culture, but because a discussion of
geomancy enabled him to make certain points about modern art.
Lewis asserts that the skills needed by a good geomancer are
parallel to those needed by a modern artist. He thus draws a parallel
between past and present, not because the parallel is exact, but because this use of the past enables a sharper perception of the
present. In other words, the past is brought to bear on the present,
which is why the past is being investigated.

In Lewis's painting of the Vorticist period, there is no hint of
any such investigation of the past. His stylistic idiom and subject
matter are purely modern, of his own time. He is joined in his
exclusive concentration on the present by the other Vorticist
painters. However, the Vorticist sculptors, Henri Gaudier-Brzeska
and Jacob Epstein, bring the past to bear on the present in a manner strikingly akin to that found in Lewis's discussion of geomancy.
There is, in short, a distinctively Vorticist use of the past.

The past Epstein and Gaudier-Brzeska use in their sculpture is
the primitive past, and their work is part—though a distinctive
part—of a much larger current of "primitivism" in early twentieth-
century art.[126] The signature of primitivism in early twentieth-
century art is the use of the simplified forms broadly characteristic
of primitive art. The most widespread and influential kind of
primitivism restricts itself to that formal borrowing. With few
exceptions, the primitivism of the School of Paris painters was of
this kind, whether that primitivism was fundamental and abiding,

as in the case of Modigliani, or relatively superficial and brief, as in the case of Braque.

Malraux's reflections on primitivism show why these painters were content with simply borrowing the forms of primitive art. European painters knew the primitive art whose formal properties they imitated only as art, something they collected or saw in museums. This statement sounds like a tautology, but it is not, as most primitive art objects have a practical function in the context in which they were made. Only when removed from that context, in Europe for sale or in a museum, is the African nail fetish or mask defined as art. The resultant gap between "our" and "their" notion of the meaning of those objects is a serious problem, but only for those who recognize the existence of such a gap, precisely what was ignored by the formalist variety of primitivism. Little enough was known in any case about the origin, function, and associations of the objects these painters were acquainted with; no wonder the artists simply responded to what they could see, to the formal properties of primitive art.

Picasso, however, presents an exception to this generalization. His use of primitive art as a source for his own art begins in *Les Demoiselles d'Avignon* (1907).[127] The faces of the two figures on the right of the painting closely resemble African masks. Obviously, more than a formal relation is involved: one is meant to feel the primitive nature of these figures. And, as others have done before and after, Picasso uses the primitive as a token of the violent, the horrible, the unspeakable. But this painting was abandoned and was not shown publicly until 1937; this kind of expressive distortion also disappears from Picasso's work until the 1930s. In the so-called Negro period, the period of his most marked interest in African art, which lies between Picasso's discovery of African art in 1907 and the inception of Cubism, his interest in African art is comparable to Braque's or Modigliani's. The example of African sculpture aided Picasso in simplifying his forms; no other feature of that art seems to have affected his use of it.

Against this kind of primitivism, Vorticist primitivism is striking in that it tries to close the hermeneutic gap between the effect primitive art has on a Western beholder and its original context. In contrast to, say, Modigliani, neither Epstein nor Gaudier-Brzeska ever developed a single consistent primitivistic style. The style of

each successive piece varied radically, both in the degree of prim-
itiveness and in the kind of primitive art imitated. This deliberate
variation is a function of the appropriateness of the style for the
piece. The Vorticist sculptors were interested in the origins and
context of the primitive works of art they imitated as well as in
the formal properties of those works. Moreover, that context is an
important component of what they hope to get across by means
of their primitivistic style.

Epstein's *Tomb of Oscar Wilde* (1912), a work of the period just
prior to Vorticism, is stylistically indebted to Egyptian tomb sculpture, because Epstein thought the Egyptian reference appropriate
for a tomb. The tomb done, he never did anything in that style
again. Epstein, like Picasso, Vlaminck, and others, collected primitive art, and, as Richard Cork has discovered, several of his works
of the Vorticist period bear a resemblance to pieces in his collection. But the critical point is that it is always possible to discern
some special reason for the formal resemblance. The mother in his
Marble Mother and Child (1915) and one of his *Marble Venuses*
(ca. 1915) are based on carvings of women in his collection; the
male figure of *Cursed Be the Day Wherein I Was Born* (fig. 12; ca.
1913–15) is based on a male Bakota figure he owned.[128] The three
sets of *Marble Doves* (ca. 1913), on the other hand, just as simplified in their forms, have no direct indebtedness to primitive art.
Instead, they bear a close formal resemblance to Brancusi's *Maiastra*
(1912) and may be deliberate imitations or evocations of Brancusi's
work.[129]

Arguably, Gaudier-Brzeska's work reveals an even greater variety.
Much of his sculpture is without any overt reference to primitive
art, but he also did a number of virtual copies of primitive pieces.
His wood carving, *Portrait of Ezra Pound,* and the bronze, *Men
with Bowl,* both works of 1914, are closer to their models than
any of Epstein's sculpture.[130] The cause of this variety is the same
concern with finding a style appropriate to the subject. His *Hieratic
Head of Ezra Pound* (figs. 10 and 11; 1914), as Cork has shown,
stylistically echoes a monumental Easter Island figure in the British
Museum.[131] The monumentality of the head is accentuated by
that echo: again, the context of the primitive artifact is consonant
with and supportive of the meaning of the modern work. Lewis
dubbed this work "Ezra in the form of a marble phallus."[132] Both

Epstein and Gaudier-Brzeska seemed to have associated virility and fecundity with the primitive, and because of that association Epstein's various birth studies are primitivistic, like the *Hieratic Head.*

One might want to fault Epstein's and Gaudier-Brzeska's ethnographic information and intuition on nearly every point. But it is significant that they are there to fault. Not content with borrowing the forms of primitive art, they tried to use those forms so as to transmit a sense of the context of that art. This awareness of the values of the primitive needs to be differentiated in turn from what one might call the programmatic primitivism of Gauguin, D. H. Lawrence, and the German Die Brücke group. The Vorticists do not quote the primitive because they consider it better than the modern—no Vorticist ended up in Tahiti or New Mexico—and their detached modernism is not these artists's attack on the modern. Programmatic primitivism sees the primitive both as Gaudier-Brzeska's "vortex of fecundity" and as Picasso's vortex of violence and irrationality, but it identifies with that sexuality and aggressiveness. D. H. Lawrence exemplifies this psychological primitivism more fully than any painter, and Lewis attacked Lawrence's preference for the primitive over and again, most notably in *Paleface* (1929) and *The Apes of God* (1930).

Epstein and Gaudier-Brzeska (and Pound, for that matter) were both more fascinated by and less detached from the primitive than Lewis, but the very way in which they put primitivism to use indicates their distance from it and from any programmatic identification with it. For Gaudier-Brzeska's focus is not Easter Island, but Ezra Pound. He uses a primitive style because it offers him a way to approach his modern subject, a language appropriate to that subject. His primitivism, in other words, is not primitivism at all, but again a kind of modernism or presentism.

Moreover, the way in which Vorticist primitivism enables an approach to the modern makes it an important development in its own right and not simply a voyage between the Scylla of Parisian formalism and the Charybdis of emotive identification with the primitive. T. E. Hulme saw the modern use of various archaic and primitive styles as a return to geometric art which would be a bridge to—but be replaced by—modern geometric forms. This view is an acute analysis of the role of the primitive in the evolution of

Braque or Brancusi, but for Vorticism primitive styles were a bridge to the modern *not* to be replaced as they offered categories for understanding the modern.

Consider Epstein's large plaster figure, now lost, entitled *Cursed Be the Day Wherein I Was Born* (fig. 12). Unlike anything else Epstein ever did in medium or style, it is based on a Bakota figure which Epstein owned and has perhaps the most authentic primitive feel of any of his pieces, at least in black and white reproduction. But its highly polished and bright scarlet surface equally mark it as highly modern. The title, words spoken by Job in the Bible, helps us grasp how Epstein combines the extremes of modernity and primitivism: he identifies them.[133] Worringer had described primitive man as being in fear of the instability of the world, in desperate search for some refuge from it, and Epstein equates Job's fear with that of primitive man by using this quotation from the Book of Job (3:3) as the title of a piece of African-influenced primitivistic sculpture. Richard Cork has also argued that Epstein meant that "I" to include the descendants of primitive man in the modern world. including the blacks in America, and hence by synecdoche all subjugated and oppressed peoples, anyone who would identify with the speaker's sentiments, anyone who would speak those words.[134] I think the speaker is, above all, Jacob Epstein himself, a maker of graven images despite the Jewish prohibition against them, and therefore cursed like Job, yet a representative of the Jewish people, who remain as buffeted by circumstance as Job himself.[135]

Epstein, therefore, matches style and subject, primitive and modern, in the interest of effecting an identification between them. Like Lewis in his account of Chinese geomancy, Epstein abstracts characteristics common to both primitive and modern as a way of presenting the modern. A perceived congruence of past and present is the Vorticists' focus, and the art work expresses that congruence as if no gap in time and space existed between them. It does not abolish time, but it creates a loop in time by equating and bringing together at least two moments in time.

Thus, the Vorticists did not evolve a generally primitivistic style because they did not want to evoke some generalized archaic or primitive sensibility. They wanted to evoke specific primitive styles and contexts, Egyptian tomb sculpture, for example, or

Easter Island figures, as a category for representing something in the present. It was Pound who was most sensitive to and influenced by the Vorticist use of the past. For this reason, I borrow the word *ideogrammatic* from him and call the loop created in time by these Vorticist sculptors the ideogrammatic loop: ideogrammatic because the two times, past and present, are simply juxtaposed to create a meaningful relationship as in the Chinese ideogram; loop because a moment in the past is identified with the present in a way that replaces historical sequence with a loop in history. This ideogrammatic loop is the essential feature of the Vorticist use of the past.

What proves that the ideogrammatic loop is a genuine aim of the Vorticists, and not simply an accidental feature of their primitivism, is that we can see them striving for an equation of past and present in works in a modern stylistic idiom as well. Epstein's central Vorticist sculpture, *Rock Drill* (figs. 5 and 9; 1913-16), is uncompromisingly modern in its subject matter, and yet the figure astride the drill is both modern and primitive, mechanistic and totemic, at the same time. Rather than stressing the presentness of the past, *Rock Drill* stresses the pastness of the present: mechanized man is primitive man. The confident treatment of mechanization found in Futurism is absent from this sinister and mutilated figure. Epstein equates the aggressive energy of the primitive with that of the modern, but is removed from and horrified by both.

Richard Cork correctly points out, though he overstates the change, that the final cut-down version of *Rock Drill* (fig. 9) is more negative in its portrayal of mechanization than the first (fig. 5). He links this change to the outbreak of the war: "this driller looks more like a war victim than a triumphant harbinger of the machine age."[136] But his programmatically modernist conception of Vorticism, his notion that the movement as a whole was such a triumphant harbinger, leads him to see the final state of *Rock Drill* as an erosion of Vorticist tenets, indeed the sounding of the movement's death-knell.[137] Rather than its death-knell, the final version is its apogee, for the doubt about the machine world and the detachment from modernolatry emphasized in Epstein's modifications to his sculpture stand at the center of Vorticism.

Rock Drill itself stands at the center of Vorticism, the movement's epitome, in spite of, or perhaps because of, Epstein's refusal to join the movement formally. Its subject matter is a modern dynamic form, man at work in the machine world, and both style and subject bear certain affinities to the latest Continental work. (Here the obvious affinities are with Archipenko and Duchamp-Villon.) But an aspect of the work's style not caught by those affinities is an element of coldness and alienation, indicative of the detached, almost antagonistic, attitude towards that subject matter. This detachment from the modern, conclusively established by Epstein's use of the past to comment on the modern, is part of a general ideal of detachment. The artist stands back from life, somewhat like the driller depicted in the sculpture. Epstein would perhaps be bothered by being linked to the wounded and unsympathetic figure of the driller, but he was soon bothered by the piece itself, never attempting its like again. In either form *Rock Drill* has had no artistic progeny as sculptors interested in mechanization have not attempted to use it as a mode of figuration nor have they been as dubious as Epstein about that mechanization. *Rock Drill* has been claimed as an influence by one person alone, Ezra Pound, who named a major section of *The Cantos* after Epstein's almost forgotten work. That influence is a synecdoche for the process that I am attempting to make manifest, the process through which Vorticism, though initially a movement primarily of painters and sculptors, has had its enduring impact on literature.

3 Vortex and Ideogram:
Pound's Vorticism from
1914 to 1920

Vorticist literature did not play a prominent role in the articulation of the Vorticist aesthetic, and the important external forces that shaped Vorticism were other movements in painting. Although in theory there was a place in Vorticism for literature, in practice the Vorticists themselves developed and defined their aesthetic in terms of the visual arts. Nonetheless, in the period of the Vorticist movement, one finds Vorticist literature, or, to be more precise, attempts to be Vorticist in literature, by Lewis and Pound, the two major figures in Vorticism.

Vorticist literature, in other words, was in 1914 rather tentative, trying to do, in a variety of ways, what painting and sculpture were doing. Hence, though the initial attempt at literary Vorticism—the subject of this chapter and the next—was contemporaneous with the developments in art already discussed, the art was decisive in shaping the evolution of the literature. Just as Vorticism in painting and sculpture must be seen with the Continental movements of its era in mind, Vorticist literature must be read with Vorticist art in mind. In each case, the direction of influence is one-way: Vorticist art played no decisive role in the evolution of painting on the Continent, and Vorticist literature played no decisive role in the evolution of Vorticist painting and sculpture. The difference is that literary Vorticism displays no hostility towards what inspired it: Lewis and Pound wanted their writing to be Vorticist in the same sense that the art was.

Lewis's Vorticist writings in the period of Vorticism are much easier to define than Pound's. Lewis's major works are the *Blast* manifestoes, the play in *Blast #1, Enemy of the Stars,* and his first published novel, *Tarr,* which though published in 1918 was substantially finished by the time of Lewis's enlistment in 1916.[1] All of these works explicitly attempt to be Vorticist. In addition to these and his writings on art, Lewis in the 1914–17 period wrote a

number of war stories and a second play, *The Ideal Giant,* which
are neither particularly interesting nor relevant to our concerns
here.

Pound's literary activities in this period, however, are more complex and diffuse. These are the years, after all, that placed Pound
at the center of twentieth-century literary history. The relevance
of the term *Vorticist* to translations of Fontenelle or campaigns
promoting James Joyce is far from obvious. The only works that
we can certainly consider Vorticist are the poems by Pound published in *Blast.* This fact more than any other has made it easy to
consider Vorticism an unimportant and rather unpleasant episode
in Pound's career. Most of these poems seem utterly out of place
in *Blast,* typical of Pound's work of the preceding years and without any conceivable relation to Vorticism. Lewis remembered these
poems years later when he described Pound's contributions to
Blast as "some nice quiet little poems—at least calculated to vex
Signor Marinetti with their fine passéiste flavour."[2] Lewis's description is apt enough of lines such as these from "Before Sleep":

> She of the spear stands present.
> The gods of the underworld attend me, O Annubis,
> These are they of thy company.
> With a pathetic solicitude they attend me;
> Undulant,
> Their realm is the lateral courses.
>
> > (*Bl* #1, 47)[3]

Lewis has forgotten, however, some strenuous attempts to rival
Marinetti (and Lewis) in polemic modernism. The first of Pound's
poems in *Blast,* "Salutation the Third," strikes a different note:

> > SO shall you be also,
> > You slut-belled obstructionist,
> > > You sworn foe to free speech and good letters,
> > You fungus, you continuous gangrene.
> >
> > > (*Bl* #1, 45)

"Salutation the Third" also contains Pound's first anti-Semitic
lines:

> Come, let us on with the new deal,
>   Let us be done with Jews and Jobbery,
> Let us SPIT upon those who fawn on the JEWS for their money,
> Let us out to the pastures.
>
> (Bl #1, 45)

Pound omitted the references to Jews when he revised the poem for inclusion in the 1926 collection, *Personae,* but even in revision this poem is extremely offensive, in tone as well as in content. Hugh Kenner has indicated that the tone points forward to the "impotent vituperation" of Pound's World War II radio broadcasts,[4] and it startled at least one reviewer who knew Pound well. Richard Aldington, reviewing *Blast* in *The Egoist,* called Pound's contributions "quite unworthy of their author":

> It is not that one wants Mr. Pound to repeat his Provençal feats, to echo the 'nineties—he has done that too much already—it is simply the fact that Mr. Pound cannot write satire. Mr. Pound is one of the gentlest, most modest, bashful, kind creatures who ever walked this earth; so I cannot help thinking that all this enormous arrogance and petulance and fierceness are a pose. And it is a wearisome pose.[5]

Pound saw this poem, one must assume, as his contribution to the Vorticist polemics, and it does form part of an extended polemic of Pound's against corrupt and socially complacent journalism which continued in *Blast* #2 in "Et Faim Saillir le Loup des Boys" and received its enduring expression in *Hugh Selwyn Mauberley.* But "Salutation the Third" has none of the wit or elegance of *Mauberley;* instead it tries unsuccessfully and painfully to match Lewis in polemic vigor. Pound's own criterion of the primary pigment should have warned Pound away from such an attempt: this central tenet of Vorticism says that one should never do in one's own art what some other art or artist can do better. And no one, I think, in this century can match Lewis in polemic intensity. Hence this poem is Vorticist only in the sense of formally imitating some property of Vorticism, but that formal imitation has not enabled Pound to write an acceptable polemic or even a good poem.

The same must be said about Pound's other attempt in *Blast* to write Vorticist poetry. His "Dogmatic Statement on the Game and

Play of Chess (Theme for a Series of Pictures)," published in *Blast* #2 (subsequently titled simply "The Game of Chess"), is Pound's most obvious attempt at a Vorticist poem. As such it has received some praise: W. C. Wees has called it "Pound's one truly Vorticist poem"; Richard Cork, calling it "an equivalent of a Vorticist painting," argues that "Pound captures the effect of a Vorticist painting in the very form of his poem."[6] But these claims by critics who, like myself, are deeply involved with Vorticism carry little conviction. "Dogmatic Statement" does describe a game of chess in terms made available by Vorticist painting:

> 'Y' pawns, cleaving, embanking!
> Whirl! Centripetal! Mate! King down in the
>   vortex,
> Clash, leaping of bands, straight strips of hard
>   colour,
> Blocked lights working in. Escapes. Renewal of
>   contest.[7]

The one interesting aspect of this poem is the relative paucity of both verbs and complete sentences. Pound uses a remarkable number of participles (such as "cleaving, embanking!"), presumably to give the poem a greater sense of motion. But reading this poem does not give one "new eyes" with which to see a game of chess. A game of chess is presented in an elaborate, mannered, and indirect way, which makes one see, if anything, Vorticist painting. A game of chess, with its geometric board and moving pieces, is a convenient formed-yet-dynamic subject with which to attempt to render the effect of Vorticist painting on the poet. "Dogmatic Statement" is a much better title than "The Game of Chess"; again, Pound has not adhered to his own notion of the "primary pigment." "Dogmatic Statement" tries to do in words what a Vorticist painting could do much more easily. For that reason, though trying hard to be Vorticist, it is neither Vorticist nor a good poem.

Vorticism, though an inspiration to Pound, did not therefore inspire him to write new kinds of poems. Pound needed no one to tell him this: he knew that "Salutation the Third" and "Dogmatic Statement" were failures, and consequently they had no successors. But nevertheless Vorticism is the crucial moment in Pound's evolution as a writer. It is under the impact of the Vorticist aesthetic that Pound becomes a major writer. Vorticism has this importance, not because it leads Pound into new territory, but because it clarifies and organizes for him the territory he had already begun to explore in his art. Pound once referred to Vorticism as a "correlated aesthetic,"[8] and it is primarily such a correlating force in his own work.

From the time of Pound's arrival in London in 1908 until the genesis of Vorticism in 1914, Pound had been exploring two radically different modes of writing poetry, one strikingly original, the other frankly and deliberately imitative. The first, of course, was Imagism, the movement often assigned the central place in Pound's development that I am assigning to Vorticism; the second, though not a movement with a name, is expressed in Pound's translations and imitations of other poets and poetry, particularly medieval European and Oriental lyrics. However, there seemed to be no focus, no common ground, to these diffuse activities. The only unifying characteristic of Pound's work was a negative one: most of these early poems strike one as poetic exercises or "warm-ups." In a sense, Pound in these years was rehearsing modes of writing poems rather than really writing them.

The importance of Vorticism for Pound was that it enabled him to continue the work he had begun but to free it from this air of the rehearsal. Pound moves, in other words, from doing preparatory sketches to painting major canvases. Under the aegis of Vorticism, the essence of *his* Imagism and explorations into other literatures emerges, and proves to be the basis for a compatible and rich aesthetic. This subtler Vorticism, combined with notions about form derived from Vorticist art, provided an aesthetic basis for the design of Pound's longer, major poems, including *The Cantos*. The example of the Vorticist artists provided Pound, as we have seen, with a catalyst; their aesthetic also provided coherence.

The history of Imagism is familiar, well-charted territory, and so a brief account of Imagism should suffice.[9] Imagism was a movement hatched virtually overnight by Pound with H. D. and Richard Aldington in the spring of 1912. In March 1913, an article on "Imagisme" by F. S. Flint appeared in *Poetry;* in 1913 Pound put together an anthology, *Des Imagistes,* which was published in

March 1914. Shortly after its appearance, Amy Lowell arrived in London and captured the movement from Pound, publishing anthologies in 1915, 1916, and 1917 entitled *Some Imagist Poets,* in which each contributor chose what would represent his or her own work. At this point, Pound quit the movement in disgust. His Imagism, as he put it, had been transformed into "Amygism," and thereafter he considered Vorticism his primary allegiance.

Pound subsequently presented Imagism as something that had started out well but had gone wrong. According to Pound, it had begun with high standards but those high standards had been diluted. Imagism began primarily as a discipline in poetic method; F. S. Flint recorded its three central tenets:

1. Direct treatment of the "thing," whether subjective or objective
2. To use absolutely no word that did not contribute to the presentation
3. As regarding rhythm: to compose in sequence of the musical phrase, not in sequence of a metronome. [10]

What gave this movement its name, however, was none of these rules, but Pound's insistence that the point of poetry was to present "images." In early 1913 he defined an image as "that which presents an intellectual and emotional complex in an instant of time." [11]

The dilution took place according to Pound when the image came to stand simply for a visual image, not an image in Pound's more abstract sense. He is not the only contemporary observer to have noted this. Conrad Aiken, writing in 1915 about the (post-Pound) Imagists, sounds much like Pound on the "Amygists": "They give us frail pictures—whiffs of windy beaches, marshes, meadows, city streets, dishevelled leaves; pictures pleasant and suggestive enough, but seldom is any of them more than a nice description." [12] A reviewer of *Some Imagist Poets, 1917* made almost the same point in *Poetry* in March 1918: "Unfortunately, imagism has now come to mean almost any kind of poetry written in unrhymed irregular verse, and the 'image'—referred solely to the visual sense—is taken to mean some sort of pictorial impression." [13]

It is difficult to disagree with the perceptions of these contemporary reviewers. Consider, for example, this typical Imagist poem:

I am weary with longing,
I am faint with love;
For upon my head has the moonlight
Fallen
As a sword.[14]

It is obviously not the kind of sensibility that will bring in a great dynasty. But this poem "Nocturne VI," by the justly forgotten Skipwith Cannell, was printed in the original *Des Imagistes* anthology, put together by Pound himself. This example alone (though there are plenty more if we need them) shows that Pound's account of an original pure Imagism destroyed by Amy Lowell cannot be accepted uncritically. Imagism had its weaknesses from the beginning, weaknesses that can be laid to Pound's original theoretical formulation of the tenets of Imagism, not just to the failure of the later Imagists to pay heed to those tenets.

Imagism was a crucial step in the evolution of Pound's aesthetic but it did not and could not provide him with a coherent aesthetic. In the cardinal notions of Imagism, there are poetic principles important and valuable for Pound's thinking. However, in his search for a viable aesthetic, Pound made absolutes out of these principles, which simply cannot stand as absolutes. Nowhere in Pound's Imagism do we find a sense of the limits to his Imagist principles or a recognition of the existence of equally important contradictory principles. In other words, in Imagism, unlike Vorticism, there is no synthesis, no recognition of the play of opposites which alone can produce a coherent aesthetic.

Let me be more specific. Consider what is probably the most important rule of Imagism, that of using "no word that does not contribute to the presentation." This is not simply a matter, as the anecdote about Pound goes, of rewriting a ninety-seven-word poem in fifty-six words.[15] Concision as a criterion forces the writer to look for the primary qualities of his subject, and we have seen that this concern endures in Vorticism. Moreover, Pound insists that transitions be cut as well. It is not absolutely necessary to say what x and y have in common: place them next to each other and the reader will try to find the connection.[16] But this method can be abused by the artist who has no connection in mind (cf. Surrealism) or whose connection is so obscure that the reader will fail to grasp it (cf. much of *The Cantos*). Hence a corollary is required: not any x should be placed next to any y. Moreover, concision cannot stand alone as a criterion. If it does, the poems honoring that criterion will get shorter and shorter. Accordingly, no one ever wrote a long Imagist poem. Concision is not an aesthetic absolute: a poem can be concise only in terms of what it is trying to do, and to consider concision as an absolute is to condemn oneself to trying only small things.

The Imagist insistence on "direct treatment of the 'thing'" is equally incomplete, containing a weakness diagnosed by Wallace Stevens. "Not all objects are equal," notes Stevens in one of his "Adagia." "The vice of imagism was that it did not realize this."[17] To praise only the mode of treating the "thing" without specifying what sort of thing one is to treat is to promote an attitude of indifference to subject matter. Lewis attacked Cubism for holding precisely this attitude, and Pound, I am sure, saw that Lewis's critique, leaving aside its relevance to Cubism, was a devastating critique of Imagism. Imagism's concentration on technical criteria to the exclusion of considerations of subject matter explains why most Imagist poems seem like exercises done according to formulas. To consider only how a thing is done means that one risks having something trivial done very well.

That was the fate of Imagism, which degenerated into a mode of writing viewy descriptive poems, images of something, not images in Pound's more austere sense. Pound repeatedly warned against this chief vice of Imagism, and against the misapprehension that by an image he meant a visual image. Herbert Schneidau has given us the best definition of what Pound actually meant by the image in the period of Imagism: "the Image of the Imagists is an attempt to combine the essentiality of the conceptual image with the definiteness of the perceptual image; this cannot be achieved, at least in poetry, through merely visual means."[18] Schneidau's emphasis on the conceptual aspect of the image is perfectly correct as far as Pound is concerned, but was not understood at the time, nor should we blame those who failed to grasp Pound's intent. Even his Imagist poems are most easily understood as perceptual. Pound was still far too caught up with mastering the discipline of rendering perception to write the poetry with a conceptual as well as perceptual dimension, Pound's aim as Schneidau correctly claims. Take Pound's most famous Imagist poem:

In a Station of the Metro

The apparition of these faces in the crowd;
Petals on a wet, black bough.[19]

It is obviously not simply descriptive: visual impressions are being ordered and transformed. Yet the poem is still wholly a matter of perceptions. Nothing here indicates that Imagism is not a discipline for recording pictorial impressions, even though those impressions may be highly individual. In fact, that only makes matter worse, as Imagism becomes a blank check for any sort of pictorial subjectivism, including the hapless Mr. Cannell's.

Pound's doctrine of the image is thus misstated (or incompletely stated) just as the other tenets of Imagism are misstated. His personal notion of an image may have been more than perceptual, but, as it runs contrary to the accepted meaning of the word, he needed to state it clearly. He needed, in other words, one more limiting principle. To say that a poet's business is to present an image without defining what one means by the term is to invite the sort of perceptual impressionism that Imagism came to represent.

Hence, though in Imagism Pound was setting forth crucial elements of his poetics, his one-sided formulation of those ideas impeded their realization. Given Imagism as a basis, how was Pound to write poetry with concepts as well as percepts? How was he to write a long poem? Or to attempt the major themes that attracted him?[20] Vorticism, which was born in 1914 just as Pound was beginning to see the limitations of Imagism, offered him answers to those questions without forcing him to abandon what was achieved in Imagism. It allowed Pound to recast *his* Imagism and rescue it from the impasse just outlined, by providing the limiting principles missing in Imagism.

The "primary pigment" is clearly such a limiting principle.

Though the assertion that the image is the primary pigment of poetry, as sound is of music and "color in position" is of painting, does not define the nature of the image with any precision, it does make it clear that the image is not simply pictorial. To present an image means to do something that a painter cannot do more easily; the weakness of many Imagist poems can be summarized as a failure to conform to this principle. Thus, Pound's definition of the image becomes somewhat more precise, or at least less susceptible of misinterpretation, as it begins to link up with Vorticism's correlated aesthetic. Pound avoids one possible misinterpretation in the opposite direction when, in the essay "Vorticism," he warns: "The image is not an idea. It is a radiant node or cluster; it is what I can, and must perforce, call a VORTEX, from which, and through which, and into which, ideas are constantly rushing" (*G-B* 92).

Calling the image a vortex helps to reinforce the aesthetic principle involved in the "primary pigment," as an image must have the density or intensity of a vortex. In a note to the same essay, Pound says that "no artist can possibly get a vortex into every poem or picture he does" (*G-B* 94). Pound, I think, meant for the image to stand for the taut presentation of essentials central to Vorticism, but the descriptive connotations of the word stood in his way. Pound's language here reveals how far away he is from an aesthetic of description.

Yet does any of this explanation prevent a Vorticist Skipwith Cannell? The most serious flaw in the Imagist program was the invitation it offered to subjectivism, and defining the image as conceptual rather than perceptual seems merely to second that invitation. How can Pound establish the difference between his poetic of the image and a pictorial poetic of impressions? The polemics of Vorticism play a crucial role in freeing Pound from this dilemma as well. Lewis, as we have already seen, attacked other art movements, the Impressionists, the Cubists, and the Futurists, for their passivity. Art, according to Lewis, is necessarily a subjective response to the world, but that response must be active, forming the world, not formed by it. Defining Vorticism in 1915, he begins by saying: "By Vorticism we mean (a) *Activity* as opposed to the tasteful *Passivity* of Picasso" (*WLOA* 96).

Passivity is exactly the word for what is wrong with the Imagism

Pound wanted to disown, and he readily takes over (though in a modified form) Lewis's polemic against passivity. Pound seeks to define the difference between his Imagism and any simple pictorial impressionism, and presents his definition as the difference between Vorticism and Futurism in the "Vorticism" essay of September 1914.

He sweepingly divides mental activity into two types, a passive receiving of impressions and an active conceiving of reality. Futurism, "accelerated impressionism," exemplifies the first type, while Vorticism, Cubism, Expressionism (by which he means Kandinsky), and Imagism (his, not Amy Lowell's) are grouped together as active and exploratory. The Vorticist in this active investigation finds the analytical form of his material, which is quite distinct from a passive impression of it (G-B 89–90). [21]

French Impressionism is not passive in the way suggested by Lewis and Pound. But the real objects of their polemics are closer at hand, the pictorial impressionism involved in both Futurism and Imagism. Pound's identification on these points with the Vorticist aesthetic is completely justified. Vorticist painting, as I have shown, requires interpretive labor just as Pound's work does, and both seek to arrive at the essence or analytic form of the subject being represented. Their conception of art may not be objective, as objectivity was not their concern, but it is active, explorative, and fundamentally concerned with what is "out there" in the material world.

Years later, in ABC of Reading (1934), Pound criticized the "diluters" of Imagism for thinking "only of the STATIONARY image," [22] and his emphasis on activity clarifies the aesthetic of Imagism in yet another important regard. The primary strategy of the Imagist poem was juxtaposition or parataxis. The poet does not specify the connection between, in Pound's poem, "The apparition of these faces in the crowd" and "Petals on a wet, black bough," or, in Cannell's poem, between the weariness and faintness of the poet and the falling moonlight. The poet places one concise perception next to another without a transition in a way that implicitly creates a connection, but it is up to the reader to fill in the transition and to make the connection explicit. The best Imagist poems had implicitly worked in this manner, but only in his writings

on Vorticist art does Pound explicitly grasp juxtaposition as an
aesthetic principle. If art could give him, in his words, "new eyes"
(*G-B* 85) and make him "see form" (*G-B* 126), then he in turn
could do this to others in his art. By withholding the connections,
by refusing to make everything clear, he would force readers into a
much more active stance, forcing them to define the poem's
statement.

Only when Pound realizes this principle does he realize how he
can write major poems that build upon the basis of Imagism.
Pound's "In a Station of the Metro" and Cannell's "Nocturne"
rely to an equal extent upon an affective, juxtapositional aesthetic.
But the reader who grasps Cannell's juxtaposition does not see anything beyond Cannell's private sensibility. Pound's reader sees
something that—if not objective—has at least an intersubjective
validity. The reader whose perceptions are oriented by Pound's
poem can see something new and interesting in the world outside
of the poem. Of course, two lines cannot effect a profound reorientation on the part of the reader, but the affective aesthetic offers
Pound a criterion by which to define major poetry: a poem's value
is a function of how interesting the work is that the reader must
do to understand it, and how profound a transformation the work
manages to effect in the reader.

Implicit in this position is the aesthetic basis for a long poem. If
one chooses a subject complex enough to require a complex process
of understanding and investigation on the part of the reader, guid-
ing the reader through that process will provide the coherence for
a long poem. With *The Cantos* in mind, one can see the major
problem in this program: what if the reader does not want to work
that hard? But one can also see how this dynamic and openly
affective aesthetic which Pound draws out of Vorticism lies behind
the design of *The Cantos.* It is therefore the necessary contrary or
limiting principle to the Imagist insistence on concision and focus
on technical criteria. For Imagism concision and technique had
been too close to ends in themselves; Pound's literary Vorticism
manages to make them, instead, the means to a long poem that
combines epic amplitude with Imagist concision.

Nothing in Imagism, however, or in Pound's Vorticist recasting
of Imagism, suggests what this long poem is going to be *about.*

Imagism's concentration on poetic method left it curiously indifferent to subject matter, but subject matter would obviously be essential for a long poem. It is therefore not to Imagism but to Pound's explorations of and borrowings from other literatures that we turn to find the sources of the subject, not the method, of Pound's major work. Here, too, Vorticism plays a crucial role in pointing out to Pound what he could do with the past he had explored so thoroughly.

The range of Pound's explorations in other languages and literatures is well known. Intent on being, as Pound later reported Yeats saying, "a portable substitute for the British Museum,"[23] by 1914 Pound had already translated Guido Cavalcanti, Arnaut Daniel, *The Seafarer,* and some Chinese poems from H. A. Giles's *History of Chinese Literature;* written poems using Cino da Pistoia, Bertrans de Born, and others as personae; and in *The Spirit of Romance* composed a full-length study of medieval literature.

Pound's interest in the past troubled his modernist associates. Richard Aldington, as we have already seen, wanted no more of Pound's "provençal feats." Ford Madox Ford was so appalled at the archaisms in Pound's 1911 volume *Canzoni* that he rolled on the floor to express his disdain and displeasure.[24] Wyndham Lewis, looking back on the Vorticist period in 1927, commented that Pound's poetry at this point "was a series of pastiches of old french or old italian poetry, and could lay no claim to participate in the new burst of art in progress. Its novelty consisted largely in the distance it went *back,* not forward; in archaism, not in new creation."[25]

Thus, in the period of Vorticism, though Pound wanted to continue his explorations of the past, he was under a certain amount of pressure—especially from Ford Madox Ford—to abandon these explorations, to be modern. Pound shared the imperative of modernity, as we can see by the terms with which he praised Eliot just after they first met: "He is the only American I know of who has made what I can call adequate preparation for writing. He has actually trained himself *and* modernized himself *on his own.*"[26] But Pound had an intuition that led him to resist direct modernization, an intuition that through a study of other literatures, one could find a way around romantic and Victorian methods of writing poetry. It was through studying the old that one would "make it new."

Pound published some translations of Cavalcanti, for example, in 1912, and Cavalcanti's poetry has a hard, direct clarity with precisely the character Pound sought for his own verse. Eliot subsequently used the first line of Cavalcanti's "Perch'i' no spero di tornar giammai" in the opening of *Ash-Wednesday* (1930), and Eliot's rendering, "Because I do not hope to turn again," reveals what it is about Cavalcanti's verse that interested Pound and (through him) Eliot. But look at Pound's 1912 version of this opening:

> Because no hope is left me, Ballatetta,
> Of return to Tuscany,
> Light-foot go thou some fleet way
> Unto my Lady straightway,
> And out of her courtesy
> Great honour will she do thee.[27]

It brings across none of the qualities that Pound found of interest in Cavalcanti. Note the archaisms, the inversions, and above all the transformation of the direct and active "perche io no spero" into the indirect and passive "Because no hope is left me." It is neither modern nor a good translation, reminding one inevitably of Rossetti's (much better) translations of the early Italian poets, precisely what Pound wanted to move away from. The judgment one must make here is that Pound knew what he wanted from Cavalcanti (and he was right to want it), but he did not know how to get it. The same judgment must be made of Pound's other early versions of other cultures' poetry. He wanted to capture the complex sonority of Provençal poetry, the clarity of Cavalcanti, and the spareness of Chinese poetry, but he did not extract these elements. He merely rendered their atmosphere, and the dominant impression the reader has of these poems is that they are, to use Lewis's word, pastiches.

But, despite Lewis's scorn and Ford's exhortation, the detached modernism of Vorticism did not require a rejection of all past styles, though it rejected the styles of the immediate past. The works of Vorticist art that Pound praised most highly, the sculpture of

Gaudier-Brzeska and Epstein,[28] suggest through their use of the past a solution to Pound's dilemma, one he quickly employed. Juxtapose the old and the new, and they will comment on and illuminate each other. As we have seen, Pound already had begun to use juxtaposition in his poetry, but the Vorticist sculptors taught him to expand his use of that technique dramatically, to juxtapose as they did styles and subjects centuries and continents apart. This temporal and cultural montage, which I have called the ideogrammatic loop, is what allows Pound to reconcile his antiquarian and modern tendencies. It allows him to be a modern poet.

His breakthrough in the use of the ideogrammatic loop is in *Cathay*, his translations of Oriental poetry based on the manuscripts of Ernest Fenollosa, which he began late in 1914 and published in 1915. The date of *Cathay*'s composition helps to explain the breakthrough: 1914 is not only the year of Vorticism and hence the period of Pound's deepest immersion in Vorticist art; it is also, of course, the year in which World War I began. The war impinges directly upon *Cathay*, which is, as Hugh Kenner has pointed out, a response to that war, "among the most durable of all poetic responses to World War I."[29] Pound uses Chinese poems about war, loss, and exile to comment on a present filled with war, loss, and exile. He sent some of these translations to Gaudier-Brzeska in the trenches in France, and his response (and that it is *his* response) was fitting: "The poems depict our situation in a wonderful way" (*G-B* 58).

Gaudier-Brzeska's comment reveals what is different in *Cathay:* Pound has a situation to depict and something to say about it. More is at stake in his investigations than simply an interest in stylistic aspects of Chinese verse. His desire to make the past comment on the present collapses the distance between them; owing to the force of the parallel the air of pastiche vanishes. Hence, though these poems are translations they are also poems by Pound in which he uses Li Po and others as speakers, as personae. In other words, these poems are both translations and original compositions. The mask that the translator takes on is a perfect fit.

The term *personae* is of course Pound's own, the title of an early volume of poems and subsequently the title for his collected short poems. Yet, as a term for capturing Pound's use of the past to

comment on the present, it is too restricted. It focuses our attention on the speaker of the poem, not on the context he brings
with him. Pound's interest in the past grows more complex after
his early poems of 1909 employing personae such as "Cino" and
"Sestina: Altaforte": his interest is not simply in the speakers or
authors of the Chinese poems he translates in *Cathay,* but in the
total situation the poems depict. The two times, the two places,
and the two civilizations are juxtaposed in addition to the two
poets. Pound has moved, in short, from a poetic of the persona to
a poetic of the ideogrammatic loop, though the new poetic does
not abandon the persona, using it instead with the purpose of
making broader, more meaningful juxtapositions.

This new poetic is perhaps easier to see in the *Homage to Sextus
Propertius,* Pound's masterpiece of 1917, than it is in *Cathay,* even
though—or perhaps because—*Propertius* would seem at first glance
to be a return to the more restricted poetic of the persona. After
all, unlike *Cathay,* it has a single speaker, Sextus Propertius, who is
important in the sequence and is well characterized. Pound obviously delights in the character of Propertius, and presenting him to
a modern audience is an important aim of this "Homage." Pound
thus clearly identifies with Propertius and uses him as a persona.
But *uses* is the key word, as Pound is interested in Propertius because (in Pound's account) he stood in essentially the same relation
to his time as Pound stands to his, and because the times they live
in have so many similarities. Both poets are more interested in love
than in war, but live in times full of war and live in the center of
an empire filled with stupidity. It is less the parallel between Pound
and Propertius that interests Pound than the parallel between the
Rome of Propertius and the London and Britain of 1917. Years
later, Pound stated the theme of his *Homage to Sextus Propertius*
in the following way:

> It presents certain emotions as vital to me in 1917, faced with the
> infinite and ineffable imbecility of the British Empire, as they were
> to Propertius some centuries earlier, when faced with the infinite
> and ineffable imbecility of the Roman Empire.[30]

Hence Pound goes to China to write about World War I and to
Rome to write about London. In both cases, the present is seen

and portrayed (critically) in terms of the past. But, as the present is Pound's concern, the accuracy of the juxtaposition is more important to him than the accuracy of the account of the past. Hence Pound's "mistranslations," Propertius's references to "a frigidaire patent" and "devirginated young ladies"—Pound puts his unmistakably modern prints on the poem to ensure that we grasp that it is really about the London of frigidaire patents.[31]

This purpose is precisely what was not grasped, amid the cries of mistranslation, and, because we have never understood Pound's use of the ideogrammatic loop, the reference to the present has seemed like an excrescence, stuck on and not really part of the poem. Pound's next major poem, *Hugh Selwyn Mauberley*, is at least in part a response to this lack of comprehension. Pound later asked himself: "I wonder how far the *Mauberley* is merely a translation of the *Homage to S.P.*, for such as couldn't understand the latter?"[32] Pound's question is rhetorical: *Mauberley* presents the same perceptions as *Propertius* about London, but through the device of a persona alone, without the temporal montage of the ideogrammatic loop.

The greater fame of *Mauberley* should not obscure the fact that, as well as being his farewell to London, it is Pound's farewell to the persona and to poetry without temporal montage. *Propertius*—not *Mauberley*—is the central work in Pound's development because its indirect method of writing about the present leads directly to *The Cantos*, an epic that continually comments on the present in the way *Cathay* and *Propertius* do. It is one long ideogrammatic loop, or rather a complex combination of such loops. The key to reading *The Cantos*, which has been grasped only sporadically and intuitively, is that the poem is always about the present. The past is investigated and represented to shed light on the present, and every canto must be read with an eye to seeing the ideogrammatic loop that Pound has in mind.

The ideogrammatic loop of course is not quite the whole story: there are changes and problems in Pound's use of the past in *The Cantos* which we will discuss. But the ideogrammatic loop is a crucial organizing principle, most obviously in the Early Cantos, and it is a signal instance of Pound's learning from Vorticist art.[33] Pound finds a true equivalent to—not a programmatic imitation of—those Vorticist works of art that are intent upon bringing the past to bear on the present.

The Vorticists, obviously, were not the first artists to investigate and use the past in their art, and a brief summary of where the Vorticist use of the past diverges and where it borrows from other such uses may help to make my discussion more concrete. To begin generally, conceptions of history can be divided into two classes, which one could call syntagmatic and paradigmatic. Syntagmatic conceptions stress historical sequence and causal connections: first this happened, then that happened, and the order is significant. The Vorticist view of history, in contrast, is paradigmatic: history has a shape or pattern or form as well as a linear order, and the significance of history lies in the patterns we find in it, not just in its linear order. Of course the Vorticists' paradigmatic view of history is only one of a long tradition of such conceptions, but it can be distinguished from many others by virtue of its modernism or "presentism."[34] Most paradigmatic conceptions of history either let the categories of the greater pattern-providing past control how we see the present, or sacrifice both past and present to a rigid scheme that determines the categories through which we look at history. Yeats provides convenient examples of both of these views. When in the elegy "In Memory of Major Robert Gregory," he calls Gregory "Our Sidney," Sidney provides a pattern, a predecessor, but the phrase betrays Yeats's awareness that Robert Gregory will seem like Sidney only to "us." Sidney is indisputably the larger figure: the past dominates the present and is introduced to shed its glory on it. Most references to a commonly shared past have this form, as what is shared is the obviously great and the present is seldom felt to measure up.

A little closer to the Vorticist sense of history is the view that history moves in circles, that, as Yeats puts it in another mood:

> Another Troy must rise and set,
> Another lineage feed the crow,
> Another Argo's painted prow
> Drive to a flashier bauble yet.[35]

The poems in *Cathay* do, as Hugh Kenner points out, "say, as so much of Pound's work says, that all this has happened before and continually happens."[36] But the difference is that Yeats, looking forward, feels that history is determined, doomed to move in cycles. The Vorticist stress on repetition or loops in history is more tentative and simply points out that history has repeated, not that it must repeat. Vorticists do not look to the past to predict the future; they look to the past to study and represent the present. The past is a parallel or an equivalent, not an exemplary pattern requiring imitation.

Neither the present nor the future needs imitate the past; it is the artist who should imitate the past (or rather the art of the past). The Vorticist use of the past is less a theory about history than a theory about art and artistic imitation. History may or may not have a pattern, but it is the role of artists to provide history with patterns, to pattern or form it in their art. One does so, primarily, by imitating past art: imitating Chinese poems about war is a way of establishing a parallel between those Chinese wars and the war one is alluding to in the present.

The aim of imitation, therefore, according to Vorticism, is the construction of a parallel or equivalence between the past and the present. This view clashes with the modern sense that imitation produces derivatives that cannot be equivalents. But the Vorticist notion is the traditional one, closer to the notion of imitation found in the Renaissance. Petrarch, for instance, defines proper, creative imitation precisely as a mode of attaining equivalence:

> A proper imitator should take care that what he writes resembles the original without reproducing it. The resemblance should not be that of a portrait to the sitter—in that case the closer the likeness the better—but it should be the resemblance of a son to his father.[37]

The notion of imitation as the creation of a family resemblance implicitly makes Petrarchan (or Humanist) imitation a mode of canon formation: one should imitate one's fathers, the writers who have produced the central texts of one's tradition, and it is by means of imitation that one defines those central texts.[38] This notion sets poetry an awesome task, that of attaining equivalence with the absolutely great, and, although Petrarch's notion remained central for the Renaissance, few have ever lived up to his standards.

The history of the imitation of Petrarch, of Petrarchism, involves far more reproduction than resemblance, far more excessively faithful imitation than attained equivalence.

Petrarch's example of weak or excessively faithful imitation is painting, but a notion of imitation close to his begins to operate in painting in France in the nineteenth century (equivalent to, though not in imitation of, Petrarch's Humanist imitation) in the art of Edouard Manet. Just as Petrarch at his most extreme included lines of Arnaut Daniel, Dante, Cavalcanti, and Cino da Pistoia in a poem, Manet in his paintings of the early 1860s, as Michael Fried has shown, appropriated figures from paintings by Velasquez, Raphael, Watteau, and others, also at least partially with the aim of defining a canon.[39] Like Petrarch, Manet provides the pattern for a new kind of painting, though few subsequent painters attained equivalence with their model as clearly as he did in *Le Déjeuner sur l'Herbe* and *Olympia*.

Imitation in the service of making things new, thus, is an ideal both of Renaissance literature and French modernist painting before it becomes the ideal of Vorticism.[40] The Vorticists, moreover, were aware of and drawing upon these predecessors. Pound may have been contemptuous of Petrarch himself but he knew the Renaissance precedents for his creative translations.[41] The Vorticist artists' fashioning of new art out of old would have been unthinkable without the models of Manet, and in more oblique ways, Cézanne and Gauguin. Vorticism is, in other words, the point at which the notion that imitation can be creative rather than parasitical comes (or comes back) to life in English art and literature.

But it is more than that. If imitation is a matter of family resemblance, for Petrarch and Manet imitation is about the definition of fathers, whereas for Pound and other Vorticists it is a matter of distant and long-lost cousins. Pound defines, not a central and ineluctable tradition, but a deliberately eccentric one. He repeatedly goes to obscure corners of the past to find models for imitation. His Renaissance paradigm is Rimini, not Florence; his Augustan poet is Propertius, not Virgil. The other Vorticists are equally bent upon promoting the obscure: Bakota art, Chinese geomancy, and Easter Island monoliths are not central to our vision of the past. Lewis did illustrate a Shakespeare play, but characteristically he chose *Timon of Athens,* one of Shakespeare's least known plays.

Some of Pound's material, as Hugh Kenner has pointed out, was not so obscure then as it is now: common readers in 1910 could be expected to be conversant with Provençal poetry and the history of the Italian Renaissance; Bertrans and Sigismundo Malatesta were both subjects of popular novels written early in the twentieth century.[42] But in virtually every subject that attracted Pound's attention, he gravitates towards the neglected corners of that subject and presents neglected figures (often correctly) as more interesting and important than those customarily taken as central. His poetry (and criticism) thus is archaeological: he digs into the past in order to change our perception of that past. Pound's great originality was that he combined this archaeological perspective with his poetic of imitation: he changes the shape of the past, as best he can, by means of his innovative and revisionary imitations. Moreover, it worked: much of Pound's material—if not Provençal poetry—is less obscure now than when he wrote, because of the industry of his critics in learning about his interests.[43]

It should be clear by now how incorrect it is to call this use of the past passéism, as Lewis did. I would like to call it presentism instead to point out both that Pound explicitly declares the present as his vantage point and that this declaration of perspective is crucial to his archaeological poetic of imitation. A major theme of modern thought has been that all historians work as Pound did, whether they like it or not: we confer importance on the past as we study it and where we stand in history inevitably affects our view and presentation of it. Pound may not have been the first to realize this fact, but he was the first, I think, to write a poetry of imitation based on his realization. It is also, one might add, much easier to attain equivalence with the past when the past imitated is comparatively obscure. The Vorticists do confer importance on the past they treat by rescuing it from obscurity as much as they reflect or borrow its glory.

The final salient characteristic of the Vorticists' use of the past is that they are perhaps as interested in the political and social context of the art as in the art itself. The difference here is perhaps one of degree, not of kind, but Petrarch and Manet quote the art of the past, whereas Pound quotes the past through its art. The influence of Victorian literature on Pound is relevant here, as works by Browning, Arnold, and Pater (among others) set in the past are really about the present and comment on it in a way that anticipates Pound. The obvious difference is that the temporal montage involved in Vorticism is not found in Victorian literature.

But using the past to comment on the political and social aspects of the present has its dangers. First, the account of the past offered in the work of art may be so slanted to contemporary concerns that its "pastness" becomes simply a polite fiction: who has ever read *Marius the Epicurean* as a portrait of Rome? (*Marius* fails to get out of the present at all, and therefore must be distinguished from the alternation between past and present characteristic of modernism.) Second, commenting on the present can slide into lecturing or even hectoring the present: why do you fit this parallel? Or, why do you not fit it? Pound gradually slides into this attitude; in the 1930s he uses the past to issue directions to the present.

This hectoring, however, should be distinguished from the ideogrammatic loop of Vorticism, whose juxtapositional technique never leads the artist to make an explicit comment on the present. It is up to the audience to complete the loop back to the present. At the earlier stage of Pound's career which concerns us now, the ideogrammatic loop is essential to the evolution of Pound's poetry, not simply because it allows him to build on his earlier "passéism" while rescuing him from the aesthetic impasse that passéism had placed him in. Pound's use of the ideogrammatic loop enables him to pull the various strands of his poetic together because the juxtapositional technique necessary for the ideogrammatic loop is also the basis of Pound's Imagism. That poetic, as should be clear, is an affective one: it is up to the reader to make Pound's juxtapositions meaningful. Moreover, the ideogrammatic loop enables *Pound* to make his juxtapositions meaningful: it provides him with a means of including serious content in his poetry. It shows him what his long poem should be about.

Nevertheless, Vorticism cannot be assigned the utterly dominant role in Pound's evolution that I have assigned it so far. The Vorticist use of the past, as seen in the work of the sculptors Jacob

Epstein and Henri Gaudier-Brzeska, is peripheral to the main thrust of the Vorticist aesthetic. Most Vorticists tried to represent the essence of modernity directly in their art, without any reference to the past through the ideogrammatic loop. For Pound, in contrast, the essence of any situation is a relation: for example, the faces in the crowd are related to petals; Pound in London is related to Sextus Propertius in Rome. Though these relations aim at the same analytic representation that the Vorticist artists wish to attain, Pound's notion that essence is relation establishes a basic difference between Pound's and Lewis's aesthetic. Pound, too, is active and exploratory, not simply passively receiving an aesthetic from Lewis and the other Vorticists.

Another source for Pound's aesthetic thinking reinforced Pound's particular borrowing from the Vorticist sculptors. Pound's famous account of how he wrote "In a Station of the Metro," in the "Vorticism" essay of September 1914, enables us to pinpoint where Pound found support for his view that essence was relational. His account is full of references to Oriental poetry, and he describes the final result, correctly, as "hokku-like" (G-B 89). Chinese and Japanese poetry is concise, juxtapositional, and relational just as Pound would like his poetry to be. One of Pound's greatest merits as a critic is the frankness with which he gives credit to whatever has taught him something. In the years of the Vorticist movement, he correctly gives the most credit to Vorticism (and modern art in general), but in the same period the Orient is another extremely important cultural resource for Pound, second only to Vorticism.[44]

Moreover, as my analysis of Cathay suggests, Pound's Orientalism and his Vorticism are far from incompatible. Pound himself saw the compatibility of the two influences, and in the period of Vorticism he constantly drew parallels between his two sources of inspiration. He compared his own writing to haiku and Nō drama, and Gaudier-Brzeska's sculpture to Chou bronzes (annoying Gaudier-Brzeska in the process).[45] The parallel that he drew most often was to note that both had made him look at things in a new and fresh manner. After making the claim in Gaudier-Brzeska that Vorticist art had made him "see form," he cited as proof the fact that "my eye is ten times as quick to discriminate between fine and mediocre Chinese or Japanese prints or paintings" (G-B 126).

The equation between Vorticism and the Orient is another example of Pound's relational perspective. Unlike Lewis's more single-minded literary Vorticism, Pound's literary Vorticism is to be found in his Orientalism as well. In his study of the Orient, Pound finds a way to be Vorticist; he finds the notions and relational techniques that allow him to construct a genuine equivalent to Vorticist art. Pound's key discovery in this regard was Ernest Fenollosa's theory about the Chinese ideogram—that the ideogram is both visual and relational in nature—and the detail that Pound often cited as proof of this theory was that Gaudier-Brzeska was able to read many Chinese characters at first sight.[46] These two ways of seeing proved wonderfully compatible.[47]

The Pound-Fenollosa relationship, like Imagism, is familiar material, so my treatment of it can, should, and will be brief. But no one has pointed out its direct relationship to Vorticism. The period of Pound's immersion in Fenollosa's manuscripts is exactly the period during which Vorticism flourished. Pound, receiving the manuscripts from Fenollosa's widow in late 1913, began his work on them in 1914, translating Nō plays and the poems that were to make up *Cathay*. He published *Cathay* in 1915, a preliminary selection of Nō texts, *Certain Noble Plays of Japan,* in 1916, a fuller selection with explanatory material, *Noh, or Accomplishment,* in 1917, and finally, in 1918, Fenollosa's essay on *The Chinese Written Character as a Medium for Poetry.*

The part of Fenollosa's own work that had the greatest impact on Pound was his famous (or infamous) essay on the Chinese ideogram. His theory that the Chinese ideogram is a kind of natural pictorial language which is a superior medium for poetry because it avoids the arbitrariness of the linguistic sign is now thoroughly discredited.[48] Only a handful of characters fit his theory, and the average user of Chinese is no more aware of the pictorial content of these ideograms than the average user of English is aware of Greek and Latin etymologies. However, this observation is at least partially beside the point, as his essay is less about the Chinese language as used ordinarily than about how it was (or might have been) created and used poetically.

Fenollosa makes it clear also that it is not simply the pictorial nature of the Chinese characters that interests him. It is that they

are pictures, not of things, but of processes and relations. Pound
called Fenollosa's essay the "big essay on verbs" because of the
stress on process, but verbs alone, in Fenollosa's view, will not
quite do the job:

> But examination shows that a large number of the primitive Chinese
> characters, even the so-called radicals, are shorthand pictures of
> actions or processes. . . .
>   A true noun, an isolated thing, does not exist in nature. Things are
> only the terminal points, or rather the meeting points, of actions,
> cross-sections cut through actions, snapshots. Neither can a pure
> verb, an abstract motion, be possible in nature. The eye sees noun
> and verb as one: things in motion, motion in things, and so the
> Chinese conception tends to represent them.[49]

Nouns, then, think like Cubists and verbs like Futurists, but both
nature and the eye think like Vorticists: they do not separate motion and things but see "things in motion, motion in things."
Fenollosa conceives of the universe as dynamic but formed and
the purpose of language is to try to represent the dynamic form of
the universe. The ideogram is Fenollosa's linguistic ideal because it
is a concrete picture that within the limits of language mimes the
motion of things, giving that motion form in its representation.
The ideogram is thus a kind of diagram that codifies the flux in a
two-dimensional rendition of reality.

   It should be easy to see why Pound would be excited about this
theory of language: it offers him a way to be Vorticist in language.
His initial excitement about the ideogram had, as Schneidau has
pointed out, nothing to do with the "ideogrammic" method of
definition that will concern him in the 1930s.[50] He was excited by
the stress on language as a diagrammatic codification of dynamic
form. In Chinese, at least, language has its equivalent to the dynamic
forms or diagrams of Vorticist painting. But Fenollosa's argument
is not just about Chinese. He discusses Chinese because it is so
much closer than Western languages are to his ideal of poetic language, but he intends the ideal to be valid for the Occident at well.
He refers periodically, in fact, to Western poetry, repeatedly citing
Shakespeare as support for his contentions. Though Fenollosa's
essay stimulated Pound's interest in Chinese, Pound understood

that Fenollosa's focus of attention was on the Western poetry that poets could write in imitation of the ideogram. Poems should work, in short, as ideograms do. They should take up the same exploratory stance towards the world and should have the same kind of reorienting effect on the reader.

Fenollosa, in other words, was not an Orientalist whose ideas allowed Pound to make a synthesis of East and West; Fenollosa had already done the synthesizing. His thinking had a tremendous impact on Pound, because, like Vorticism, it provided Pound with correlations or syntheses of so many things, not just East and West, the aesthetic of painting and literature, but most of all Pound's Orientalism and his modernism.[51] The ideogram, moreover, sharing elements both with Pound's doctrine of the image and the dynamic forms of Vorticist painting, helps to reinforce Pound's perception of a relation between them. In brief. Fenollosa's aesthetics, not his Sinology, are crucial for Pound, and those aesthetics are remarkably consonant with the aesthetics of Vorticism.

But in one important respect Fenollosa differs strongly from Vorticism. The model aesthetic act for Fenollosa is the creation of language. The purpose of art is to create something that, though based on an individual perception, will be valid for others and pass into common currency. We are not far away here from a familiar romantic notion, and indeed Fenollosa's theory that Chinese is a naturally poetic language is a recasting of romantic notions about natural folk poetry in terms of the Orient.[52] Fenollosa's praise of language for being simultaneously mimetic and inventive bears a close resemblance to the anti-Cartesian theories of language of Giambattista Vico, the original theorist of naturally poetic folk language. Joyce used Vico to construct his modernist aesthetic in *Finnegans Wake* just as Pound uses Fenollosa: they both go to theories about the origins of language to justify their own innovations. But the comparison with Joyce's use of Vico exposes one area in which the ideogram does not give Pound an equivalent to Vorticist painting. Vico is as oriented towards particulars as Fenollosa; the unit of linguistic speculation for Vico, like Fenollosa, is the individual word. (And, I might add, his etymologies are about as accurate as Fenollosa's.) But his aesthetic unit is not the individual word but the "epics" of Homer, Moses, and Dante that preserve and allow us to see the linguistic world of the culture in which they wrote. Vico's concern with epics naturally oriented Joyce towards large forms (or rather reinforced his orientation in that direction), but Pound, with an equal orientation towards large forms, had a problem, because his aesthetic was based on one-word units. A poetic of individual words and haiku-like fragments works best for poems of haiku length. Can Pound write the modern epic, or its equivalent, using the ideogram as his aesthetic model? If not, are there any other compatible models he can build on?

Pound wrestled with this problem through *The Cantos,* but in 1914 he thought he had an answer, characteristically one provided by Fenollosa, in the Nō drama of Japan. Fenollosa left incomplete at his death an essay on the Nō and a number of translations of Nō plays. Pound edited this material into a book, *Noh, or Accomplishment,* published in 1917, which for a number of perfectly good reasons has never received the attention the other Pound/Fenollosa collaborations have.[53] Fenollosa's manuscripts were a long way from final form and the state of Western knowledge about the Nō was so sketchy that Pound was almost on his own in putting this material together. As a result, he knew less about the Nō than he did about Chinese poetry though he needed to know more about the dramatic form in order to translate it adequately.[54] Hence, the translations are often jumbled and incomprehensible. They lack the sustained beauty of *Cathay* and often fall into a pastiche of the Anglo-Irish idiom of Synge and Yeats.[55] The major impact these translations had was to inspire the dance-drama of Yeats, and consequently what attention Pound's versions of the Nō have had has come from readers of Yeats, not of Pound.[56]

But in the "Vorticism" essay of 1914, Pound cites the Nō in a note as an example that shows that the Oriental poetic of moments of intense insight can be utilized in works longer than haiku:

> I am often asked whether there can be a long imagiste or vorticist poem. The Japanese who evolved the hokku, evolved also the Noh plays. In the best "Noh" the whole play may consist of one image. I mean it is gathered around one image. Its unity consists in one image, enforced by movement and music. I see nothing against a long vorticist poem. (*G-B* 94)

In this passage Pound is obviously thinking about *The Cantos* (or of the already projected long poem that will become *The Cantos*). But note how he equates his own aesthetic with an Oriental one. He tries to explain his own art (and that of his friends) through a constant resort to Oriental parallels. But he does not call his own art Oriental: the parallel provides examples, not categories, to aid understanding. The categories he advances are his own, with which he then proceeds to categorize the Orient. Nō drama is a useful parallel to Pound's yet unwritten long Vorticist poem, but *The Cantos* will not be a form of Nō drama. Instead, if anything, Nō drama is an example of Vorticist literature.

Only thirty years later will Pound find that the Oriental world view has a still center; otherwise the analogy between Fenollosa's Orientalism and Vorticism is complete. However, though Pound equates the two, his own culture is fundamental. Pound's ideogrammatic loop always returns to the present. By 1914, because of Vorticism, he has put pastiche firmly behind him.

Fig. 1. Wyndham Lewis, *Timon of Athens: Alcibiades,* 1912. Process engraving, whole sheet, 29.5 by 28 cm. Private Collection.

Fig. 2. Henri Gaudier-Brzeska, *Red Stone Dancer,* 1913. Red Mansfield stone,
43 by 23 by 23 cm. Tate Gallery, London.

Fig. 3. David Bomberg, *In the Hold,* 1913–14. Oil on canvas, 198 by 256.5 cm. Tate Gallery, London.

Fig. 4. David Bomberg, *The Mud Bath,* 1914. Oil on canvas, 152.5 by 224 cm.
Tate Gallery, London.

Fig. 5. Jacob Epstein, *Rock Drill*, 1913–15. Plaster and ready-made drill. Now dismantled.

Fig. 6. Wyndham Lewis, *The Crowd*, 1914–15. Oil on canvas, 200.5 by 153.5 cm. Tate Gallery, London.

Fig. 7. Wyndham Lewis, *New York,* 1914. Ink and watercolor, 31 by 26 cm.
Private Collection.

Fig. 8. Wyndham Lewis, *Workshop*, 1914–15. Oil on canvas, 76.5 by 61 cm.
Tate Gallery, London.

Fig. 9. Jacob Epstein, *Torso in Metal from the "Rock Drill,"* 1913–16.
Bronze, 70.5 by 58.5 by 44.5 cm. Tate Gallery, London.

Fig. 10. Henri Gaudier-Brzeska, *Bust of Ezra Pound* (also known as *Hieratic Head*), 1914. Marble, 92 by 45 cm. Private Collection.

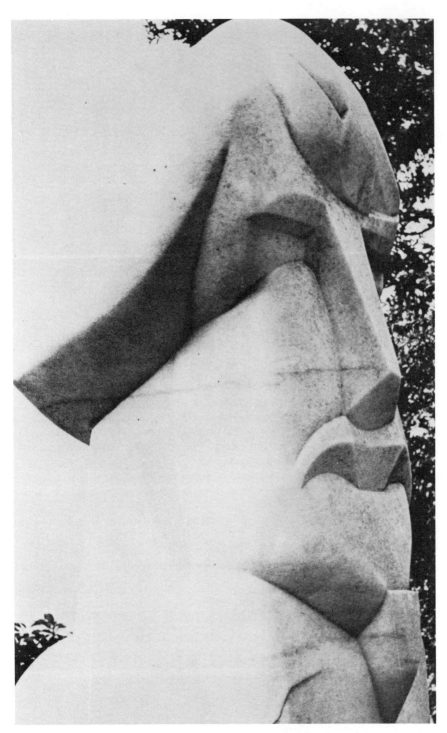

Fig. 11. Henri Gaudier-Brzeska, *Bust of Ezra Pound* (side view).

125

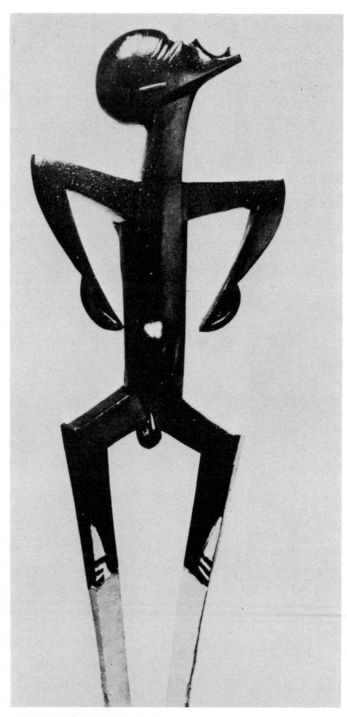

Fig. 12. Jacob Epstein, *Cursed Be the Day Wherein I Was Born,* ca. 1913–15. Painted plaster, height 115.5 cm. Lost.

4   Lewis's *Enemy of the Stars* and Modernism's Attack on Narrative

To discuss Pound's literary Vorticism is, as we have seen, to trace and weigh a multitude of influences, and the influence of Lewis was only one of a number of potent influences on Pound in these years. In contrast, Lewis the writer, just like Lewis the painter, never sympathetically accepted influences of any kind. Other writers, like other painters, were above all to be reacted against. Lewis, in his second autobiography, *Rude Assignment* (1950), recollected that in the period of Vorticism it was Pound in particular whom Lewis was reacting against:

> At this distance it is difficult to believe, but I thought of the inclusion of poems by Pound etc. in "Blast" as compromising. I wanted a battering ram that was all of one metal. A good deal of what got in seemed to me soft and highly impure. . . . My literary contemporaries I looked upon as too bookish and not keeping pace with the visual revolution. A kind of play, "The Enemy of the Stars" (greatly changed later and published in book form) was my attempt to show them the way.[1]

Enemy of the Stars was Lewis's literary contribution to *Blast* #1, and as the most extensive work of literature published in *Blast* and as Lewis's first major literary publication, it stands out as Lewis's central attempt during the Vorticist movement to be Vorticist in literature. As he later recalled, poets such as Pound struck him as simply not doing the job, so Lewis had to show them how things ought to be done. Lewis's programmatic invention of a literary Vorticism, *Enemy of the Stars,* demands attention and, I would like to argue, ultimately repays such attention. But, perhaps because of its origins as a polemical demonstration, it is a peculiar, almost unreadable work. Nevertheless, it has had—as I should like to demonstrate in this chapter—a large (if previously undiscovered) impact on other writers. Moreover, its difficult style has been responsible for this influence.

Thus, to understand this influence, we need first of all to examine the peculiar style of *Enemy of the Stars* and then to understand what motivated these peculiarities. The play contains passages of straightforward dialogue and narration, but it also contains sentences that are unprecedented in the extent to which and the manner in which they evade any specification of the temporal relations that exist among the various parts of the sentence. Conjugated verbs are as sparse as possible, punctuation is used to conceal syntactical relations as well as to establish them, and subordinating conjunctions are suppressed almost completely. In short, these are odd sentences indeed, and we need to examine the details of these sentences carefully before we can see what Lewis was up to in writing them.

Lewis's reinvention (or destruction) of English grammar produces a large number of sentences that are ungrammatical. Many are simply clusters of phrases: "Bastard violence of his half-disciple, métis of an apache of the icy steppe, sleek citizen, and his own dumbfounding soul" (*CPP* 100). The second phrase attaches itself to the first as a description of his "half-discipline" because of the semantic echo of half by métis, but otherwise we are given no clues about how to connect these phrases. Other sentences contain verbs, but contain only infinitives or participles, neither of which allows the reader to resolve the puzzling syntax. The sentence that in the play follows the one just quoted exemplifies this: "Fungi of sullen violent thoughts, investing primitive vegetation." If one could replace the comma with "are," the sentence would be a grammatically straightforward—if rather obscure—simple sentence. But the presence of the comma prevents us from assuming that an "are" might be understood and forces us to read "investing" as the present participle of a separate participial phrase. The sentence is therefore a verbless assemblage of two ambiguously related phrases.

Lewis often uses commas in this curious fashion: "His criminal instinct of intemperate bilious heart, put at service of unknown Humanity, our King, to express its violent royal aversion to Protagonist, status-mirage of Liberty in the great desert" (*CPP* 96). "Put" at first would seem to be the verb of the sentence, but once again the comma immediately preceding it clearly marks it as a (past) participle. The sentence therefore has no verb and also breaks apart into a cluster of phrases. "Our King" and the final phrase seem to be in apposition to "Humanity" and "Protagonist," though semantically it is unclear how they could be in apposition.

The colon is a particularly favored form of punctuation in *Enemy of the Stars,* and it is also used to obscure relations, not to point to them:

> Harsh bayadère-shepherdess of Pamir, with her Chinese beauty: living on from month to month in utmost tent with wastrel, lean as mandrake root, red and precocious: with heavy black odour of vast Manchurian garden-deserts, and the disreputable muddy gold squandered by the unknown sun of the Amur. (*CPP* 101)

Even when Lewis writes a sentence with an apparent subject and verb, he is likely to surround these with a flood of phrases that stand in an uncertain relation to them: "Throats iron eternities, drinking heavy radiance, limbs towers of blatant light, the stars poised, immensely distant, with their metal sides, pantheistic machines" (*CPP* 100). This sentence, like the others we have looked at, is most easily read simply as a series of seven phrases, linked in series by commas. One can construe the third phrase and, I suppose, the first as in apposition to the stars. The second phrase then attaches itself to one of these two as a description of the stars, and the fifth and sixth modify the subject. The sentence, thus, can be marshaled into a syntactic order (of a kind), but only by dint of considerable attention. Moreover, this resolution assumes that "poised" is a conjugated verb in the past tense; once again, "poised" is more satisfactorily read as a past participle, making the sentence also verbless.

In order to understand why Lewis would write in this way, one should return to his retrospective critique of Pound already quoted from *Rude Assignment.* Lewis saw his literary contemporaries as "not keeping pace with the visual revolution." In Lewis's account, the center of that revolution was its rejection of mimesis and the mimetic theory of art. Whether or not painting continued to be representational (as Vorticist painting did), it would no longer faithfully reproduce appearances; it would no longer aspire towards the condition of photography.[2] Lewis, I think, deliberately set out while writing *Enemy of the Stars* to identify the feature of writing that was equivalent to representation in painting. Ignoring the obvious choice of reference which the *transition* group years later would repudiate in an analogous attempt to bring literature "up-to-date," Lewis seems to have decided that the sequentiality or temporality of literature was the central aspect of traditional literature and therefore was outmoded and ought to be done away with. Therefore, as fully grammatical sentences with conjugated verbs unavoidably involve temporal reference, Lewis moved in *Enemy of the Stars* towards a new type of sentence (or perhaps non-sentence) in which the basic unit is the phrase, not the sentence. Though Lewis does gather these phrases together into sentences, he does not join them together by any of the syntactic devices that produce an intelligible or grammatical order. The readers must perform the task, if they wish to put these phrases in some kind of order. In other words, readers must puzzle over these sentences as beholders must puzzle over Vorticist paintings (if they wish to read them as representations), and just enough semantic, syntactic, and punctuative clues are present that they can "resolve" these sentences, determine their relation to the world, and make them fit into a coherent narrative sequence.

But Lewis was a much less thorough revolutionary than I have made him seem so far, as not all of *Enemy of the Stars* is written in this style. As the following passage shows, Vorticist sentences are surrounded by passages of quite straightforward narration:

> Arghol crosses yard to banks of the canal: sits down.
> "Arghol!"
> "I am here."
> His voice raucous and disfigured with a catarrh of lies in the fetid bankrupt atmosphere of life's swamp: clear and spendid among Truth's balsamic hills, shepherding his agile thought.
> "Arghol!"
> It was like a child's voice hunting its mother. (*CPP* 99)

The contrast between the plain style and the virtuoso style we have been examining makes the Vorticist sentences seem even more mannered and showy, more like objects put in a window to catch our eye than functional parts of an artistic whole. The net effect of this contrast is to let us know that the Vorticist style is not Lewis's natural style, but something deliberately constructed for the occasion. This contrast is one more sign that Lewis's style stems above all from a programmatic necessity, from his own desire to be in the artistic vanguard.

Therefore Lewis as a writer is firmly in the camp of Futurism or programmatic modernism. Innovating simply to be modern, he imports a revolution in one art into another without concern for the validity of that importation. Yet the stylistic direction that Lewis would take literature is diametrically opposed to Futurism. Futurism celebrates movement above all, and Lewis's new prose style cannot move at all. A sentence that is a series of ambiguously connected phrases is static and immobile; though Lewis criticized what he saw as the deadness and immobility of Cubist painting, his Vorticist prose has those very same attributes.[3] In his attempt to avoid specifying temporal relations, he has suppressed not only the ways in which sentences represent motion or change, but also the way in which they move, from one topic to another or from one aspect of a topic to another.

One would not want to call this style "Cubist," as I think it most unlikely that Lewis was trying to duplicate the effect of Cubist painting in words. Despite Lewis's unkind remarks about Pound's poetry in this period, one could call it Imagist or at least imagistic. Like the weaker products of Imagism, the showcase sentences of *Enemy of the Stars* break down into a series of static images, though the kind of image Lewis presents is more akin to Surrealist than to Imagist poetry: "A canal at one side, the night pouring into it like blood from a butcher's pail" (*CPP* 98). This image—though quite startling—is utterly static in the sense that nothing leads up to it, and it in turn leads up to nothing else. It could occur at any moment in *Enemy of the Stars* without ever seeming out of place or really in place, and the "showcase sentences" of *Enemy of the Stars* are a chain of such self-contained images, the presence and order of which seem utterly arbitrary.

Consequently Lewis can use the Vorticist style only intermittently, as it cannot be used to introduce any new topics.[4] Only when the reader understands what Lewis's subject is can he follow Lewis's treatment of it. If one isolates a "blast" from the *Blast* manifestoes, for example, one often finds the same kind of sentence structure:

Quack ENGLISH drug for stupidity and sleepiness.
Arch enemy of REAL, conventionalizing like
                gunshot, freezing supple
                REAL in ferocious chemistry
                of laughter.   (*Bl* #1, 17)

The graphic design here supplies emphasis and makes grammatical syntax seem less crucial, but reading it still poses some of the same problems encountered in *Enemy of the Stars.* It appeared in *Blast,* however, with a title: "BLAST HUMOR." With the title serving as a clue both to subject matter and to the attitude taken towards that subject matter, it now works as a stunning description of the effect of humor.

The title, therefore, provides the clue that allows the reader to coordinate these phrases into a meaningful whole. We have seen titles work in this way before, in Vorticist paintings such as Lewis's *The Crowd* and David Bomberg's *In the Hold,* and in poems by Pound. Despite an enormous and readily apparent difference in sensibility, Lewis is working here on principles close to those operative in, for example, "In a Station of the Metro." Unlike Pound, Lewis is not concerned with seizing a moment, but both writers condense their statements to the point of ungrammaticality, both count upon graphic design to indicate some of the connections that syntax would ordinarily indicate, and both depend, finally, in a characteristically Vorticist fashion, upon the reader to do the work necessary to render their statements intelligible.

But to note this comparison is to note the greater audacity of Lewis. By 1914 Pound had employed "this hard, telegraphic sort of writing," as Richard Aldington called it in a review of *Blast,* only in tiny fragments;[5] Lewis, in contrast, employs it in a narrative of considerable length. For the word *audacity,* we might wish to substitute words such as "perversity" or "obstinacy," for the basic thrust of his style is to block the sense of duration absolutely essential to narration. In this way Lewis manages to create quite a problem for himself: how does one write a narrative in a style incapable of narration? Lewis's solution is to narrate around his Vorticist style. Sections of flat, non-Vorticist prose advance the narrative a little, and then Lewis switches into a Vorticist set piece during which the narrative comes to a dead halt. Then, the pyro-technics over, the narrative progresses once again. The alternation between the glittering Vorticist prose and the remnants of narration that surround that prose is both bizarre and unsettling, as there is no functional relationship between the two elements. The show-case sentences make the narrative intermittent and extraneous, whereas the simple declarative sentences that advance the narrative make the Vorticist sentences look a little ridiculous. Each com-ponent makes the other look unnecessary and perverse.

But it is the very perversity manifested in *Enemy of the Stars* that makes it repay attention so richly. Lewis had a superb gift for narrative, as he had already shown in the posthumously published *Mrs. Dukes' Millions* (written ca. 1908–10) and in his sketches which would later be collected in revised form in *The Wild Body*. Nor had he lost the gift, as later novels would show. But *Enemy of the Stars* shows him deliberately refusing to employ this gift. It is a terrible botch of a narrative, because the narrative is deliberately botched. That deliberateness or willfulness is the source of the fascination of *Enemy of the Stars*.

Lewis subsequently revised the play, publishing it in book form in 1932, and a comparison of the two versions is revealing. Though only a few substantive additions were made, the revised version is considerably longer (48 pages versus 25 in the recent *Collected Poems and Plays*), and Lewis extensively revised the "showcase sentences." He added conjugated verbs and relational indicators, introduced unambiguous subjects and verbs, and removed enough of the contrapuntal punctuation so that these sentences are no longer a frozen constellation of images. The sentence quoted above ("Throats iron eternities, drinking heavy radiance, limbs towers of blatant light, the stars poised, immensely distant, with their metal sides, pantheistic machines") becomes in the 1932 revision:

> Throats iron eternities (drinking heavy radiance)—limbs towers of blatant light—the stars poise, stupendously remote. Metal-sided, meteoritic, they are the pantheistic machines fashioned by the astronomer. (*CPP* 148)

What forms one sentence in 1914 is divided in the later version into two sentences. Each sentence has an obvious subject and verb, and these stand in an obvious relation to each other. The first three phrases, linked by nonrelational commas in the first version, are now ordered through parentheses and dashes. Though the referential meaning of these phrases remains quite obscure, their syntactic role is clear enough that the reader can put these phrases to one side.

This example is representative and shows that with the 1932 revision it is possible to discern what it was that Lewis was trying to say in 1914. The later version provides a guide to the Vorticist text in much the same way that preparatory sketches for Vorticist paintings help immeasurably in identifying the representational content of those paintings. This analogy is not exact, of course, because the condensed, "abstract" text is prior; the later version, in fact, was produced by revising a copy of the printed text of the 1914 version.[6] But there is some evidence that a "preparatory" text existed. A note accompanying the 1932 edition tells us:

> This version of *Enemy of the Stars* differs in detail from that to be found in *Blast No. 1*. There were several versions—the author has restored passages removed from, or not used in, the *Blast* version, and has added new ones. In other respects it is substantially the same. (*CPP* 221)

This note suggests that an ur-*Enemy of the Stars* existed from which the *Blast* version was condensed. How close the 1932 version is to this ur-text is unclear, as the ur-text has not survived, but the 1914 version does often read like a condensation of a more readable prior text. We can assume, I think, that though this hypothetical ur-text would not have had some of the thematic complexities Lewis injected into the 1932 version, it would have shared its greater degree of syntactic regularity.[7]

The 1932 text thus reveals that Lewis deliberately disfigured the narrative in 1914. He had a coherent, legible narrative in mind but rewrote the play suppressing the elements that would have allowed a reader to follow that narrative readily. Only in 1932 did Lewis make available the parallel text that enabled readers to make sense of *Enemy of the Stars,* but by then no one was particularly interested.

However, to focus one's discussion of *Enemy of the Stars* on the sense that it makes is to miss Lewis's point altogether. The real significance of the play is as a gesture. Lewis wanted to start a revolution in literature that would be equivalent to the modernist revolution in painting, and he conceived of *Enemy of the Stars* as a gesture that would show writers the path and get them moving along it.

In one respect, the gesture was far from successful. He wanted his Vorticist prose to be the equivalent of his painting; its narration was designed to be problematic in the same way that the representational aspect of Vorticist painting was problematic. However, this analogy is not particularly profound; nor, judging from the result, was it particularly fruitful. Lewis's initial attempt at Vorticist literature, one must conclude, was not much more successful than Pound's: *Enemy of the Stars* is Lewis's "The Game of Chess."[8] Both resemble Vorticist painting in too superficial a manner, imitative of—not equivalent to—the art.

However, the gesture of *Enemy of the Stars* may not have been as empty as I have just implied. For the central stylistic innovation of *Enemy of the Stars* was to replace the sentence with the phrase as the central unit of meaning; and the style of *Enemy of the Stars*, with its paratactic concatenation of phrases, anticipated the subsequent stylistic direction of Pound, Eliot, and Joyce, all of whom also replace the sentence with the phrase as their basic building block. Thus, in its assault on the conventional sentence, despite the fuzzy thinking and programmatic extremism that inspired it, *Enemy of the Stars* announces a central theme of modernist literature.

Lewis himself sensed that *Enemy of the Stars* had helped inaugurate a line of development that he had not pursued. Consequently he made claims about its influence even though he derided the work itself. According to Lewis, *Enemy of the Stars* "was responsible for the manner here and there" of Joyce's *Ulysses*, particularly the "Circe" episode.[9] As Joyce owned a copy of *Blast*, he could have read *Enemy of the Stars* in time for it to have influenced *Ulysses*, but I see no signs of such influence. Lewis's claim, moreover, obscures the real relation of *Enemy of the Stars* to *The Cantos*, *The Waste Land*, and *Finnegans Wake*, which is that each of these works, like *Enemy of the Stars,* moves towards a style in which the phrase, not the sentence, is the fundamental unit of meaning.

The manner in which the phrase, not the sentence, is the fundamental unit of meaning in *The Cantos* and *The Waste Land* should be obvious. Parataxis or juxtaposition is the outstanding feature of Pound's and Eliot's poetic syntax. There are, of course, fully grammatical sentences in these works; but syntactic continuity always breaks down, giving way to montage or juxtaposition. The poems of Eliot and Pound, as they themselves tell us, are collocations of shored fragments, and what relation the shored fragments have to one another is a matter of inference, not something established by syntactic connectives.

Finnegans Wake is less obviously an assemblage of phrases. It is in prose, after all—one sentence follows another, divided by periods—if a very odd sort of prose. But syntactic continuity and coherence are under attack in *Finnegans Wake* in a manner that has some parallels with the work of Pound and Eliot. In the early drafts of *Finnegans Wake,* both those published as *Work in Progress* and the still earlier drafts subsequently published as *A First-Draft Version of Finnegans Wake,* the language used is essentially normal English, both in syntax and semantics.[10] But as these passages underwent anywhere up to seventeen revisions, the text grew ever more elaborate. The process of elaboration was twofold: each sentence became more complex syntactically and more dense semantically. The end result of these revisions is that the unit of meaning in *Finnegans Wake* becomes the phrase, or even the individual word, because the meaning of the parts of these endlessly elaborated sentences has nothing to do with the syntactic structure in which they are embedded. The sentences break of their own weight, and syntax no longer sets anything in an intelligible relation to anything else. By eschewing parataxis, Joyce avoids the problems in continuity and transition that plague a paratactic style, but his sentences in *Finnegans Wake* are collocations of shored fragments with as little continuity as any comparable section of *The Waste Land* or *The Cantos.*

Thus Lewis's shift from a style based upon sentences to one based on phrases is the beginning of a pronounced trend in modernist literature. But this observation only raises a new question in turn: what are the attractions of such a style? Why move away from the sentence and from the coherence provided by syntax in this way? Lewis wanted to move away from the sentence, in essence, because he wanted to move away from narration. Because grammatical sentences necessarily involve temporal reference, they are the building blocks of narrative. They place and order events in time, and this temporal sequence enables the larger temporal sequence we call narrative to take shape. The phrase, in contrast, is a non-narrative unit because it avoids any such temporal reference, and a style built up of phrases avoids or prevents any such temporal sequence from taking shape. Lewis's style, built up of phrases, hindered the emergence of a coherent narrative in *Enemy of the Stars;* what we now need to grasp is that this was the whole point. Modernist painting had reacted strongly against the tradition of narrative painting and if literature was to aspire towards the condition of painting, Lewis in 1914 thought that it, too, was going to have to move away from narration.

A number of different points need to be made about the impact of Lewis's 1914 assault on the canons of narration. The first is that in his later work Lewis abandons the ideal of a non-narrative literature towards which he was groping in *Enemy of the Stars.* Either because he diagnosed the strain of programmatic modernism in his play, or because he saw rightly that his gifts ran in another direction, the main line of Lewis's development is away from the antinarrative modernism of *Enemy of the Stars,* though *The Childermass* (1928) is a conspicuous exception to this generalization. The evolution is not simply an antimodernist return to traditional novelistic procedures, as Lewis and some of his critics have claimed.[11] As we shall see in the next chapter, he continued to attack the temporal suppositions of narrative from ever more subtle and sophisticated positions that allowed him, at the same time, to make use of his tremendous gift for narrative. But he moved away from the frontal asault on narration found in *Enemy of the Stars,* and consequently (as we shall discuss in more detail later) he presented his 1914 experiments as a programmatic dead end. For him they were, but we should not let his account obscure the fact that for others they were not a dead end.

My second point is that just as the later works of Pound, Eliot, and Joyce follow Lewis in his shift towards a style based on the phrase, so too do they follow him in his shift away from narrative. The discontinuities we have already traced in *The Waste Land, The Cantos,* and *Finnegans Wake* are discontinuities in narration as well as in syntax. Just as syntactic continuity always breaks down, so too does narrative continuity, and these are really aspects of the same thing. *The Cantos* is the longest poem ever written, I suspect, with no "story" or plot line, and though *The Waste Land* is not nearly so long, it even more spectacularly possesses no narrative coherence, no story line that unites the fragments of Eliot's poem.

It is much less obvious that *Finnegans Wake* represents an attack on narration, just as its attack on the sentence is less obvious. An abiding impulse of criticism of *Finnegans Wake* has been to reassert narrative coherence, to provide a synopsis or "skeleton key" that would establish the narrative thread of the text. Moreover, the early drafts of *Finnegans Wake* which are in fairly ordinary language often offer just such a skeleton key, as a narrative is far more obviously present in these drafts. One can read *Finnegans Wake* through these earlier drafts, and if one does so, one can find the narrative thread that dominates the earlier drafts in the final version as well.

The existence of these parallel, less problematic texts should remind us of *Enemy of the Stars.* In both cases, one can read the difficult text through the easier and in both cases the later version is much longer, as it elaborates or fleshes out the original. But in *Finnegans Wake* the additions swamp the narrative thread; narrative clarity progressively disappears as the text grows ever more elaborate. As the sentences of *Finnegans Wake* no longer hold their elements in an intelligible relation, any sense of narrative in *Finnegans Wake* disappears.

This view of Joyce's arcane masterpiece is not without challengers. There are those who still call it a novel and speak confidently about plot and characters.[12] These critics insist that the skeletal narrative of the early drafts (or that which they uncover themselves) is the key to unlocking the whole, that underneath the polysemous and chaotic suface is a thread of narrative continuity that is crucial. Obviously, I cannot argue the matter here, but I would like to suggest that the path to understanding Joyce's last work is to follow—not to try to reverse—the direction of Joyce's revisions. That direction is similar to the direction of the revisions of *The Waste Land* and the evolution of *The Cantos:* it is away from linearity, away from the ready coherence provided by a single line of narrative development, and away from the ready coherence provided by English syntax.

But one cannot describe these innovative works simply in terms of what they dispense with, just as one cannot innovate in any serious sense simply by dispensing with things. This is one of the lessons taught by *Enemy of the Stars.* Lewis wanted to move away from narrative but he had no idea what to move *towards.* In a sense what their reading of *Enemy of the Stars* probably told Pound, Eliot, and Joyce was that Lewis had not been radical enough. His onslaught was against the means of narration, not against the notion that literature narrates. Lewis simply disrupted the narrative that he had in mind, without allowing anything else to take its place. The later works of Pound, Eliot, and Joyce are far more successful than *Enemy of the Stars* in their move away from narrative because they move towards something else as well. They see that they must create a new source and sense of coherence to replace the old narrative sense of coherence they are discarding.

It is therefore not to *Enemy of the Stars* that they turn for what they use to create that new sense of coherence. From *Enemy of the Stars,* they take only the project of replacing narrative. But Vorticism does not only contribute Lewis's imperative of non-narrative modernism. For other aspects of the Vorticist aesthetic play an essential role in the complex development of an alternative to narrative coherence.

Not many critics have tried to define what takes the place of narrative in providing coherence in modernist literature, partly, as the criticism of *Finnegans Wake* shows, because we have tended to bring our old reading habits to bear on these works, and partly, I expect, because the question is so daunting. The one critic who has seen the turn away from narration as central to modernist literature and who has spelled out his notion of what it was moving towards is Joseph Frank, with his notion of spatial form, defined long ago in his 1945 article "Spatial Form in Modern Literature" and eloquently defended and restated more recently in *Critical Inquiry*.[13] Frank would agree with what I have said so far, that the narrative sequence of the text in modernist works is disrupted as part of an attempt to create an alternative to what he might call the "temporal form" of narrative. Frank's argument, put briefly, is that the time-logic of conventional narrative, in which the order of the text by and large conforms to a sequence of events referred to in the text, is replaced in the works of Eliot, Pound, Joyce, Proust, and others by a space-logic, in which, to quote Frank's most succinct formulation:

> syntactical sequence is given up for a structure depending on the perception of relationships between disconnected word-groups. To be properly understood, these word-groups must be juxtaposed with one another and perceived simultaneously. Only when this is done can they be adequately grasped; for, while they follow one another in time, their meaning does not depend upon this temporal relationship.[14]

This space-logic is directly opposed to the sequential time-logic of narrative: "Past and present are apprehended spatially, locked in a timeless unity that, while it may accentuate surface differences, eliminates any feeling of sequence by the very act of juxtaposition."[15] Frank here links the time-logic of narrative or temporal form to historical consciousness and spatial form to an ahistorical and atemporal consciousness. He concludes his essay by describing what has happened in modern literature as the transformation of "the time world of history into the timeless world of myth."[16]

In contrast, Wyndham Lewis in *Time and Western Man* claimed that much the same group of writers was obsessed by time. He presented Joyce, Pound, Proust, and Stein, in particular, as exemplars of a larger time-mind that permeated modern literature and culture. Eliot, Joyce, and Pound cannot logically be both exemplars of a time-mind and fervent opponents of a time-logic, and Frank and Lewis are really pointing to the same phenomenon, though calling it by different names. Lewis's fellow modernists were obsessed by time, and in fact the best evidence for Lewis's polemic—*Finnegans Wake, The Cantos, A Vision,* and *Four Quartets*—had barely begun to appear by the date of *Time and Western Man* (1927). The form this obsession took was an attack on the sequential time-logic Frank correctly presents as the basis of narrative. As I have already argued, the central works of modernist literature in English break with linear continuity on the syntactic plane as a way to break with linear continuity—Frank's sequential time-logic—on a narrative plane.

Frank and I therefore seek to explain precisely the same phenomenon, and our discussions have certain key landmarks in common, Worringer, T. E. Hulme, and modernist painting. It would therefore be both easy and persuasive to argue simply that Frank's argument has a missing middle which I supply. The initial attempts at literary Vorticism that I have been discussing could easily be presented as the first instances of spatial form. Vorticism is, after all, the means by which Worringer's ideas and the influence of modernist painting enter English literature. Frank notes a difference between Eliot's first major poem, "The Love Song of J. Alfred Prufrock" (written ca. 1910-11 and published in 1915) and *The Waste Land* (1922) and between *Mauberley* and *The Cantos* in that the earlier works of both Eliot and Pound still depend upon at least a semblance of narrative continuity. Arguably, the difference is attributable to the impact of Lewis and his attack on narrative. Thus, Frank and I might find common ground in arguing that narrative is replaced in modernist works by spatial form as the source of coherence, and it is literary Vorticism that is responsible for the articulation of spatial form in literature in English.

Nevertheless, despite the convergence of our perspectives, I think that Frank's account stands in need of amendment. Frank's view is close to Lewis's in 1914 in that neither makes a distinction between sequence and narrative sequence. In Frank's view, spatial form replaces narration as a source of coherence in modernist works by removing sequence itself as a source of coherence. Readers of these works, according to Frank, must fight their customary assumption that the order of the text has a meaning or function. Though the "word-groups" of *The Waste Land,* for instance, "follow one another in time, their meaning does not depend upon this temporal relationship. . . . Modern poetry asks its readers to suspend the process of individual reference temporarily until the entire pattern of internal references can be apprehended as a unit."[17] Hence, in contrast to narrative works in which sequence is meaningful, in modernist works utilizing spatial form, only a pattern of reference is meaningful, a pattern quite divorced from the sequence of the text.

Frank's notion that sequence is meaningless in modernism is an astonishing misunderstanding. The order of a modernist text is not referentially directed, but affectively directed: modern poetry asks its readers to understand that "word-groups" follow one another in the text because they stand in a meaningful relationship, not because they follow one another in historical time. When, to use Frank's example of *The Waste Land,* the line "These fragments I have shored against my ruins" is followed by "Why then Ile fit you. Hieronymo's mad againe," the reader who recognizes the allusion to *The Spanish Tragedy* does not wait until the end of the poem to start making sense of the juxtaposition. Remembering that Hieronymo's play in *The Spanish Tragedy* is a mishmash of languages that no one in the audience understands, the reader makes a connection between that play-within-a-play and this poem, also composed of fragments of various languages that bewilder the audience. One might also want to push the connection and see the two lines as an oblique reference to Eliot's own mental breakdown prior to composing *The Waste Land.* That interpretation would probably depend upon one's critical allegiances and does not affect my point here, which is that the sequence of *The Waste Land* is very different from a narrative sequence, but sequence remains an important clue to significance. One would simply not connect Eliot's and Hieronymo's fragments if the line from *The Spanish Tragedy* were moved fifty or even ten lines.

Pound, to provide another example, begins Canto 31, the first of a number of cantos concerning Thomas Jefferson, with Sigismundo Malatesta's Latin motto, *tempus loquendi, tempus tacendi.* We should immediately make sense of the juxtaposition (after all, waiting for the end of the poem is, in several senses, a physical impossibility); for Pound, Thomas Jefferson is another Sigismundo Malatesta, and he stands in much the same relation to his time that Malatesta does to his. Both, in fact, exemplify the type of the Great Ruler. This statement may seem like a great deal to grasp in two lines, so let me put it more precisely. The juxtaposition should establish a working hypothesis in the reader's mind that Jefferson is a Malatesta figure and the cantos that follow should confirm it.

These examples from *The Waste Land* and *The Cantos* show, I think, two things. First, they show that modernist literature does not, as Frank supposes, cancel or suspend the order of its texts. Far from being irrelevant to the meaning, the order or sequence establishes meaning, and it does so by juxtaposing heterogeneous items in a way that forces the reader to see a connection between them. This juxtapositional technique is, of course, characteristic of Pound's Imagism, but something new has come into play, for the material juxtaposed is far more heterogeneous—comprising material from different times, cultures, and languages—than anything juxtaposed in Imagism. Part of what is behind this development is the historical juxtaposition Pound learned from the Vorticist sculptors and used first in *Cathay*. However, in those earlier poems, the time of the poem's setting was merely juxtaposed with our own; later, Pound and Eliot expand the technique dramatically, juxtaposing many times within the poem as well as drawing large-scale juxtapositions between past and present. In other words, juxtaposition or the ideogrammatic loop is now controlling local relations, specific juxtapositions, as well as the large-scale structure of the poem as in *Cathay* or *Propertius*. What enables Pound and Eliot to do this is a stylistic fusion of the historical juxtaposition Pound took from Vorticist sculpture and the paratactic syntax of Lewis's literary Vorticism in *Enemy of the Stars*. This fusion enables them in turn to move beyond the simple parallelism of *Cathay* towards a style of writing in which the sequence of the text created by juxtapositions is powerfully determinant of meaning.

Second, Frank's mistaken notion that the juxtapositional sequences of modernism involve a cancellation of textual sequence leads him to make the second, related mistake of insisting that this cancellation of sequence is an attempt to cancel historical time and represents an escape into the timeless world of myth. Frank is correct in seeing an identity between modernist ideas about textual and historical sequence (or between their ideas about syntax and their ideas about history), but his misunderstanding of the first leads him to misunderstand the second. I would grant that the logic of Pound's presentation of an analogy between Malatesta in Rimini and Jefferson in America differs from the assumption implicit in narrative that events have a significant relation (a causal relation, in essence) only in terms of sequence. But that assumption represents only one possible time-logic, the syntagmatic time-logic of narrative and historical chronicle. Lying behind the temporal montage of modernism is another time-logic that I have already referred to as paradigmatic. History for Pound and the other modernists is a pattern, not a line. History is not simply a chronicle of unrelated events but, like a work of art, it has meaningful repetitions and patterns. In their art, the modernists point out those repetitions in a way that enables a complex series of historical patterns or analogies to emerge.

Modernist writers establish these analogies in two quite different ways. Pound and Eliot, as we have already seen, do so by utilizing the temporal montage of *Cathay*. Sections of *The Cantos* and *The Waste Land* work as fragments of narration but one fragment—as we have seen—is followed by another that has no relation to it in a temporal and narrative sequence and may very well be set in a different time (and in a different language). In other words, relations among times predominate, not relations within any one time. Canto 1 begins with Odysseus, Canto 2 with Robert Browning, and Canto 3 with Ezra Pound in Venice as a young man, though of course many more historical moments, characters, and civilizations are included in just those three cantos. These juxtapositions create the historical pattern that we should grasp. Joyce, again in contrast to Pound and Eliot, tends to meld discrete historical moments together instead of placing them in juxtaposition. HCE, the "protagonist" of *Finnegans Wake*, is Parnell, Christ, and Noah (among others); he is not simply placed in an intelligible relation to them.

Note how the "historical syntax" of these works is identical to their actual syntax: in *The Waste Land* and *The Cantos*, juxtaposition or parataxis is reinforced by historical parataxis, the juxtaposition of different times, cultures, and languages. In *Finnegans Wake*, Joyce unites different words, phrases, languages, and times in the same syntactic unit in a polysemic compression. When he wishes to connect St. Augustine's reference to the Fall as a "felix culpa" with a crime in the Phoenix Park in Dublin, he simply

unites them: "O foenix culprit."[18] But the net effect of Pound's
and Eliot's parataxis and Joyce's paranomasia is the same: each,
by replacing the sentence with the phrase and narration with
pattern, replaces syntagmatic modes of organization with paradigmatic ones. In *Finnegans Wake,* Joyce refers to HCE as "that
patternmind, that paradigmatic ear,"[19] and though I would want
to argue that for modernism the eye—not the ear—is the primary
source of paradigms, all of the modernists betray such a patternmind and an orientation towards paradigms.

It is this paradigmatic representation of history in modernist
works of literature that replaces narration as a source of structural
coherence. Both syntax and narrative sequence are disrupted
sufficiently so that the order of the text has no referential function, unlike the order of a narrative which corresponds roughly (or
at least allows us to construct) a linear order outside the text. But
the absence of a referential function neither denies a meaning to the
order of the text nor makes these works primarily self-referential.
The order of these texts creates a series of historical juxtapositions
which establish a series of meaningful relationships. As one reads
and continues to make the connections implicit in the juxtapositions, one constitutes the paradigmatic representation of history
that underlies the text. One sees the form of history that the artist
is trying to present, and that form is what provides the work with
coherence. The modern world is the waste land; Bloom is Ulysses;
Maud Gonne is Helen of Troy; Jefferson is Malatesta—once we
grasp that these analogies or equations form the underlying logic
of *The Waste Land, Ulysses,* Yeats's poems about Maud, and Cantos
31–34 of *The Cantos,* we understand what it is that brings the
disparate aspects of these works together. We understand their
principle of coherence.

From this perspective, we can see how we need to modify
Frank's conception of spatial form. In their works, as we have
seen, the modernist writers seek to give time and history itself
a shape or form. This aim can only be achieved spatially, as form
or shape is a property of space, not of time. Paradoxically, therefore, modernist literature uses spatial form to represent the form
of time. If time has a form, it is dynamic, not static, and the spatial
forms used to represent history in modernist literature are really

dynamic forms codified diagrammatically in spatial terms. Frank himself uses such a form as a title for the volume in which his essay on spatial form was collected, *The Widening Gyre*. The title comes from "The Second Coming," of course, and the works of Yeats, Joyce, Pound and Eliot are full of such diagrams—the diagrams of *A Vision* and the map of *Finnegans Wake*—and more prominently, of concrete images that are nearly as schematic— the gyring birds of Yeats's lyrics, Chinese ideograms, Pound's favorite image of the rose in the steel dust, and the patterns created by birds, stars, the dance, and the "Chinese jar" in *Burnt Norton*. What these represent are dynamic forms, comparable to and in many cases derived from the dynamic forms of Vorticist art; many of these dynamic forms in turn are representations of the dynamic form of history itself, or rather, to be as precise as possible, of the dynamic forms through which modernist writers perceive and present history.[20]

Among the modernist writers, Yeats was most explicit about history being a pattern that one can represent by means of dynamic forms and he was also most explicit about what the form or pattern of history was. Joyce, regretting that explicitness, said of *A Vision* that it was a pity Yeats had not put all of this "colossal conception" into a "creative work,"[21] and Joyce here is speaking for modernism in general in preferring such patterns to be implicit and drawn out by the reader (as they are in *Finnegans Wake*), not explicit in the manner of *A Vision*. But Yeats saw, I think, that his project in *A Vision* was closely related to the modernist enterprise, as he went to some trouble to ensure that we place *A Vision* in a modernist context. The Preface to the second edition of *A Vision* (1937) was entitled "A Packet for Ezra Pound." It contains one of the earliest—if also one of the most confused—discussions of the form of Pound's *Cantos,* and Yeats obviously is trying to draw an analogy between his work and Pound's in that both—according to him—have a "mathematical structure."[22] He draws a much more explicit analogy when he is discussing how he expects the whole system of *A Vision* to be taken. His instructors, he tells us, said that they came to give him "metaphors for poetry."[23] This statement does not clear up every difficulty, as Yeats did not want his historical references to be taken as mere metaphors, at least not always, but the formulation is pertinent: his historical patterns are means to poems, not ends in themselves. Moreover, he goes on to say that he regards his "circuits of sun and moon," his dynamic forms, "as stylistic arrangements of existence comparable to the cubes in the drawing of Wyndham Lewis and to the ovoids in the sculpture of Brancusi."[24] Yeats, in other words, frankly subjects his historical material to stylistic constraints and considers his arrangements of history to be comparable to the severe geometrical shaping of modernist and specifically Vorticist art.

Yeats's analogy is worth exploring for a moment: how might his arrangements of history be comparable to the formal arrangements of the drawings of Wyndham Lewis? He refers to them as containing cubes, not vortices, an interesting modification, particularly as the vortex, or as Yeats calls it, the gyre, is Yeats's central model for the representation of history. Clearly he sees an analogy between the way Lewis abstracts the complexity of experience in a two-dimensional diagram or dynamic form and the way he has reduced or abstracted the complexity of history to his series of dynamic forms, the whirling vortices that for Yeats express the dynamic form of history. Moreover, these works share a theory of representation as well as a preference for dynamic forms. Yeats's theory of representation, like that of the Vorticists, is frankly essentialist. Making no pretense of being complete in its coverage, it treats the high points of history, the moments of greatest intensity, and it aims to produce, not a point-to-point resemblance, but a map or diagram of history. Each modernist in his own way presents in his work a representation of the pattern of history, a stylistic arrangement of experience comparable to the diagrammatic and dynamic forms of Vorticist art.

One should speak, therefore, not of spatial form but of spatio-temporal form, for the spatial form one finds in modernist literature is always the form of something in time, not something that tries to be, in Frank's terms, "one timeless complex of significance."[25] The scientific, Einsteinian connotations of the term *spatio-temporal,* whether or not they could stand up to rigorous examination, are salutary as a corrective to the automatic assumption that the modernist concern with pattern and form in history expresses a desire to escape from history into myth.

Far from escaping their historical moment, the modernists should probably be distinguished for their obsession with it. What I have called their presentism is an index of their desire to come to grips with their historical situation, even though the paradigmatic conception of history from which they operated led them to study and portray that situation largely through juxtapositions with other times, through the ideogrammatic loop. The modernists were pessimistic, by and large, about their historical situation, and they did tend to be nostalgic for various "golden ages." But they placed these "golden ages" in history, England before the "dissociation of sensibility," or the Italy of Sigismundo Malatesta, or at the farthest remove the Byzantium of Justinian. No simple formula of antimodernism will explain either their faith in the possibility of renewal or their dedication to the concrete present:

> Time past and time future
> What might have been and what has been
> Point to one end, which is always present.[26]

I hope by quoting Eliot here to indicate the limits to my argument without undermining it. Eliot does aspire to the timeless world that Frank posits as the modernist ideal, but—no Arnoldian—he is aware that poetry cannot get him there. For Eliot as for his fellow modernists, whatever their religious persuasion, religion is not an art, nor is art a religion. The modernist aesthetic is to be distinguished from the romantic aesthetic precisely by its acceptance of such limits. For those of us who are not saints, and Eliot knows that neither he nor his fellow poets are saints, "there is only the unattended / Moment, the moment in and out of time."[27] The "unattended moment" is what art can provide, not an escape from time but detachment from time *in* time. Furthermore, history for Eliot is not something one tries to escape from, for it is an agent of redemption:

> A people without history
> Is not redeemed from time, for history is a pattern
> Of timeless moments.[28]

Those timeless moments are beyond the reach of art; what art can do is articulate the pattern of history, and in articulating that pattern leave a place in the pattern for that which is beyond time and history.

Eliot's stance is representative, I would argue, of the stance of his fellow modernists: in their very different ways, Pound, Lewis, Joyce, and Yeats would accept this distinction. The dynamic forms of modernist art leave a place for the artist in the center, the still point of the vortex, which is where a detached perspective is available. This stance does not conflict with the historical nature of their art, as their search for the form of time is a search for a detached perspective on it. They search for the still point of the modern world, a place of repose from which they can best study and represent their own point in time. At moments in the careers of most of the major modernists, they have wanted to find something beyond that still point "in and out of time," to seek something "timeless." But at that point they fall silent, aware that what they wish to say cannot be said. We shall see two occasions in succession, in the chapters that follow. Modernists may seek "the intersection of the timeless and time," but their art does not and cannot.

In conclusion, I am suggesting that there is such a thing as a High Modernist Mode, to use David Perkins's term.[29] The works of the major modernists in English have a distinctive signature, found in the collocation of themes and forms brought together here; in the last analysis they are really aspects of each other on different planes. These works share:

1. Their presentism, a commitment to understanding the present by means of historical patterns and parallels
2. The presentation of such patterns through dynamic forms, either abstractions such as gyres or vortices or concrete images of dynamic forms in nature
3. A fracturing of narrative which is a fracturing of linearity equivalent to the replacement of history as line with history as pattern
4. A fracturing of syntax in which the sentence is either

replaced or endlessly elaborated until it loses all coherence and therefore all structural power.

The matrix of these innovations, if not their combination into
works of masterpiece status, was the attempt at literary Vorticism
by Pound and Lewis around 1914. If the Vorticist movement is
not exactly the vortex of modernism, it is its seedbed or labora-
tory; one finds little achieved stillness, but a good deal of furious
and creative innovation. An argument against the seminal role I
have assigned these works would be (and has been) that they are
not works of the highest quality, but Pound himself, well aware of
the cost of innovation, has supplied an answer to that objection.
In *ABC of Reading* he divided writers into inventors and masters,
those "who found a new process" and those "who combined a
number of such processes."[30] Pound and Lewis around 1914 are
inventors par excellence and only later, in the 1920s and the 1930s,
are these new processes combined in the masterpieces of modernism. Pound, of course, was not simply an inventor, as *The Cantos*
should be included with *Ulysses* and *Finnegans Wake*, *The Waste
Land* and *Four Quartets*, and the lyrics of Yeats in the list of those
masterpieces.

Vorticism is a key locus of innovation, I think, because the
Vorticist writers were uniquely positioned to learn from and be
influenced by painting.[31] The deepest sense in which Joseph Frank's
term, spatial form, is useful is that it suggests that, in moving
against narration and syntax, modernist literature aspired towards
the condition of painting; and, in its attempts, sometimes heroic,
sometimes foolish, to see whether literature could change its nature
as fundamentally as painting had, modernist literature was aspiring
towards the condition of modernist painting.[32] From the perspective of the 1980s, the attempt seems misplaced: nonrepresentational painting, itself under attack, looks far more firmly established
than the non-narrative literature of modernism. Lewis's relevance
to the contemporary situation is that he was the first figure with a
major role in modernism to begin to call the modernist enterprise
into question. Even before the innovations discussed here were
carried through, Lewis had decided that they were fundamentally
misguided. In his novels, he moves away from the modernist move

away from narration, and it is this complex and fascinating development (which is not quite the same as a return to narrative) that we shall consider next.

I have been speaking of modernism as if it were a single entity and indeed have been trying to define that entity. But I should be the first to admit that there are limits inherent in the unification or consolidation of modernist literature which I have attempted here. Beyond the crucial but skeletal points of convergence that I have outlined, the works of the modernists diverge drastically, and not every piece of modernist literature necessarily exemplifies the four categories of innovation. *Four Quartets,* for example, is far more conventional in its syntax and sequentiality than *The Waste Land* yet it is also more concerned with historical and temporal patterns; it is only in the second version of *A Vision* (1937) that Yeats sees that his diagrams of history are comparable to Vorticist art and are not the absolute, gospel truth. Moreover, Vorticism is a generative matrix, but not the only one; *Ulysses,* for instance, moves away from narrative in a manner parallel to, but not in any way derived from, the earlier experiments of Lewis.

To trace the full ramifications of the innovations I have just sketched would be to write the history of twentieth-century literature, for if Lewis and Pound influenced Eliot, Joyce, and Yeats, whom did Eliot, Joyce, and Yeats not influence? I have preferred in what follows, therefore, to keep my focus on the works of Lewis and Pound, the two literary Vorticists, in order to show how their later work developed out of the matrix of literary Vorticism I have just discussed. Implicit in what follows, moreover, is a sense that their work continued to be seminal and innovative. Though virtually unrecognized, Lewis's later novels are the prototype for the contemporary postmodernist attempts to move beyond the modernist attack on narrative without simply returning to premodernist modes of narration. As is widely recognized, Pound's attempt to write a paradigmatic, non-narrative epic in *The Cantos* remains the primary model for the contemporary long poem. Their literary Vorticism, in short, though seminal in the development of High Modernism, also helps initiate the movement beyond High Modernism, as I shall attempt to trace in the chapter on Lewis's later fiction and the chapter on *The Cantos.*

5   Wyndham Lewis and the Trial of Man

If there is a single reason why Lewis's role in the turn away from narrative in modernist literature has remained obscure, it is because Lewis himself obscured it so well. In the late 1920s and early 1930s, as he formulated his critique of Joyce, Pound, and others and presented himself as the enemy of every orthodoxy, his own earlier modernism and his role in Vorticism became, I suspect, something of an embarrassment. The Enemy, as Lewis liked to refer to himself in the late 1920s, had friends (or had had them), and this would never do. So Lewis, in the midst of his most productive period (1927–32), took the time to revise his early work. In 1927, *The Wild Body,* a collection and revision of his early sketches, was published; in 1928, a revision of *Tarr* appeared; and, in 1932, *Enemy of the Stars* was published in book form, expanded, and, as we have seen, heavily revised.

As Hugh Kenner has noted, "In none of these reprints except that of *Tarr* in 1928 is there any adequate indication of the amount of reworking that has been done."[1] Even in the case of *Tarr,* the revision is described in Lewis's preface to the revised edition as simply a matter of polishing an imperfect first draft:

> But in turning back to [*Tarr*] I have always felt that as regards form simply it should not appear again as it stood, for it was written with extreme haste, during the first year of the War, during a period of illness and restless convalescence. Accordingly for the present edition I have throughout finished what was rough and given the narrative everywhere a greater precision. A few scenes have been expanded and some material added.[2]

But the "roughness" of *Tarr,* such as it is, cannot be ascribed simply to compositional haste. Lewis began *Tarr* intending another "abstract" work on the model of *Enemy of the Stars,* but he abandoned that aim according to his own later account. In *Rude Assignment* (1950), Lewis traces the transformation:

> It became evident to me at once, however, when I started to write a novel, that words and syntax were not susceptible of transformation into abstract terms, to which process the visual arts lent themselves quite readily. The coming of war and the writing—at top speed—of a full-length novel ("Tarr") was the turning point. Writing—literature—dragged me out of the abstractist cul-de-sac.[3]

Tarr, thus, takes on a pivotal importance in Lewis's *oeuvre*, as writing it enabled him to see the flaws in the programmatic modernism of *Enemy of the Stars*. His road out of the "abstractist cul-de-sac" was a compromise with the temporal and referential nature of syntax:

> In the course of the writing, again, I grew more interested with every page in the life of my characters. In the end—apart from the fact that I abstained from the use of any clichés (even the inoffensive mates of more gregarious words) eschewed sentimental archaisms, and all *pretty language* as it might be called—"Tarr" turned out a straightforward novel.[4]

The prodigal son returns, the rake reforms, the revolutionary accepts a post in the government—such is the tone of this account. And, in contrast to *Enemy of the Stars, Tarr* does seem the "return to normalcy" recollected in this passage.

But the first version published in 1918 retained quite enough moments of waywardness to make Lewis's subsequent revisions necessary. The rough spots smoothed out in 1928 are precisely those points in the original where the reader is reminded of *Enemy of the Stars* and its peculiar Vorticist narration. In the 1918 version a view of Paris from Kreisler's window is rendered in this manner:

> The late spring sunshine flooded, like a bursted tepid star, the pink boulevard. The people beneath crawled like wounded insects of cloth. The two-storey house terminating the Boulevard Pfifer, covered the lower part of the Café de Berne.[5]

The 1928 version subtly but consistently transforms this view:

> The late spring sunshine flooded, like a bursted tepid star, the pink boulevard: beneath, the black-suited burgesses of Paris crawled like wounded insects hither and thither. A low corner-house terminating the Boulevard Kreutzberg blotted out the lower part of the Café Berne.[6]

Lewis joins the first and second sentences with a colon, which, with the new location of beneath, relates the two and creates a smoother transition between them. The arresting image, "wounded insects of cloth," is clarified, as "of cloth" is replaced by "black-suited" and the "wounded insects" are described as crawling "hither and thither," a clear and comprehensible image of the ebb and flow of people in city streets. The semantic revisions in the final sentence seem insignificant. "The two-storey house" becomes a "low corner-house," "Pfifer" becomes "Kreutzberg" and "covered" is replaced by "blotted out." But the comma present in the first version works in the way commas often do in *Enemy of the Stars,* separating the subject from the verb and making that verb resemble a participle. Removing that comma makes the sentence as conventional in syntax as it is in other respects.

These passages are representative, I think, and readers of Lewis have not been of one mind about the diminution of revolutionary zeal they represent. Robert Chapman and William Pritchard, neither of whom even discusses *Enemy of the Stars,* consider the revised version far superior. They praise the process of syntactic accommodation traced in the evolution of Lewis's prose, and Pritchard explicitly claims that in the 1928 version Lewis "has become the novelist rather than the abstractist innovator in prose."[7] In contrast, Timothy Materer and Hugh Kenner, far more interested in, though ultimately critical of, *Enemy of the Stars,* see the first version of *Tarr* as superior to the later version, because the first is a fascinating balance between the intensity of *Enemy of the Stars* and the demands of narrative. *Tarr* in its second version is too complete an accommodation to those demands; as Kenner remarks, "in the process of firming up the narrative, Lewis has inadvertently wafted much of the magic away."[8]

Though these critics evaluate Lewis's development quite differently, they agree that the direction of his development is towards narrative, towards a "truce with time," in Kenner's memorable phrase.[9] On the level of syntax, this is clearly so; a tendency running through his *oeuvre* is a slow but steady return to a less eccentric style that functions much less problematically as a vehicle of narration. However, there is no compelling reason why the evolution of Lewis's syntax should be an accurate index of the evolution of his work as a whole. Indeed, though the first version of *Tarr* is a syntactic return to (relative) conventionality, it contains one peculiar nonsyntactic innovation whose existence suggests that at least a partial qualification of the received image of *Tarr* is in order.

The innovation I speak of is Lewis's invention of a new form of punctuation, the equal sign. It has aroused little comment, probably because the reason for its employment remains obscure. Lewis only uses it after a period to link complete sentences; therefore it is always possible to ignore the equal sign.[10] Moreover, Lewis never discussed what the equal sign was supposed to accomplish. Hugh Kenner, the only critic to venture an explanation, has called it "yet another device for preventing the prose from flowing."[11] Just the opposite would seem to be the case. A logical assumption would be that the equal sign was intended to be a connective device, which by bringing two sentences together would enable the prose to flow. Initially, it does work this way, functioning as a replacement for other forms of punctuation. In the following passage it functions (approximately) like a colon:

> This was Allan Hobson's outfit.=A Cambridge cut disfigures his originally manly and melodramatic form.[12]

It can also make an entire sentence function parenthetically:

> "How is London looking?"
> "Oh, very much as usual.=I wasn't there the whole time.=I was in Cambridge last week."[13]

And it can be used in the middle of what could ordinarily be a single sentence, as if it were a semicolon:

> It seems to me you know more German than I do.=But *you're
> ashamed of it.* [14]

In these cases, all culled from the first conversation in *Tarr,* the
equal sign knits together the staccato sentences of the clipped
conversation of Tarr and Hobson. One feels the need of connection,
and the equal sign adequately—if oddly—fulfills that need.

Elsewhere, however, the function fulfilled by the equal sign is
much less clear. In passages that stand in no need of such knitting
together, Lewis sprinkles equal signs seemingly at random:

> She felt his hand on her arm as though it had been she he had seized.
> This rough figure disappeared in the doorway, as incapable of ex-
> plaining anything. She shivered nervously as she grasped her partner's
> arm again, at this merely physical *contact.*="What's the matter with
> that chap?"—her partner asked, conscious of a lameness, but of some-
> thing queer going on.=This question had been asked a few minutes
> before elsewhere.="Herr Kreisler is behaving very strangely.=Do you
> think he's been drinking?" [15]

Here the effect is exactly as Kenner suggests. The presence of the
equal sign creates more discontinuity than continuity. Even if it
serves to bring together the sentences it connects—and I am not
sure this is true—it only heightens the gap between those sentences
and the rest. Moreover, an expectation is created that an equal sign
will follow a period. When that is not fulfilled, a visual gap is
created between sentences as one begins to feel the absence of the
equal sign. The absence of the equal sign reinforces the sense of
discontinuity between sentences that Lewis's abrupt style is prone
to create. The effect would be the same even if there were an evident rationale for the placement of the equal sign, as there is in
a limited number of instances. But far more often, the placement
of the equal sign seems utterly arbitrary. In these cases, whatever
Lewis's intention, the equal sign serves only to separate sentences
and to highlight the absence of any continuity between them.

The equal sign, in fact, has much the same effect on the relations
between sentences that the suppression of conjugated verbs and
the contrapuntal punctuation in *Enemy of the Stars* had on the
relations within the sentence. The effect of both is to block con-

tinuity; certain phrases and sentences become more visible in their splendid isolation, but overall the effect is that the prose becomes more static and idiosyncratic. One might assume, therefore, that Lewis's invention of the equal sign dates from a time close to the writing of *Enemy of the Stars,* from the period of extremism that he moved beyond while writing *Tarr.* But this is not the case. The first appearance of the equal sign in Lewis's published correspondence is in a letter written in the summer of 1915. It remains a feature of his epistolary style until August 1919, after the publication of *Tarr.*[16] Moreover, *Tarr* began to be serialized in *The Egoist* on 1 April 1916, and the Egoist Press published the first English edition in June 1918. Neither contains an equal sign. Only the contemporaneous but textually independent first American edition, published by Knopf in June 1918, contains the equal sign.[17]

Despite Lewis's evolution away from eccentric syntax during the writing of *Tarr,* Lewis was therefore still striving for the effect he had tried to achieve earlier through such eccentric syntax. Defeated in his attempt to block the linear continuity of prose on the level of syntax, he shifted his attention to the connections between sentences and attempted to block continuity there. The rejection of syntactic innovation in *Tarr* is therefore not representative of a broad rejection of innovation, as Lewis implied in *Rude Assignment.* Instead, after *Enemy of the Stars,* syntax is no longer the locus of innovation in Lewis's fiction. He may continue to obey the rules of English syntax (albeit in his own fashion), but not because of some broad return to conventionality. He does so because he has varied his method of achieving the aim that previously had motivated his eccentric approach to syntax.

I do not suggest that Lewis's use of the equal sign in *Tarr* succeeds where his verbless sentences in *Enemy of the Stars* fail. Neither succeeds particularly well and the equal sign has as short a life as the verbless sentence. But more important than the success or failure of these innovations is the pattern that the shift from one to the other reveals. The reason why I have depicted the interplay of formal invention and acceptance of convention in *Tarr* in such detail is that I consider it to be paradigmatic for the evolution of Lewis's career as a novelist. In matters of syntax Lewis does make a "truce with time." But the desire on Lewis's part to write fiction that would somehow win the war with time persists beyond the writing of *Enemy of the Stars* and *Tarr*.

In Lewis's fiction, the locus of innovation will continue to shift, as he tries to realize his aim of atemporal fiction by means of innovations with a successively vaster area of application. His formal maturity as a novelist dates from his realization that the proper ground on which to fight his "war with time" is not the individual sentence or the place where sentences join, but something much broader, the formal design of the entire novel. But this realization is not the end of his literary Vorticism, for it is precisely to Vorticism that he turns both for the forms with which to defeat time in the novel and the aesthetic rationale for desiring such an aim in his art.

The text in which we can see Lewis coming to this realization is his 1922 "Essay on the Objective of Plastic Art in Our Time," published in the second (and final) issue of his magazine *The Tyro*. Let me quote the pivotal passage in full:

> If you conclude from this that I am treading the road to the platonic heaven, my particular road is deliberately chosen for the immanent satisfactions that may be found by the way. You may know Schopenhauer's eloquent and resounding words, where, in his forcible fashion, he is speaking of what art accomplishes. "It therefore pauses at this particular thing: the course of time stops: the relations vanish for it: only the essential, the idea, is its object."
>
> That might be a splended description of what the great work of plastic art achieves. It "pauses at this *particular thing*," whether that thing be an olive-tree that Van Gogh saw; a burgher of Rembrandt or Miss Stein. "The course of time stops." A sort of immortality descends upon these objects. It is an immortality which, in the case of the painting, they have to pay for with death, or at least its coldness and immobility.
>
> Those words are, however, part of a passage in the World as Will and Idea that it may be useful to quote fully:
>
> "While science, following the unresting and inconstant stream of the fourfold forms of reason and consequent, with each end attained sees further, and can never reach a final goal nor attain full satisfaction, any more than by running we can reach the place where the clouds touch the horizon; art, on the contrary, is everywhere at its goal. For it plucks the object of its contemplation out of the stream of the world's course, and has it isolated before it."

> We might contrast this with a Bergsonian impressionism, which
> would urge you to leave the object in its vital *milieu*. Again, the
> "presence of mind" in the midst of the empirical reality which
> Schopenhauer cites as the characteristic of genius, this coldness is
> a self-isolation, in any case; for he who opens his eyes wide enough
> will always find himself alone. Where the isolation occurs, of subject
> or object, outside or inside the vortex, is the same thing. The im-
> pressionist doctrine, with its interpenetrations, its tragic literalness,
> its wavy contours, its fashionable fuss, points always to one end: the
> state in which life itself supersedes art: which, as Schopenhauer points
> out, would be excellent if people knew how to use their eyes. But if
> they did it would no longer be "life" as we commonly mean it.
> (*WLOA* 208-9)[18]

It is not known what led Lewis to Schopenhauer in 1922, but
Schopenhauer actually helps to establish an element of continuity
in Lewis's thinking. For there is a close connection between
Schopenhauer's "eloquent and resounding words" and the work of
Worringer whose relevance to the Vorticist aesthetic we have already explored. Worringer cites Schopenhauer with approval in
Abstraction and Empathy, and his notion of the "urge to abstraction" is obviously influenced by Schopenhauer's notion of art.
The difference between the two is that for Schopenhauer all art
obeys Worringer's urge to abstraction: what he opposes to the urge
to abstraction is science, though what he has to say about science
makes it resemble Worringer's "urge to empathy." This one-
sidedness weakens the descriptive force of Schopenhauer's aesthetic, as one can easily find art that does not obey the urge to
abstraction. But it also intensifies its polemic force. Art that does
not satisfy these canons is not simply another kind of art, as in
Worringer's and Hulme's system of categories, but is the opposite
of what art should be.

   Schopenhauer's position, in fact, dovetails nicely with the Vorticist polemics of 1914, and Lewis shows his awareness when he
contrasts Schopenhauer's aesthetic ideal "with a Bergsonian impressionism, which would urge you to leave the object in its vital
milieu." According to Schopenhauer's categories, Futurism and
Impressionism seek to attain the condition of science, not of art.
In their aesthetic of empathy, they follow "the unresting and
inconstant stream"; Schopenhauer's ideal, on the other hand, is

to move out of that stream and take "the object of its contemplation out of the stream of the world's course."

The aesthetic is an implicitly antivitalist one, and Lewis makes his own antivitalism perfectly explicit in this passage. The artist, in plucking the object out of the stream of time, makes it timeless by killing or, in Worringer's phrase, "deorganicizing" it. The art object thus attains an immortality that it pays for with the "coldness and immobility" of death. But this transformation into Vorticist hardness and bareness should not occasion Keatsian pangs about the tragic cost of art. Lewis's ideal has always been that the artist should find the detached still point, distinct from the world around him. This ideal finds support from Schopenhauer, whose remarks on the self-isolation and presence of mind of the artistic genius sound distinctly Vorticist. Schopenhauer's contribution is to insist that the art work, as well as the artist, should attain that still point, and it does so by taking "the essential, the idea" for its object.

This aesthetic is quite close to what I have called the essentialism of Vorticism. In each case, the artist wishes to take the object he depicts out of the flux of time in order to arrive at its essence and in order to attain a still point. One difference is that for Schopenhauer that still point is more than a moment or attitude of repose: it is the mode of entry into the higher world of the eternal Forms or Ideas. Lewis's position is distinctly less Idealist. The artistic examples he chooses ("an olive-tree that Van Gogh saw; a burgher of Rembrandt or Miss Stein") should demonstrate that he is not talking about an unequivocably transcendental art. The art work may be dead or immortal but it does not lose contact with the sphere of the vital. It represents an essence, but the essence of something alive and subject to time.

If we put this difference (which will concern us later) to one side, Schopenhauer's aesthetic is completely consonant with the essentialism, detachment, and antivitalism of the Vorticist aesthetic; and Lewis, in 1922, although the Vorticist movement is dead and buried, is interested in establishing this consonance and in grounding the Vorticist aesthetic in Schopenhauer's neo-Kantian and Idealist philosophy. Vorticism remains, therefore, a relevant context for Lewis's aesthetic, given the continuity between his position here and that of 1914 and given the presence of both the word and the image of a vortex in this passage. Moreover, as we shall see, the presence of the vortex in this passage heralds the reappearance of the vortex in Lewis's aesthetic thinking in a new and striking form.

Nonetheless, the language used by Lewis and Schopenhauer to describe art contains a significant ambiguity. "The course of time stops"; "a sort of immortality descends"; art "plucks the object of its contemplation out of the stream of the world's course." The use of the present tense is evasive. All of these clauses refer to a state in which motion has ceased: time has stopped, immortality has descended, and the object has been plucked. Presumably, this state of repose would be the world of the Forms where Schopenhauer wants to place art. Yet the present tense implies motion, if only the motion involved in coming to a halt. Time is stopping, immortality is descending, and the object is being plucked.

It is unclear, therefore, whether the object is still or is passing from the flux of time to the condition of stillness. This ambiguity is not a minor point of grammar, but a crucial point of aesthetics. Does art pluck the object out of the stream and portray the passage from the vitality of life to the deadness of art? Or is its concern only the stillness achieved after the course of time stops? Is its focus immortality or the process of immortality descending? The image of the vortex contains exactly the same potential for ambiguity. If the course of time stops for the art object, then it finds its way from the stream of time to the still point of the vortex. But is its concern the finding of the still point or the still point once found?[19]

Unlike either Lewis or Schopenhauer here, Worringer in *Abstraction and Empathy* came down clearly on one side of this opposition. In his view, art is the process of wresting the object from the flux, the process of de-organicization or abstraction. He stressed the movement from flux to stillness, not the stillness itself. However, this point is precisely where his English spokesman, T. E. Hulme, misread him. Hulme replaced Worringer's subtle and dialectical "geometricization of the vital" with a dichotomy of vital art and geometric art. Hulme praised art that was quite dead, not art that portrayed the passage from life to the death of art.

Hulme's celebration of the geometric, one should remember, led him to attack Vorticist art and its concern with dynamic forms. He preferred the more static and geometric art of David Bomberg. Therefore, if Lewis's aesthetic preference in 1922 is simply for the dead or the still, he is adopting a position at variance with that of Vorticism. I think we can see by the paintings Lewis mentions as examples that he has moved towards Hulme's position of 1914. In 1922, he approvingly mentions Picasso's *Portrait of Gertrude Stein,* a work that—though pre-Cubist—exemplifies the deadness he castigated in 1914.

In comparison with the paintings of the Vorticists, Lewis is now praising quiet and still paintings. Stillness, therefore, not the passage from flux to stillness, is the proper concern of art. Lewis's own development as a painter in the 1920s and 1930s is consonant with this shift in aesthetic preference. His own paintings grow quiet and still. What Lewis realized was that the earlier Vorticist attempt at harmonizing motion and form was at variance with the nature of the medium of painting. Paintings are necessarily still and Lewis makes this fact the prime constituent of his style of painting until he goes blind in 1951. As Hugh Kenner has remarked, Lewis "presents us with pictures which are *about* their necessary condition of silence and immobility."[20]

One could not call these paintings Vorticist, as they turn their back on Vorticism's concern with forming the flux. But that detached zone which Vorticism claimed for the artist is where Lewis now tries to place the art work, which is and should be detached, cold, and still just as the Vorticist artist was. In short, the stylistic concerns of Vorticist painting are not carried forward by Lewis in his later work; what is carried forward is the aloofness or isolation implicit in the image of the vortex. As Lewis puts it, "He who opens his eyes wide enough will always find himself alone." Lewis's portraits are, if this is not too strong a claim, an allegory of that process: the sitter who stares out at the beholder has an overpowering awareness that he is alone. The paintings convey an awareness that this isolation is necessary, that it is part of the discipline and nature of art.

Although Lewis came increasingly in the years after Vorticism to be regarded and to regard himself as a writer, painting continued to be his primary aesthetic frame of reference. Nothing shows this emphasis more than the way his aesthetic of stasis and isolation, indebted to Schopenhauer and formulated in Lewis's "Essay on the Objective of Plastic Art in Our Time," directs his polemics in *Time and Western Man* (1927), even though these are against philosophers and writers, not painters. His position in *Time and Western Man*, essentially, is an extrapolation of his preference for the still point against the flux or the stream of becoming that surrounds this point.

He attacks the "Time-mind" in *Time and Western Man* because, in short, it makes the world look like a Futurist painting, blurred, in motion, and impalpable. More opposed than ever before to Futurism's stress on dynamism, Lewis insists that stability, not movement, is the goal of both art and life; and his "wanting things *solid* and wanting them *dead,*" as he puts it, clearly derives from his painterly aesthetic.[21] Nor does Lewis attempt to disguise this origin. He admits in the Preface that "it is the criticism of this view, the Time-view, from the position of the plastic or the visual intelligence, that I am submitting to the public in this book."[22] Later in the book, he admits his bias in even plainer terms: "whatever I, for my part, say, can be traced back to an organ; but in my case it is *the eye*. It is in the service of the things of vision that my ideas are mobilized."[23] Such a frank confession of partisanship tends to disarm further inquiry, but Lewis can hardly be said to be speaking for painting itself, as he claims. He is speaking for a particular kind of painting, that praised in his 1922 essay.

The literary criticism in *Time and Western Man* and the later *Men Without Art* (1934) even more directly applies criteria derived from painting to literature. In *Time and Western Man*, Lewis speaks of "the painter's heaven of exterior forms,"[24] and much of his criticism of the period 1927–34 can be summarized as an attempt to convince his fellow writers that it was "the writer's heaven" as well. With obvious self-satisfaction, he argues in *Men Without Art* that "for *The Apes of God* it could, I think quite safely, be claimed that no book has ever been written that has ever paid more attention to the *outside* of people."[25] Paying attention to the outside of people is a criterion of value for Lewis only because literature in his view ought to aspire towards the condition of painting in direct fashion. "Dogmatically, then, I am for the Great Without, for the method of *external* approach—for the wisdom of the eye, rather than that of the ear."[26] Hence, when he attacks Pound, Joyce, and his other illustrious contemporaries for their adherence to time, his grounds are really aesthetic, not philosophical. Art ought to be antitemporal (and therefore spatial), and painting, not music, ought to be the art to which literature turns for direction.

I have already argued that this was precisely what the writers whom Lewis attacked were doing. Therefore it is crucial to realize that Lewis was not presenting the position or point of view of painting per se (as if that were possible) but of a particular kind of painting. Lewis's position all too often can be reduced to an assertion that literature ought to aspire towards the condition of *his* painting. Let me cite as an example a brief dismissal of D. H. Lawrence in *Men Without Art:*

> To put this matter in a nutshell, it is *the shell* of the animal that the plastically-minded artist will prefer. The ossature is my favorite part of a living animal organism, not its intestines. My objections to Mr. D. H. Lawrence were chiefly concerned with that regrettable habit of his incessantly to refer to the intestinal billowing of "dark" subterranean passion. In his devotion to that romantic abdominal *Within* he abandoned the sunlit pagan surface of the earth.[27]

Lewis's characterization of Lawrence's "devotion to that romantic abdominal *Within*" is acute. But it fails to rise above the level of brilliant ad hominem attack because the supposedly general consideration Lewis brings forward, that "the plastically-minded artist will prefer" the shell, collapses so quickly into a personal preference. It "is my favorite part," Lewis says, and the implied continuation is, "it ought to be yours."

It would be possible to argue, however, that it is precisely the fluctuation between the personal and the abstract that constitutes the permanent interest of Lewis's criticism. A more serious problem, I think, is that Lewis attacked his contemporaries for failing to conform to principles that he himself ignored. His own practice as a novelist was much more flexible than the polemical rigidity of *Time and Western Man* and *Men Without Art* would indicate or seem to allow. His mature style of painting and his literary theory, as I have rapidly characterized them, find their rationale in Lewis's Schopenhauerian aesthetic. But both Schopenhauer and Lewis share a fundamental ambiguity as to whether art's subject matter is the condition of timelessness or the passage from time to timelessness. In Lewis's painting and criticism, he insists upon the former, whereas in his novels he resolves this ambiguity in the other direction. His fiction depicts the voyage out of the stream of time to the still point. In Schopenhauer's terms, it plucks its subject out of life's stream and analyzes it while it spins to a stop. The passage out of time, from the vitality of life to the deadness of art, is figured forth time and again in Lewis's novels. A group of characters is isolated and analyzed as their doomed world grinds slowly to a halt.

The Apes of God (1930), *The Revenge for Love* (1937), and *Self Condemned* (1954) all show a similar pattern. The design of these novels has baffled readers because of the lack of continuity and linear direction they display. Our sense of which characters are central to the plot keeps shifting, as does our sense of the plot itself. The original title of *The Revenge for Love* was "False Bottoms," which would be a suitable title for any of these novels.[28] One's experience while reading these novels is like a process of continually discovering false bottoms in something that had seemed solid and familiar. At the beginning of practically each section, our expectations about where the novel is heading must be drastically revised, and these new expectations must be revised again, in a process that lasts as long as the novel itself.

The Apes of God begins at Lady Fredigonde Follett's, and the Prologue is an incredibly detailed portrait of the ninety-six-year-old Lady Fredigonde dressing. In Part I, her relative Horace Zagreus comes to visit and, after we follow Zagreus out, we see and hear nothing of the Folletts for nearly six hundred pages, until the novel's close. With Zagreus is his protégé, Dan Boleyn, a moronic young "genius" Zagreus has collected. The tenuous thread that links the successive episodes together is that Horace is showing Dan the apes of God, the pathetic but pernicious imitators of the artist who populate Chelsea and Bloomsbury. He is doing so supposedly on the instructions of Pierpoint, a mysterious figure resembling Lewis whom we are never shown. Otherwise, there is little connection among the episodes of this urban picaresque: each part introduces a new set of apes, until Part XII, which is a nearly three-hundred-page account of a huge gathering of apes, "Lord Osmund's Lenten Party."[29] In the brief and final Part XIII, "The General Strike," set in a London virtually paralyzed by the General Strike of 1926, we return with Zagreus to Lady Fredigonde's. She has induced a fatal stroke in her husband and now proposes to Horace Zagreus, at least thirty years younger but in dire need of money. He accepts, but as they embrace she dies and the novel ends.

The Revenge for Love displays even less of a coherent plot. It begins in a Spanish prison, where the English Communist Percy Hardcaster is contemplating escape. He is shot in the attempt, loses a leg to amputation, and is repatriated to England. The next five sections are set in England, and Percy is only intermittently the center of attention as we are shown the world of Bohemian and Communist circles in London. Parts II through V are each titled with the name of a character, "Victor Stamp," an impoverished Australian painter, "Jack," a skirt-chasing tax expert who is helping the young Communist Tristan Phibbs with his financial affairs, "Sean O'Hara," an Irish gun-runner and Communist, and "Gillian Communist," Tristan's wife who in this chapter undergoes a violent apostasy. By the end of these sections, something draws these characters into relation with one another, but the next part then begins with a new character as if the novel were beginning all over again. Finally, in the penultimate part, "The Fakers," a plot begins to jell. O'Hara is arranging to smuggle some arms from France into Republican Spain and proposes to employ Victor Stamp and Percy Hardcaster. The last section, "Honey-Angel," is set on the Spanish border and then returns to Spain, ending tragically with Victor and his wife Margot dead and Percy Hardcaster again in a Spanish jail.

Self Condemned, Lewis's novel about his wartime experiences in Canada, is not so purely circular. It begins when René Harding, a distinguished historian in England, resigns his professorship in an English university and moves to Canada with his wife Hester, just as Lewis and his wife went to Canada in 1939 at the onset of World War II. Once in Canada their life becomes claustrophobically confined to a single hotel room; the middle chapters of the book seem to drift chaotically in exactly the same manner that the middle parts of *The Apes of God* and *The Revenge for Love* do. Then, again as in the other two novels, the plot tightens. First, their hotel burns down. Then, when René shows signs of planning to stay in Canada permanently, Hester commits suicide rather than stay there any longer. René, in shock, goes in retreat to a Catholic seminary, only to emerge at the very close of the novel. When he emerges, he accepts a professorship in the United States and thus goes back to the situation, if not the place, he was fleeing at the novel's opening. But this similarity should not conceal a great difference. His wife is dead and he is "a glacial shell of a man," though, as Lewis says in the closing words of the novel, his new colleagues did not realize René's condition "mainly because they were themselves unfilled with anything more than a little academic stuffing."[30]

From these three summaries, it should be possible to see a certain pattern in what seems at first to be sheer disorder. At the end of each of these novels, one has returned full circle to the situation of the beginning, and in all but *Self Condemned* to the exact location. (Lewis, in fact, drafted a synopsis for an alternative ending to *Self Condemned* in which René did return to England after the war.)[31] But everything has changed. The characters at the beginning were full of hopes, plans, and plots. At the end, Lady Fredigonde is dead, Horace Zagreus's schemes have collapsed and he has no one to turn to for money, and England in a gigantic objective correlative is paralyzed by the General Strike. Victor and Margot Stamp discover, too late, just before they die in an accident while fleeing the Guardia Civil, that they were not even running guns across the border, only bricks. In one more false bottom, their activities were merely a cover for the real gun-running elsewhere. But this fact does not save their lives or keep Percy Hardcaster from ending up back in his Spanish prison, this time mutilated and without hope of escape. At the end of *Self Condemned*, René's wife is dead, and he is a hollow man living among hollow men.

To speak as critics tend to do of the course or the plot or the development of these novels, therefore, is to apply the wrong descriptive terms. The characters begin these novels full of life but by the end they find themselves in a situation in which any possibility of further movement or development seems to be blocked. It is difficult to imagine anything happening to the characters in a Lewis novel after the novel's end. The world the characters inhabit is a world that has died, a machine that has seized up. The development, in other words, is the precluding of development, the plot is the ending of plots, and the course is the course of time stopping. These words (and virtually our entire terminology for describing novels) are appropriate for novels that stay in the stream of time. These novels do not tell a linear story so much as they describe a circle (or more precisely a diagonal approximation to a circle) while dissecting a group of figures with Lewis's characteristic detachment and analytic scrutiny.

The formal design of these novels is exactly that found in Lewis's 1922 discussion of Schopenhauer. The circle they describe is from life to the death of art. By the end, the characters in these novels, like Rembrandt's burghers and Miss Stein, have attained an immortality that they have paid for with death or complete immobility. They have been plucked out of the stream of time and now stand isolated, abstracted, out of time. The circularity of Lewis's novels is the circularity of the vortex itself: the novels depict a group of characters being spun or taken off the stream of time; they end when the bubble that the artist has plucked out of the stream comes to a halt. The apparent indirection and lack of continuity, thus, are strategic and intentional. The Lewis novel really is not going anywhere, in the conventional sense. It is circling around itself, eddying, as the stream of life abandons these characters and leaves them in the splendid isolation of art.

What conclusively demonstrates that Lewis's formal model is the vortex is that these novels speed up as they approach their end, as if they were approaching the center of the maelstrom; they do not slow down, as if they were simply approaching death. These three novels all lose their way in the middle. Even the most enthusiastic Lewisian wonders how long one is going to spend in the dens of the apes, following the vagaries of "parlour-pinks," or in that hotel room. But in the final third the pace speeds up and the plot thickens: the events at Lord Osmond's Lenten Party in *The Apes of God* grow increasingly bizarre and out of control; the dénouement of *The Revenge for Love* has the elements and moves at the speed—

though not exactly in the style—of a thriller; and Hester's death marks a real quickening of the pace in *Self Condemned* that persists until the end. I do not mean to imply that these three novels are similarly paced and move in lock step. *The Revenge for Love*, at its most lethargic, is paced more quickly than the often tedious *Apes* or what Hugh Kenner has acutely called the "slow and terrible wind" of *Self Condemned*.[32] But in every case the pace quickens as the dénouement approaches, until, suddenly, the still point is reached and the excitement of the close is revealed to be a death rattle, with corpses littered across the stage like the end of a revenge tragedy. But, in Lewis's vision, no Fortinbras arrives to provide an illusion of continuity and renewal. The end is truly an end, a close, and the doomed world we have followed has ground to a dead halt.

It is by making the thrust of his novels this attainment of immortality at the cost of death or immobility that Lewis finally constructs a coherent antitemporal aesthetic for his novels. No one could write a novel according to the painterly principles outlined in his criticism. Fiction cannot suppress the element of time and depict simply the timeless or even simply the spatial. But it can, as Lewis showed, depict the course of time stopping, immortality descending, the attaining of the still point. The process takes time and can be the basis of a narrative sequence, even though the end point is something out of time. Thus, though Lewis's explicit aesthetic pronouncements urge a very different, more static aesthetic, the formal pattern implied in Lewis's discussion of Schopenhauer in 1922 underlies the form of at least three of Lewis's major novels; moreover, they should be seen as the successful accomplishment of Lewis's desire to write an antitemporal narrative.

This desire, which goes back to *Enemy of the Stars*, had been balked because he could find no alternative between the temporal sequence of narrative and his desire to halt that sequence. The image of the vortex offers such an alternative, as it is in motion but does not really go anywhere. By making the vortex the formal pattern for his novels, Lewis could generate an impression of sequence which was both true and false. "Only through time time is conquered," Eliot would write in *Burnt Norton;* Lewis might restate that as "only through sequence sequentiality is conquered."

In the novels after *Tarr,* Lewis manages to give time and sequence their due so that his novels work as novels with a temporal sequence; yet in the last analysis they do nothing of the sort. They manage through their formal pattern to depict the course of time stopping in a manner that is a striking departure from the entire tradition of the novel.

Nonetheless, the impression should not be left that Lewis's novels have been left in isolation like their subjects, barred from any interaction with futurity. Lewis's concern with stopping time in his novels clearly runs parallel to the concern of his contemporaries with finding the form of time. The difference is that he, unlike Pound, Yeats, Eliot, and Joyce, found narrative of use though the use he made of it was to put narrative into question. Lewis's innovative use of narrative constitutes one source of his relevance for contemporary writing, which has lost the traditional novel's confidence in the logic of narrative and does not have modernism's confidence in an alternative. What remains if one rejects those two alternatives is a self-reflexive and auto-critical use of the traditional tools of the novelist; and Lewis's auto-critical and self-destructing use of temporality anticipates the subsequent explosion of such self-reflexivity in recent fiction.

The way in which the pattern of the vortex shapes *The Apes of God, The Revenge for Love,* and *Self Condemned,* though not seen before, exemplifies both the impact of Vorticism on literature and the tenacity of a kind of Vorticism in Lewis's work. This general pattern is, of course, merely that and is not rigidly executed in all of Lewis's novels. *The Human Age* forms a problem all by itself which we will be concerned with later. Lewis's lesser, though by no means negligible, novels, *Snooty Baronet* (1932), *The Vulgar Streak* (1941), and *The Red Priest* (1956), also proceed with a disconcerting lack of linear sequence. Their dénouements involve the deaths of central characters and are marked by a sense of entrapment and enclosure. But these novels do not move around in a full circle and their ends are less claustrophobically final than those we have discussed. They may strike us as less satisfactory precisely because they lack the formal closure involved in the return of the major novels to their point of departure.[33] But I do not claim either that the pattern of a vortex revealed in that formal closure is the key to the interpretation of every Lewis novel or that the presence of this pattern is a criterion of worth. My more modest claim is that this pattern is significant because it enables Lewis to achieve aims that he has been trying to achieve as long ago as his initial attempt at a literary Vorticism in 1914.

But those aims at least as reformulated in the 1922 passage about Schopenhauer are ambiguous in yet another absolutely fundamental way. It is clear that Lewis asserts that art is opposed to life and that the art work is ontologically separate from life. The image of the vortex offers one representation of this separation, as the artist and art work attain the still point, leaving the flux of the external world behind them. But the nature or status of that still point remains unclear, partly because it remains unclear to what extent Lewis endorses the Idealist and transcendental philosophy implicit in his aesthetic formulations. Lewis, following Schopenhauer, uses death and immortality as synonyms, but equating those two states requires an act of faith that neither Lewis nor his contemporary audience is quick to make. In the absence of this equation, a real ambivalence is created. Let me define that ambivalence in a series of questions that it raises: Does art immortalize its subject matter or kill it off? Is Lewis, in his portraits and novels, attempting to immortalize the people he depicts or to kill them? Is he attempting to redeem them from the flux or to satirize their essential deadness? These questions lead us towards others that explicitly involve ethical values: should man be redeemed or damned? What is the system of values expressed in this antitemporal, antivital art? Towards what end is Lewis stopping time?

The "Essay on the Objective of Plastic Art in Our Time" gives us no clue, or even a hint that Lewis sees the ambivalence I am pointing out. Yet, without an answer to these questions, even the reader who has grasped Lewis's formal design will have no clue as to what values are being advanced by that design and will therefore be baffled about how to take these novels that trace a vortex spun off of the stream of time. Moreover, these questions are crucial to an understanding of Lewis's whole *oeuvre,* as they involve themes that run throughout almost all of his work. Thus they become even more difficult to answer; if one looks elsewhere in Lewis's work for an answer, the problem quickly becomes that one finds too many. For example, when Tarr defines the nature of art for his mistress Anastasya in a conversation we have already discussed, he has to do it twice, and the two definitions correspond to the two sides of the question about the nature of art. First, Tarr insists that art is "ourselves disentangled from death and accident," ourselves, in other words, made immortal.[34] Then, striking a more characteristically Lewisian note, he insists that "soft, quivering and quick flesh is as far from art as an object can be. . . . *Deadness* is the first condition of art."[35]

The fact that Lewis revises this conversation in 1928 to exclude Tarr's first definition indicates the direction taken by Lewis in the 1920s and 1930s. Deadness, not immortality, becomes what art should stress. Lewis saw himself as a satirist whose business it was to satirize man's lack of vitality and freedom. As Lewis defines his aesthetic purpose in *Men Without Art:*

> *Freedom* is certainly our human goal, in the sense that all effort is directed to that end: and it is a dictate of nature that we should laugh, and laugh loudly, at those who have fallen into slavery, and still more, those who batten on it.[36]

However, Lewis later reconsidered the propriety of that loud laughter. His last major work, *The Human Age,* is centrally about the question of whether the artist's role should be to attempt to redeem man or to satirize and castigate him for his deadness. Lewis's answer, to anticipate a little, was that redemption and immortality should be the artist's concern; and implicit in *The Human Age* is a severe critique of his earlier satiric castigation of man.

Thus, the ambivalence found at the center of Lewis's discussion of Schopenhauer is an enduring ambivalence, one acted out at great length in his work. Just as his works seem to arrange themselves on one side or the other of the issue, so do his critics. Hugh Kenner, Timothy Materer, W. K. Rose, and others see Lewis's commitment to the tough, antihumanist view of *Men Without Art* as a tragic mistake and favorably present Lewis's evolution as a softening of that misanthropic austerity. Others, such as Fredric Jameson and Geoffrey Wagner, consider the unpleasant Lewis the

the important Lewis.[37] Perhaps the often arrogant and misanthropic Lewis of *The Apes of God* is the "important" Lewis: he is certainly unique. Perhaps the "important" one is the chastened and humane Lewis of *The Human Age:* he is certainly more likable. But instead of taking sides, I am going to try to connect those sides, to show that though Lewis does evolve from a concern with man's deadness to a concern with his immortality, the second concern grew out of the first. Both, moreover, are implicit in the image of the vortex and in the antivitalism of Vorticism. There is much more continuity in Lewis's aesthetic than is customarily granted, a continuity provided by his literary Vorticism. Detachment, the aesthetic ideal of Vorticism, remains Lewis's ideal throughout his career. Thus, just as the image of the vortex runs throughout his novels, creating a continuity in their formal design, the Vorticist ideal of detachment provides a thread of continuity in the aesthetic and ethical values advanced by his entire *oeuvre,* the nonfiction and the lesser novels as well as the major novels we have already examined. However, his notion of what constitutes detachment continues to change; that change, in fact, is probably the best index of the interplay of schism and continuity in his development as a writer.

In the period of Vorticism, to recapitulate briefly, detachment meant above all that the artist was something quite distinct. As Lewis advises in *Blast #2:*

> There is Yourself: and there is the Exterior World, that fat mass you browse on.
> You knead it into an amorphous imitation of yourself inside yourself.
> Sometimes you speak through its huskier mouth, sometimes through yours.
> Do not confuse yourself with it, or weaken the esoteric lines of fine original being.   (*Bl #2*, 91)

Proposition #6 of "The Code of a Herdsman" (1917) similarly insists: "Yourself must be your Caste."[38] Lewis published a story (of sorts) called "The Crowd Master" in *Blast #2*, and, according to Lewis at this point, both herdsman and crowd master are appropriate metaphors for the artist, who is both distinct from and above his fellow man.

He cannot be utterly distinct, of course, for he possesses the same physical apparatus as other men. But whereas other men essentially are their bodies, the artist has one, and does not identify with it. As Ker-Orr puts it in *The Wild Body:* "This forked, strange-scented, blond-skinned gut-bag, with its two bright rolling marbles with which it sees, bull's eyes full of mockery and madness, is my stalking-horse. I hang somewhere in its midst operating it with detachment."[39] The artist's attitude towards his own body is a mirror-image of his attitude toward other men. Man's physical nature, "the wild body," is mechanistic and absurd; man's artistic nature is "the laughing observer," linked to a body but as distinct as possible from it and its values.[40]

This Nietzschean assumption of superiority gradually modifies itself into an intense awareness of otherness, superiority having proved difficult to establish. One can see this modification most clearly in *The Lion and the Fox,* Lewis's 1927 study of Shakespeare. Given the notion that the artist is a crowd master, one would have thought that the tragic heroes, isolated in their superiority to other men, would hold the most fascination for Lewis. But he is far more interested in the figure of the railer or the malcontent, and he obviously identifies with figures such as Apemantus, Thersites, and Jacques. They are the professional malcontents, disaffected out of principle, not because of happenstance, and it is clear from *The Lion and the Fox* that for Lewis the role of the artist is to be just such a railer.[41] In other words, the artist for Lewis at this point is not necessarily above society, but he is certainly outside society and against it.

In *Time and Western Man,* Lewis explicitly equates his own role with that of the classical Cynic. He quotes a long discussion by Edward Caird from *The Evolution of Theology* about the role of the Cynic and then applies it to his own position, quoting the phrases from Caird that seem to apply:

> Now I have supplied you with an analogy against myself for practical reasons, although it has no literal application, as I remarked above. I am doing a very different thing from what the Cynic was doing, and I am very differently placed. But certainly I am issuing a "challenge" to the community in which I live. I am "criticizing all its institutions

and modes of action and of thought." I "create disgust," that I have
proved, "among the ordinary respectable members of the community," that is to say among the established orthodoxy of the cults of
"primitivist" so-called "revolution": what I saw is "violently re-
sented," and I very sincerely hope will "awaken thought."[42]

It was precisely this sense of his own role that led Lewis to call
himself the Enemy and title his last one-man magazine (published
between 1927 and 1929) *The Enemy*. Lewis's presentation of himself in this role could become quite bizarre. In "What It Feels Like
to Be an Enemy" (1932), for example, Lewis describes how an
"Enemy" begins his campaigns in the morning:

> After breakfast, for instance (a little raw meat, a couple of blood-
> oranges, a stick of ginger, and a shot of Vodka—to make one see
> Red) I make a habit of springing up from the breakfast-table and
> going over in a rush to the telephone book. This I open quite at
> chance, and ring up the first number upon which my eye has lighted.
> When I am put through, I violently abuse for five minutes the man,
> or woman of course (there is no romantic nonsense about the sex of
> people with an Enemy worth his salt), who answers the call. This
> gets you into the proper mood for the day. (*WLOA* 267)

But, beneath this self-dramatization, Lewis thought that what he
was doing was normal and should be exemplary. As Lewis developed the persona of the Enemy, he came to insist more and
more that the role of the artist is to oppose and unmask, not to
approve of anything, lest his objectivity be compromised. To be an
artist was to be an enemy, to have a critical and free-thinking spirit.
Few of his contemporaries had this critical detachment, according
to Lewis, and it was precisely the abdication of this role by his
fellow artists that led him, or so he maintained, to take it up with
such vigor.[43]

Hence, his attacks on his time do logically come out of his attacks
on time, for it is the aloof, detached still point occupied by the
artist that enables him to see through the deceptive appearances of
contemporary culture. Lewis's polemics of the 1927–34 period
(the most important of which are *The Art of Being Ruled* [1926]
and *Time and Western Man* [1927], though Lewis published the

astonishing number of seventeen books in these eight years) are an incredibly complex and rich elaboration of what he can see from that detached perspective. What he sees is that modern thought is governed by a rigid orthodoxy. The key figure standing behind that orthodoxy is Bergson, and its presentation of time, change, and flux as the only reality is the vitalism of Bergson and Futurism taking new form. Lewis's position is thus little more than an update of his Vorticist art polemics of 1914: he is again asserting the value of art against those who would have us worship life as the only reality and source of value. Lewis insists against that orthodoxy that man's greatness is in the attempt to escape (not deny) the reality they worship. It is through art that man can escape: in its very stillness and immobility, art shows that there are values beyond those of the flux.

Yet at other points Lewis turns the dichotomy of life and death inside out. The objects of Lewis's satire, in *The Apes of God* and *Snooty Baronet*, are obsessed with vitality only because they utterly lack it. They are dead, mechanical puppets, reminiscent of the mechanistic figures in Lewis's drawings of the Vorticist period. Those who obey the "group-rhythms" of the crowd are dead; only the detached critical observer is alive. Hugh Kenner has called Lewis "the necessary antidote to everything,"[44] and the phrase captures perfectly his stance of total opposition and his emerging sense in the late 1920s that the detached artist is the figure of life and vitality. But Kenner's phrase assumes that he wanted to keep his opponents alive. The tone of his polemics and satires would suggest that he wanted to kill them off, but that desperate tone comes from the fact that he thought they were dead already, "only pretending to be alive for form's sake," as in 1927 he remarked of Pound.[45]

In *The Childermass* (1928), the Bailiff says at one point, "I like to see a few corpses about, it makes the others seem almost alive."[46] Lewis's work of the late 1920s might be summarized as an investigation into how alive those others are. For "alive" we might want to substitute words like *autonomous* or *independent* or *free*. For Lewis most people's personalities are bogus, as he would choose to put it, cobbled together out of shoddy mass-produced elements, and their lives are completely controlled by large forces. His polemics set out to demonstrate how everyone in the modern world is controlled by forces beyond his control. His satiric novels show this in a different way, through their plots. No one ever succeeds in achieving what he wishes in these novels; everyone's plans are always thwarted. The plots reinforce Lewis's point that no one is in control of his destiny, no one is free. Lewis grants that this fact is as true of him as of everyone else, but he at least recognizes that he is not free, and this recognition in turn is a form of freedom. As he seems to be the only figure to perceive this situation, he is forced to the conclusion that he is the only one left completely alive. Everyone else has succumbed to the dead group-rhythms of the mechanized crowd.

Lewis's novels also carry out the investigation into the vitality of those around him by means of their astonishing and extreme style. This style has been both highly praised by critics as diverse as T. S. Eliot and Fredric Jameson and dismissed by many as intolerably tedious. Perhaps the most balanced assessment is Hugh Kenner's when he speaks of the vices Lewis "coerced into a style."[47] Let me provide a sample of those vices and that coercion, from a description of a party in *The Apes of God:*

> A greater volume of sound immediately rose from beneath, and after a few feints and deceptions, materialized in four people. It became still darker with increasing fog and storm. At length nineteen persons were gathered in the obscurity of the long apartment, with the fire flashing its lightnings at their feet, as if struggling with them for the oxygen required by both—the matches for their cigarettes sporadically illuminating their faces, a half-dozen cigarette-tips pricking the opaque atmosphere. Their voices produced a booming volume of sound. Most began by tuning-up the complicated round or sphenoid wind-instrument they had brought with them, that is their respective headpieces—in which the air trumpeted and vibrated in the darkness. But the tumult increased. At length each guest (with the help of his sinuses and with a possible auxiliary trumpet in the laryngeal pouch, and the neatly-ranged teeth) got really started. Soon all were working their bellows forcibly. When most in form, the hard palate could be heard producing its deafening vibrations in the buccal cavity. Eagerly they thrust their heads forward, and launched their verbal symbolizations upon the puffs of deoxydized air, in the direction of their neighbours. These responded—broke across, out-trumpeted their opposites.[48]

It should be obvious how Lewis's posture of satiric detachment governs the style. Lewis is looking for signs of life among the apes of God, but turns up no signs of it, no evidence to disturb his assumption that he alone is alive. These figures are puppets or machines who are comic in the rigidity and formality of their movements and yet tragic in the degree of depersonalization they manifest. It would take a few corpses about to make these others seem alive.

Yet there is a fundamental problem here: if Lewis is the only one left alive in a world of apes, who is he writing for? What kind of an audience can he have? This question is of obvious practical importance, and it should come as no surprise that *The Apes of God* was far from a bestseller. Few are likely to wish to read such unflattering descriptions of themselves. But this is also an important critical question. For if Lewis's descriptions are to be taken as true, no one is left who will be able to see their truth, as everyone except Lewis is part of the "group-system" that Lewis is attacking.

Hugh Kenner has the best available account of how Lewis moved towards the posture of solipsism:

> *Time and Western Man* had argued that the behaviorist, in reducing the person to a set of predictable gestures, was insulting the human race. In the same year Lewis was producing a body of fiction on the premise that people were nothing else. This fiction started by being satire, employing the strategy of appearing to know no more about the characters than a set of behaviorist's Tests would reveal. Lewis came gradually to doubt if there were in fact any more to know, and forgetting the concealed "bitter ferment" he had postulated beneath the froth-forms in "Inferior Religions," came to accept the satiric premises as truth. The only person the behaviorist had insulted, it appears, was Wyndham Lewis.[49]

Thus both reader and writer are left in a deeply paradoxical situation, though one common to many misanthropic works. The premise of *The Apes of God* seems to be that it can have no readers. If we accept Lewis's description of man, we must see ourselves as apes. But apes are apes precisely because they have no such self-knowledge. The gesture of publication implies the existence of a readership which the novel seems to deny.

The path out of this double bind is to see that Lewis's novels, like his nonfiction, are less empirical propositions than polemical acts. Lewis writes and publishes in the hope of being proven wrong. The premise of his work is something like, "This is the way it looks to me: show me that it isn't so." Time and again, in his polemics, Lewis allows for and invites the occurrence of something that would prove him wrong. As he confessed in his attack on Joyce, "I insert this last time-clause because there is no reason at all to suppose that he may not be influenced in turn by my criticism; and indeed, I hope it may be so, for he would be a very valuable adherent."[50] Lewis is therefore correct in comparing his polemic intentions to those of the Cynics, who in Caird's account created disgust in order to awaken thought and transform the situation that they opposed so violently. To return to a metaphor advanced earlier, Lewis's art is not mimetic so much as emetic, but disgust alone is not his aim. He wants to create a disgust that will transform and remove the sources of disgust. Seeing a few corpses around may make his readers wonder how alive they are. Man is on trial in Lewis's work and, though presumed guilty, is invited to prove himself innocent.

Lewis's satire is, as he himself claimed in *Men Without Art,* a metaphysical critique of man.[51] The unflinching seriousness and bleakness of this critique lead me to argue that, despite the tendency of critics to make analogies between Dante's *Commedia* and the works of Joyce, Pound, and Eliot, Lewis alone among the modernists produced an *Inferno,* in the puppet-fiction of *The Apes of God.* Lewis depicts a hell on earth, but as in Dante these figures are in hell because they have lost "il ben de l'intelletto," though Lewis would obviously define that "good" differently from Dante.

I would not, however, push this analogy very far. Dante possesses an imaginative sympathy with the damned that is utterly foreign to Lewis. One feels an identification with Francesca or Farinata or Ulysses that creates an understanding of them (and their sin) which Lewis cannot express. Lewis, instead, laughs at those he places in hell, and creates quite a different effect. But what he hopes to achieve through this laughter is what Dante hopes to achieve, a reorientation on the part of the reader towards *il ben de l'intelletto*. Confronted by the spectacle of the living English death of the apes, one instinctively wishes to avoid this condition and looks to the artist to discover how.

What we might call Lewis's polemic aesthetic is, therefore, an openly affective one. Whether Lewis depicts his situation as that of the only live man amid a pile of corpses or the only figure who sees beyond purely vital animalistic concerns, the opposition established between the detached critical artist and the crowd remains unchanged. But that opposition is not absolute, for the effect Lewis wants to have on his readers is to make them join Lewis in his posture of independence. It must be said, though, that Lewis counted on being ineffectual: he would have been quite surprised to find any converted apes joining him in his grim and solitary vigil.

That, at any rate, is the way Lewis's satiric fiction of the late 1920s and early 1930s was intended to work. I am not at all sure, however, that it has worked that way. Again, what I have been expounding here is a program rather than an accomplished fact. No one has taken his works quite so seriously as Lewis would have liked, though the mind shrinks from asserting that someone should.[52] Lewis's work of this period has not induced the metaphysical disgust he would have liked for a number of reasons. First, *il ben de l'intelletto* that he would have us embrace is too vague and ill defined. Lewis keeps pointing us towards an alternative to the deadness he depicts, but he never describes that alternative. In *Blasting and Bombardiering* (1937), in the midst of a discussion of art, he makes this typical aside: "In considering art here I am not complicating the matter by going on to consider how life also is brutal and empty without the heightening it acquires through the metaphysical or religious values."[53] The dichotomy Lewis establishes here is precisely that which governs his work as a whole: there is the "brutal and empty" life of his novels and the alternative, "the metaphysical or religious values." The definite article is startling, as it implies that only one set of such values exist. But, typically, Lewis does not go on to specify those values.

The reason why he would never be specific on this point is, I think, that he was aware, perhaps overly aware, that religion could be (and was) just as dominated by a "group-rhythm" as everything else. "And though the artist is certainly not devoid of religious emotion," Lewis writes in *Time and Western Man*, "it is exercised personally, as it were; and he is in temper the opposite of the religionist."[54] Lewis's position is consistent if somewhat self-defeating: if the artist's role is to be the enemy of every orthodoxy in the social and political sphere, he cannot abandon that role in matters of religion. But the personal nature of Lewis's alienation is a second reason why his works do not communicate that alienation effectively. Like his aesthetic critiques, his metaphysical critique too often takes the form "Be the way I am."

Finally, Lewis's critique is unsuccessful because Lewis's vision, inasmuch as he communicates it, is particularly bleak and unappealing. Being the way Lewis is is not an attractive proposition. It is significant in this context that Lewis approved of both Schopenhauer's deeply pessimistic philosophy and, possibly influenced by Schopenhauer, the metaphysical pessimism of Indian Idealism. References to Indian philosophy are scattered through Lewis's works of the 1920s, and his one attempt to be explicit about what lies beyond the flux, his 1925 essay "The Physics of the Not-Self," does little more than Westernize the Indian concept of the *atman*.[55] Only what lies beyond the self and human personality is of value according to Lewis at this point. Yeats saw this aspect of Lewis's work, when he made the point about *Tarr* that "there is the feeling, almost Buddhist, that we are caught in a kind of steel trap."[56]

Even the Devil finds Lewis's portrait of man depressing, according to *Malign Fiesta,* Book III of *The Human Age.* The protagonist of *Malign Fiesta,* James Pullman, obviously stands for Lewis himself, and Sammael, as Satan is known in *Malign Fiesta,* has been reading Pullman's "largest and best-known book" (*The Apes of God,* I would assume). Sammael confesses to Pullman: "It depresses me. Is the world so evil . . . and so ignoble?" Pullman's defense is Lewis's defense in *Men Without Art:* "I fear, sir, that it is. Often I have had that said to me, almost in your words. My answer must always be the same: I did not make the universe: if I had I should have made it differently."[57] But of course Lewis did make the "universe" of his works. Pullman's defense does not change the fact that the vision of man offered in Lewis's work is too black a vision to have the effect on its readers that Lewis wished. Lewis's satiric fiction seeks both to vex man and to convert him, but, though many have been vexed, few have been converted.

My point is not that we should convert, but that the ethical and metaphysical bases of Lewis's satire and his polemics must be recognized if we are going to make sense of Lewis's evolution. For Lewis moves away from the satiric, even misanthropic presentation of man as a living corpse towards a less extreme, more conventional style and mode of presenting character. Many critics have read this shift as an index of a change in values away from the satiric detachment of *The Apes of God*. This evolution has been greeted with enthusiasm by these critics who present the later Lewis as chastened, more humane and more agreeable. W. K. Rose's portrait may be taken as representative: "Lewis *vieux* is not less discriminating or satirical than he ever was. But he is less at the mercy of anger and bitterness, more in tune with the good spirits and humanity that were instinctive to him."[58] Passages such as this remind me of Jery Melford's description of Lismahago's transformation in *Humphry Clinker:* "His temper, which has been soured and shrivelled by disappointment and chagrin, is now swelled out and smoothed like a raisin in plum-porridge."[59] Though I would not deny a certain swelling out and smoothing in Lewis's character in his late years, his final work in the 1950s should not be presented as a recantation of his earlier anger and bitterness.

Instead, he shifts the ground of his attack on time and the conditions of existence once again. Or, rather, he shifts from that attack to a concern with the only alternative he sees to temporality and mutability, which is "the world of metaphysical or religious values." I have tried to show how his earlier satire implied a concern for those values. James Joyce saw this concern at the time: when *Time and Western Man* was published, Joyce predicted that Lewis was "preparing to make a clamorous conversion" to Catholicism.[60] That conversion never occurred, but towards the end of his life he became much more explicit about what he would oppose to time. That new explicitness indicates a major transformation in his work and thought. The detached still point of the vortex is now explicitly outside of time and the artist's concern is now the "higher death" of immortality, not the living death of Lewis's hell on earth.

This transformation clearly necessitates a shift in the formal design of the novel, and *The Human Age* reveals just such a shift. (The first book of *The Human Age*, *The Childermass*, was published in 1928, but the second and third book, *Monstre Gai* and *Malign Fiesta*, which are the crucial books for my argument here, were published together in 1955.) At first, it seems not to, for the first three books display a familiar pattern of dropping through false bottoms. The protagonist, James Pullman, hopes that he is en route to Heaven, but in each volume he is farther away than ever before. If the work had ended with Pullman back outside Third City where he began, the formal resemblance to *The Apes of God* and *The Revenge for Love* would be complete. Lewis initially ended the third book, *Malign Fiesta,* with Pullman's accidental death, caused by an angel stepping on Pullman in his garden. This end is certainly in the spirit, if not exactly in the cast, of the other endings: Pullman has ended up in Hell, has collaborated with the Devil, and now dies without any opportunity for restitution.

However, Lewis revised *Malign Fiesta* on the galley proofs: the Angel steps, not on Pullman, but on a peony. Pullman is carried off to Heaven and the novel ends on this superb note: "As he passed through the door he could hear the telephone ringing, and Borp's voice as he answered it. He imagined his servant saying, 'Mr. Pullman is being carried away by two of God's soldiers.' "[61] Lewis had projected a fourth and final book, *The Trial of Man,* which would have concerned Pullman's doings in Heaven. It was not completed but even without the final book *The Human Age* departs significantly from the formal pattern of Lewis's earlier novels. It ends in an analogous closing off of future possibilities and a stopping of the course of time. But the atmosphere of claustrophobia is replaced by an atmosphere of release. One of the angels whispers to Pullman as he is carried away, "No harm will come to you," and for the first time in Lewis's work one believes this to be true.[62] Pullman, like the previous Lewis protagonists, is plucked out of the stream of time and whirls in a vortex until he finds a still point. But the blind circle is replaced by an ascending spiral and the attained still point is now both transcendent and an object of desire.

The revision in formal design is accompanied by a revision in the values advanced by that design and a critique of the values of the earlier satiric fiction. A complete account of that shift would go back all the way to *Snooty Baronet*, I think; in *Snooty* and the novels that followed, *The Revenge for Love*, *The Vulgar Streak*, and *Self Condemned*, Lewis began to criticize the system of values that *The Apes of God* and the other works of its period present in unalloyed form. But a thorough discussion of that process would only fill out, not in any significant way contradict, the critique of Lewis's earlier work manifested in *The Human Age*. This critique is developed in several different ways.

First, though the protagonist of *The Childermass*, James Pullman, was initially a figure for James Joyce,[63] by the time Lewis wrote the next two books, twenty-five years later, Pullman has obviously become a figure for Lewis himself. The story of Pullman's collaboration first with the Bailiff in *Monstre Gai* and then with the Devil himself in *Malign Fiesta* is Lewis's reflection on his own involvement with totalitarian politics. Hyperides, who in *The Childermass* was the spokesman for Lewis's ideas, is in *Monstre Gai* unambiguously labeled a Fascist.[64] And if Third City, the setting of *Monstre Gai*, owes something to the postwar London of the Welfare State, Sammael's Hell in *Malign Fiesta* is directly indebted to the death camps of Hitler. Just as the politics of the hereafter in *The Human Age* echo those of earth, Pullman's involvement with those politics echoes his (and Lewis's) career on Earth. We know this only because of Pullman's anguished realization that this is the case. Pullman is forced to realize that his role on earth had been "essentially diabolic": "he had lived with the Bailiff upon the earth but had not recognized him."[65]

Pullman is not the only figure who resembles Lewis in *The Human Age*. Sammael, the Devil, justifies his actions in torturing man in ways that may and should remind us of Lewis's justifications of the extremity of his satire. As Hugh Kenner has said, "If the Bailiff is all that in the old days Lewis had opposed, Sammael is very nearly the Lewis who had opposed it, in satire which he described in *Men Without Art* (1934) as a metaphysical, not a moral, criticism of man."[66] "I approve of punishing Man just for being Man," the Lord Sammael tells us and his punishment of man is a literal embodiment of the figural chastisement man receives in Lewis's novels.[67]

Thus *The Human Age* is a deeply autobiographical work; however, it is not simply an allegory of Lewis's support for fascism in several of his nonfiction works of the 1930s. For though Sammael is prepared to defend the torture of man intellectually, he is laying plans to disband Hell and stop punishing man for his sins. He decides that he has been helping God all along by doing his dirty work; now he wants to create a human age, by humanizing his angels and by bringing Hell up to date. Pullman becomes Sammael's adviser as Sammael begins to implement these plans. Pullman is invaluable to Sammael because as a human being he far exceeds Sammael in his capacity for devious thinking and intrigue. Pullman helps Sammael set up the necessary human institutions, like a university and a secret police. And he convinces Sammael to hold the fiesta that gives *Malign Fiesta* its name. It is given for the express purpose of inducing the human traits of drunkenness and sexual desire in the angels. Sammael wants his fellow angels in Hell to take human wives and create a new mixed race; and Pullman draws upon the resources of modern publicity to achieve this end.

It should be clear, therefore, that Lewis's recoil from totalitarianism and from the totalitarian elements in his own earlier thinking does not lead him towards any relaxed acceptance of the realities of Western democracies or of man as Lewis find him in the twentieth century. Sammael's plans are aimed at producing a society far closer to our own than to fascism. But this aim is precisely what upsets God and leads to the dénouement in which Sammael is injured, Hell is occupied by God's forces, and Pullman is carried off by angels. If there is political allegory in *The Human Age,* it is that the potential for evil in politics did not go away with the demise of fascism. Slavery can be packaged as freedom, but it remains slavery. But this perception does not lead Lewis back to his old "plague on both your houses" posture of detachment, the posture of his satiric fiction. For he now sees that, too, as a form of slavery packaged as freedom. This lesson is brought home to Pullman in *Malign Fiesta,* when, while out for a ride with the Devil, he witnesses Sammael throwing a woman to a pack of beasts. Pullman, who is careful not to say anything, is nevertheless deeply shaken.

> His sympathy for the woman grew and subterraneously developed; and when he *saw* (with unexpected suddenness) the unsurpassable horror of her punishment he started trembling as in response to horror, because of the violent conflict in his psyche. . . . The woman, praying and crossing herself, was doing what he ought to have been doing. She was defying the superhuman strength of the infernal power.[68]

Damnation, for Pullman, had previously been something that happened to other people.[69] At this point he realizes that detachment will no longer do. He, too, is in Hell, even if in a consulting capacity, and he had better do something about it.

What Lewis now means by Hell is power and the exercise of power, and the term he now opposes to power is value. For Lewis the only source of this opposition to power is divine, which is what Pullman grasps when desperately looking for a way out of the powerful position he is in as the Devil's bright young man: "God *values* man: that is the important thing to remember. It is this valuing that is so extraordinary. There are men who only value *power*. This is absurd, because power destroys value."[70] What Lewis means here by value is not so clear as it might be, but God's brief appearance in the extant fragment of *The Trial of Man* offers a clue. Sammael is in the hospital after having experienced the characteristically Lewisian fate of amputation, and God stops by his hospital room. The nurse who is the only witness to this encounter (not much of one: Sammael is apparently unconscious) describes God in these terms:

> There was nothing personal pressing on her from this big machine: and this indifference, or this apathy, delighted her, without her knowing what was responsible for such a reaction. Here, at last, was someone asking nothing of her personality, who was a selfless expanse, of indifference (free of the selfish pressures which are emitted by all men and women, who are so unrelievedly functional).[71]

God values man, it seems, precisely by being indifferent to him, by having no designs on him. The difference between the Divine and the Diabolic is to be located here, in the divine absence of self and of selfish designs.[72]

There seems to be a contradiction, however, between this vision of the Divine as uninterested in exercising power and God's invasion and occupation of Hell at the end of *Malign Fiesta*. The purpose of that invasion was benevolent, as God wished to block Sammael's Machiavellian designs, but it nonetheless involved an exercise of power. The problem is an artistic as well as a theological one: it is hard to imagine a novel about Pullman's immersion in the Divine (with or without God as a character) because plot or action seems rigourously excluded from the divine realm. This dilemma may indicate why Lewis found *The Trial of Man* difficult to write. "God is a big problem," as he confessed in a 1951 letter.[73]

But as a problem He has a familiar form for Lewis. The problem is that it is hard to portray "indifference" in action, in time, in a plot, because it is really outside of those things. *The Apes of God* had a similar problem, which was how to portray detachment in action. Lewis solved it there by leaving his detached figure, Pierpoint, off stage, and I expect had Lewis finished *The Trial of Man* he would have adopted this stratagem again. It may sound ludicrous or blasphemous to compare Pierpoint to God but the comparison is instructive: Pierpoint stands in the same relation to God that Lewis's earlier concept of detachment stands to the new divine "indifference." The earlier concept falls short precisely where Pierpoint falls short. Pierpoint (and for him we can substitute Lewis) is supposed to be detached, selfless, and disinterested, and Lewis had opposed the detached vision of the artist to the selfish concern for power of the politician. But that detached vision was far from selfless, far from disinterested: Lewis's insistence on his superiority to the mass of people, on the superior status of his detached perspective, was highly self-centered and self-serving. Detachment, we can see from the perspective of the "higher indifference," was really an excuse for what we ordinarily call indifference, whereas the indifference of the Divine is a purified and more profound concept of detachment.

The distinction Lewis is working with is exactly that established by Eliot in *Little Gidding* in a passage I quote for the second time, though the terms are reversed:

> There are three conditions which often look alike
> Yet differ completely, flourish in the same hedgerow:
> Attachment to self and to things and to persons, detachment
> From self and from things and from persons; and, growing between
>   them, indifference
> Which resembles the others as death resembles life. [74]

Lewis's supposedly detached posture of his satiric fiction was really indifference as Eliot uses the term here, resembling detachment "as death resembles life." What is so chilling about *The Apes of God* is that indifference, the absence of the sympathy found in Dante's treatment of the damned. Pullman achieves this sympathy in *Malign Fiesta,* and his achievement of it is a figure for the sympathy of his author, who comes to "value man," though that valuation, like Dante's, coexists with astringent judgments and austere standards.

Eliot is apposite here because one way of presenting Lewis's development would be to say that he was moving towards the positions and attitudes of Eliot's later work. Lewis was certainly aware that, in *The Human Age,* he was poaching on Eliot's territory. As he expressed it in a letter, "As a theologian I am inferior to what Eliot is supposed to be. That must be remedied!" [75] Eliot, moreover, played an important role in the writing of *The Human Age,* working with the now blind Lewis virtually as an editor in an attempt to compensate for Lewis's inability to read his own manuscripts. Eliot and Lewis were closer the last few years of Lewis's life, both in personal and artistic terms, than they had been since the time forty years earlier when Lewis in *Blast #2* was the first to publish Eliot's work in England. [76] Just as Lewis preceded and influenced Eliot in his development of a modernist aesthetic, Eliot in turn preceded and influenced Lewis in his shift towards an explicitly theological aesthetic. After this turn, a theological vision of man replaces a satiric vision of man in Lewis's work just as it had in Eliot's. In this vision, man is to be valued despite his fallibility, not, as in the earlier work of both men, castigated for that fallibility.

Yet this shift can be overstated. It was, after all, the bias against time and towards detachment that carried Lewis to this point. The formal design and concern for detachment of his earlier work are transformed in *The Human Age,* not abandoned. Pullman, we should remember, is rescued and saved, despite his cooperation with Sammael. Lewis's new position is a development out of the old, not a complete break with it.

We may be inclined to wonder whether Lewis tilted quite as decisively to the Divine as my account thus far has suggested. Like Pullman, Lewis may be accused of doing the Devil's work though ostensibly favoring the Divine. The project of Pullman that raised God's ire was the humanization of the angels. Lewis, always a firm believer in dichotomies, insists that the Divine and the human should not be mixed. To mix them, as Pullman realizes, would mean annihilating the Divine.[77] However, in *Malign Fiesta,* Lewis successfully humanizes the angels, and in what we have of *The Trial of Man,* admittedly a rejected fragment, he even humanizes God himself. Lewis cannot write about the Divine, in short, without mixing the human in, just as he cannot write about the hereafter without mixing in elements of earthly politics.[78] It should therefore occasion no surprise that after concluding *Malign Fiesta,* he did not go on to write *The Trial of Man,* but returned to earth, completing *The Red Priest* and almost completing another novel, *Twentieth Century Palette,* before he died. Even though Lewis thought that he ought to be writing about transcendence and the life after death, politics and art continued to be what he could write about. The protagonist of *The Red Priest,* Father Card, is implicitly criticized by Lewis for replacing his proper spiritual concerns with the earthly concerns of politics, but Lewis—as so often in his works—could have been (and implicitly was) talking about himself as well. Despite his desire to escape time, Lewis could not do it, but instead went on analyzing and attacking the time he lived in and wanted to escape.

Part of his reluctance to embark on *The Trial of Man* may have stemmed from the fact that its composition would have forced him to be explicit about the shape of his belief. Lewis retained his old reluctance to be explicit about those "metaphysical or religious values" he embraced. The language of *The Human Age* is, for the most part, Christian, but its theology is, if anything, Zoroastrian.[79] Lewis would have found it hard to write a volume set in Heaven that would not have upset the religious orthodoxies as much as *Time and Western Man* upset the critical orthodoxies and *The Art of Being Ruled* the political. No matter what the theological stance of *The Trial of Man* would have been, we can rest assured that it would have retained the truculent independence of the Enemy.

Lewis remained a heretic, a member of a party of one, to the end of his life, and this attitude demonstrates the remarkable continuity of aims in his work, a continuity that nonetheless coexists with a great flexibility in means. Those aims, most fundamentally, consisted of (1) a desire to stop time; to write and paint as if it did not exist; (2) a desire to find a detached still point from which the (malign) order in the flux could be perceived, described, and denounced; (3) a desire to make his art a forum in which supporters of that order could somehow be brought to accept Lewis's views and consequently to move towards his stance of opposition. All three aims, as I have tried to show, are implicit in his Vorticist painting and attendant notions about that painting; they then find their way into Lewis's writing, growing in complexity and changing in complexion as they do so. The final change in complexion is the explicitly transcendental cast that these aims were given in *The Human Age,* but, as I have also tried to show, that was implicit from the beginning, in the neo-Kantian bases of the Vorticist aesthetic.

A local or efficient cause of these aims, particularly the first, was Lewis's métier, painting. Yet, there seems to have been a deeper underlying cause, which is whatever impelled Lewis's fierce drive to independence. It is easy to see the cost of that drive, in terms of its effect on Lewis's career and work; however, it is as the antidote to everything, the complete and utter heretic, that Lewis remains of permanent interest and value. True heretics are always in short supply.

6 Excellent Sausage and the Smell of Mint:
The Cantos in the Context of Vorticism

The subject of this final chapter, *The Cantos* of Ezra Pound, has had no dearth of commentary of late, and anyone proposing to add to that commentary needs, I think, if not actually to excuse himself, then at least to explain himself at the onset. Why add another word? What remains to be said?

The fact is that, as Michael Harper has recently and eloquently said, "*The Cantos* is a poem we have yet to read."[1] If one considers the amount of work that has been done on the poem, there is remarkably little consensus about it. Harper's remark itself serves to indicate at what a basic point the disagreements begin, for I at least would want to write "*The Cantos* are," which concedes the poem's unity in order to preserve agreement in number. Harper's "is" is polemical, designed to deny the widely held view that, as Leon Surette has put it, "Pound's epic is more a collection of poetry than a single coherent poem."[2] That two of the better recent commentators would disagree so completely is not, in my opinion, a sign of vitality in Pound criticism but one of confusion and chaos. No one agrees about what *The Cantos* really are (or is). Are they (is it) little more than a collection of poems or do they form a unified work?

Given this situation, many critics prefer to ignore the question of the poem's unity and structure and concentrate instead on the task of explication. Obviously, a poem as dense as *The Cantos* needs a great deal of explication. Yet explication cannot be more than a means to an end, the end of understanding the poem. A full explication of *The Cantos* (and this is conceivable in the case of *The Cantos,* unlike, say, *Finnegans Wake*) will do little or nothing to deepen our understanding of the work when considered as a whole. What kind of a poem is *The Cantos*? What was Pound up to? How do the various cantos and the various sections or groups of cantos connect? Does the poem hold together and form a

191

unified structure in any nontrivial sense? These questions, though ignored by the explicators, cannot be ignored if we hope to discuss units of *The Cantos* larger than the individual word or phrase.

The critics who try to answer the difficult questions about the form of *The Cantos* can be divided into two groups, those, to use the language of Canto 116, who think that it coheres and those who think that it does not. At first glance, certainly, it does not seem to, as *The Cantos* are a bewildering assemblage of different narratives, different styles, and even different languages. From the beginning, they were attacked as incoherent and jumbled; for this reason the sympathetic elucidation of *The Cantos* which began with Hugh Kenner's *The Poetry of Ezra Pound* (1951) argued in response that the work had an underlying coherence. Kenner, it must be said, has never committed himself to any "map" of *The Cantos;* in fact he has attacked at length the assumption that for a work to be coherent it must have a structure that can be diagrammed.[3] Yet when he has seen a connection of the kind such diagrams are made of, he has pointed it out, and the incomparable assurance of his discussion of *The Cantos* has made it seem as if one could go on making formal or structural connections until one had indeed constructed a diagram of the whole.[4]

Inspired by that assurance, a number of critics, less careful or perhaps less shrewd than he, have tried to make that formal coherence explicit. None of these attempts has proven to be generally persuasive: *The Cantos* do not, for example, divide into the neat "Inferno," "Purgatorio," and "Paradiso" posited by Daniel Pearlman in *The Barb of Time.*[5] Yet later critics continue to provide us with diagrams or master keys of the kind Kenner warned against; Forrest Read's '76 which sees *The Cantos* as a gigantic hermetic code that Read cracked is only the most recent example. One of the driving forces behind these total or holistic readings has been a desire to promote *The Cantos* as well as explicate them. Pearlman argued in *The Barb of Time* that an "integrative" view of *The Cantos* offers the only possible basis for a favorable evaluation of the poem; a "disintegrative" reading which denied *The Cantos* "major form" was in his opinion necessarily a hostile reading.[6] Perhaps this was so when serious discussion of *The Cantos* commenced in the early 1950s. But by now *The Cantos* have an assured place in the modernist canon; moreover, current literary theory is far less likely to equate structural coherence with greatness.

For these reasons and because the integrative readings have failed to do justice to the complexity of the poem, the best recent work on *The Cantos* has by and large argued that attempts to "find the form" of *The Cantos* are necessarily futile. Critics such as Ronald Bush, Leon Surette, Wendy Stallard Flory, and Michael André Bernstein have attacked the earlier criticism for its tendency to look for a master key that will reduce the complexity of *The Cantos* to an ordered scheme.[7] These critics insist that their more cautious and reasonable approach will simply explore the ramifications of a particular aspect of *The Cantos,* as no master key for *The Cantos* exists. Yet as they proceed, this disclaimer seems simply a clever anticipatory refutation. Eleusis does become the central motif for Leon Surette, personal struggle becomes the aspect that subsumes every other for Flory, and Pound's epic ambitions explains and in a sense reconciles what is otherwise irreconciliable in *The Cantos* for Bernstein.

The problem with the position of these younger critics is that it cannot be the basis for a reading of *The Cantos*. Their work is exemplary in pointing out the protean, shifting, and provisional nature of *The Cantos*. However, the minute one begins to speak of *The Cantos* as a whole, unless one glories in the chaos of the text, one must necessarily begin to try to provide paradigms that reduce the complexity of the poem to some sort of manageable order. One must, in short, try to make *The Cantos* seem less protean, less shifting; the inevitability is best shown by the way these critics, after warning against holistic, single-minded readings of *The Cantos,* end up providing fairly single-minded readings of their own. In other words, once we begin to speak about the poem as a whole, we are all doomed to be integrative critics like Daniel Pearlman even if we see the problems in that stance.

The only alternative is, as I have said, to glory in the chaos of the text. The problems inherent in a more traditional, "integrative" approach to *The Cantos* would seem to make a disintegrative, deconstructive reading of *The Cantos* such as that proposed by Joseph Riddel attractive.[8] If the poem is chaotic, let us accept that chaos and not deform the poem as we have it by trying to form it.

However, there are two signal objections to such an approach. First, it is clear that order or form was a central preoccupation of Pound. Pound's conception of the form of his poem may have changed, as the younger Pound critics have shown us, but he always had a conception of its form. Pound, at any rate, would not have us glory in the chaos of his text. Second, the reason why poetic form was important for Pound was that he had a mimetic conception of poetry completely at odds with deconstruction's skepticism about the possibility of representation or signification. The function of art, according to Pound, is to form something outside of the text, out in the world, to codify the complexity of the world into a form or a pattern. Moreover, form is crucial to a reading of *The Cantos,* for Pound saw his poem as forming or codifying the complexity of history itself.

Here I think we can see that the dilemma of Pound criticism mirrors Pound's own dilemma. Pound wanted to form the chaos of the world in his poem, just as Daniel Pearlman wanted to form the chaos of Pound's poem. But, just as the rest of us see what refuses to fit Pearlman's form, so, too, at moments in the evolution of his poem, Pound saw what refuses to fit his forms. When his forms became palpably inadequate, he set off in a new direction, recasting the form of the poem as he proceded. However, even though he kept risking incoherence by changing his poem's form, form and coherence remained his central concern. They did so for exactly the same reason that he had to keep changing his forms: he was not simply forming a poem but was trying to form (or find the form of) history itself. We therefore risk trivializing the poem if we ignore its concern with form and accept its chaos, for we ignore the central theme of the poem. But we risk rewriting the poem if we try to find its organizing form, as our search for form, like Pound's search for history's form, seems to necessitate a reductive approach to the complexity of the poem as we have it.

We can find a way beyond this double bind if we allow two principles to govern our reading of *The Cantos,* and these two principles are the basis of the reading of *The Cantos* that follows. First, one must approach *The Cantos* historically. *The Cantos* cannot be reduced to a single form or structure because Pound's ideas about the form of the poem kept changing. Those changing notions of the poem's form are the best guide to the poem, and I will attempt to chart those changes. Second, we need to consider Pound's notions of form in any case, even though they are never quite adequate to the complexity of the poem, because the adequacy or inadequacy of form, the possibility of forming reality or of finding its form in a poem, is a central concern of *The Cantos*. While writing *The Cantos,* Pound engaged in the process or mental action of codifying forms and using them to portray and interpret the flux of reality, and we need to engage in the same process in order to read and understand the poem.

This is not to say that the poem's own flux is consistently artful, carefully designed to imitate the world's. We must recognize that Pound always wanted to form the flux and write a poem with "major form" as Pearlman puts it. But that form kept changing. He began with notions about form that came out of the aesthetic of Vorticism. He subsequently moved away from his initial assumptions about the form of the poem, towards new assumptions that in turn underwent revision. The end result, the poem as we have it, is in some ways extremely chaotic, but Pound abandoned neither the hope that the chaos would be formed nor his search for forms and order. Later poets such as Charles Olson have taken this search as the most impressive feature of *The Cantos* and have taken the improvised, provisional character of Pound's epic as their formal (or rather informal) model.[9] But this "open form" of *The Cantos* was an accident occasioned by Pound's failure to find a "closed form" that satisfied him. Pound, it seems safe to say, did not set out to write *The Cantos.*

What he did set out to write was a poem whose lineaments are indebted to Vorticism. Pound began *The Cantos* in a state of uncertainty about his aims and methods, but this period of uncertanty, expertly chronicled by Ronald Bush in *The Genesis of Ezra Pound's Cantos,* ended in 1923 when Pound made his version of the *nekuia* from Book XI of the *Odyssey* the beginning of his poem.[10] To begin with a visit to the dead implies an imitation, formally speaking, of Dante's *Commedia* rather than the *Odyssey.* This implication is strengthened, moreover, by the way Canto 1, like Canto I of the *Inferno,* functions as a prologue to the rest: it ends "So that:" as if the rest of the poem were an extension of

Odysseus's descent. Indeed, when Pound summarized the themes of *The Cantos* in a letter of 1927 to his father, his first theme was "Live man goes down into world of Dead."[11] Pound's world of the dead, it should be clear from the rest of the poem if not from Canto 1, is the past and, as Odysseus largely disappears from the poem after Canto 1, the poem is Pound's voyage into the world of the dead, just as the *Commedia* is Dante's.

Yet Pound has good reasons for beginning with the *nekuia* as Odysseus's descent differs from Dante's in a number of pertinent ways. First, he descends alone; likewise, Pound will have no Virgil to guide him through his poem. Second, he descends, of course, to Hades, not to Hell, and this indicates that the world of *The Cantos* is essentially pagan, not Christian. Finally, Odysseus descends for quite a specific reason. Beyond a natural curiosity, he has no interest in the dead; his interest is in what they can teach him. He is trying to learn about his present and future situation, to learn what he will have to do to make it home.[12]

This aim is the most important sense in which Pound's voyage through the dead is Odyssean. For the investigation into the past in *The Cantos* is always directed and purposive. The poem's purpose is to tell us something about the present, and it does so by providing instructive parallels with that present. Pound learned how to do this, as I have already shown, from the Vorticist sculptors, and *Cathay* and *Homage to Sextus Propertius* are early and straightforward examples of the use of historical parallelism, which I have called the ideogrammatic loop. Pound himself referred to this structural principle as the "repeat in history" and in that letter of 1927 to his father he put it as the second major theme of *The Cantos*.[13] Pound's term, however, is slightly misleading: in his poetry, Pound never explicitly says that history repeats. The reader, as in *Cathay* and *Propertius*, completes the loop by seeing the repeat in the present; the reader interprets the known world by means of the paradigms or forms the poet provides.

Though the historical patterns or repeats that concern Pound in the Early Cantos are considerably more complex than those of *Propertius* or *Cathay*, his investigations are more focused than they have seemed to other critics. The pattern or repeat in history that fascinates Pound is the pattern of the close interrelation between cultural achievement and violence. After quickly and sketchily establishing that this interrelation is indeed a pattern (the fall of Troy; Greek myth; the troubadours), Pound in Canto 5 begins his investigation of the Italian Renaissance which remains the primary concern of *The Cantos* until Canto 31.

The Renaissance is a good period, obviously, in which to show the puzzling and troubling relation, and Pound quickly focuses in Cantos 8–11 on perhaps the key figure to demonstrate it, Sigismundo Malatesta. At an early stage in his research into Malatesta, Pound wrote, "If I find he was TOO bloody quiet and orderly it will ruin the canto."[14] This comment indicates, as I am arguing, that what he wants Malatesta to show is precisely the tension or ambivalence between creativity and violence. The choice of Sigismundo Malatesta as the key figure to represent the energy of the Renaissance is significant in other ways. It is an eccentric choice, as Rimini is not ordinarily seen as one of the crucial centers of the Renaissance, but it is an acute choice, as anyone who has seen the Tempio Malatestiana that Sigismundo had built in Rimini will testify. Here as always, Pound is consciously revisionary, intent on challenging conventional maps and notions of cultural history. Rimini is not customarily seen as central, I expect, because what was achieved there was so utterly dependent upon the personal efforts and will of Sigismundo himself. But that initiative is precisely why Pound considers it exemplary. Any notion that cultural achievement is ever broadly based is an illusion according to Pound. Enough activity took place in Florence to help to sustain that illusion; Sigismundo's one-man whirl of activity is far more representative of the conditions that usually obtain in history.

Pound portrays the Renaissance as complex, violent, divided, and fragile. This portrait is not an entirely new one: Cesare Borgia fascinated many before Pound. But Pound wants to ensure that we do not divide the Renaissance into a bad turbulent side and a good artistic side. These sides are intimately connected in the many small groups or bursts of activity that made up what we join together as the Renaissance. Pound's own term for a cultural concentration like Rimini is the vortex; in his 1915 essay, "The

Renaissance," he refers to "the numerous vortices of the Italian cities, striving against each other not only in commerce but in the arts as well."[15]

Vortex is actually quite a good word for the cultural centers of the Italian Renaissance as it captures their energy, instability, and tendency to dissipate. Their tendency to dissipate concerns Pound; for this reason, Pound balances his portrait of Malatesta creating a Rimini Vortex with the later account of the dissipation of the Venetian Vortex. Just as the Malatesta Cantos occupy the (far from still) center of Cantos 1-16, an account of Venice in Cantos 24-26 is the most extended sequence in the next section of the Cantos to be published as a unit, Cantos 17-27.[16] It should be understood that these two accounts are directly comparable. They treat the conditions in which the state in Italy bought art, and the comparison is instructive. Sigismundo, for all his political problems, brought art into being; in the far more secure Venetian Republic, great artists like Titian cheated the government and did not do the work they had been paid for. Something went wrong between the time of Malatesta and that of Titian, as Pound's juxtaposition reveals, though what exactly caused this decline is an open and unanswered question at this point in *The Cantos*.

Pound joined these two blocks of cantos together with three additional cantos to form the first enduring block of cantos, *A Draft of XXX Cantos,* published in 1930, and if these cantos have a unifying theme it is the conception of cultural history as a series of vortices. Hugh Kenner has put it this way: "for theme (he now had his theme) the coming and going of vortices in time's river."[17] Pound had said in a note on the Nō drama that a long Vorticist poem would be possible if it had unity of image; the unity of the Early Cantos depends upon the image or concept of the vortex itself. This dependence is never directly stated, of course, for it is up to the reader to see what organizes the work and to grasp its form.

Pound had used the vortex in this way in 1913-14 to describe the Vorticist movement itself. In a letter of 19 December 1913, he wrote to William Carlos Williams: "You may get something slogging away by yourself that you would miss in The Vortex—and that we miss."[18] Here the vortex stands both for a geographical place, Lon-

don, and, more importantly, for the concentration of talent and
sense of excitement that London offered at that time. In keeping
with this usage, *Blast* was subtitled *Review of the Great English
Vortex*. Whose idea it was is not known, but it was Pound, not
Lewis, who was especially alive to the importance of cultural centers or vortices. His 1915 essay, "The Renaissance," moves directly
from the discussion of the vortices of the Italian Renaissance
already quoted to a discussion of the consequences for American
cultural life of the fact that it had no such capital as London,
nothing to serve as a vortex.[19]

Pound's orientation towards vortices should help clarify his particular interest in the Renaissance. Once again, Pound's center of
interest is not the past-as-past but as a parallel to the present: he is
using the past to construct an ideogrammatic loop that the reader
must complete. Pound is exploring the possibility that this century
may be a new renaissance and that he and his friends may be a cultural vortex analogous to one of the centers of activity of the
Italian Renaissance such as Rimini. There are some attractive
parallels, which suggest in my opinion why certain material is
included in the Early Cantos. Both are periods in which cultural
horizons expand dramatically. The quattrocento learned to see
classical civilization anew, without Christianity standing in its line
of vision.[20] Pound's century has discovered Oriental culture and
has found fresh ways of seeing Mediterranean culture from Homeric
Greece through Provence to Malatesta's Rimini. Both are periods
of chaos and violence and this parallel gives a point to Pound's
interest in the possible connections between the turbulence and
brilliance of Renaissance Italy. The twentieth century has the
turbulence; the implicit question is, has it the brilliance? Or, to
put it another way, who is the Sigismundo Malatesta of our time?

Thus I would argue that it is the confluence of two separate
ideas, the notion of cultural vortices and the ideogrammatic loop,
that shapes the portrait of the Renaissance that dominates the
Early Cantos. These ideas are not completely separate, however, as
both are expressions of Pound's paradigmatic conception of history. For Pound, cultural "vortices have analogous structures," as
Hugh Kenner has noted,[21] and one vortex can best be understood
by means of another. I have already argued that this paradigmatic

conception of history—shared by other leading modernists—must be seen as an attempt to find an ordering principle for art different from the linear sequence of narrative. Appropriately, if these Early Cantos are less than completely successful, even when taken on their own terms, it is because sequence cannot be dispensed with quite so summarily. The problem of sequence reappears in a variety of ways.

The most immediately noticeable way it reappears concerns how the poem moves from one moment in time to another. Such movement had not been a problem in the *Homage to Sextus Propertius* or *Cathay* which reflect upon only two moments in time, one of which is implicit. The Early Cantos share the implicit reference back to the present, but in addition the explicit temporal setting of the poem shifts so often that successive cantos set in the same time (the Malatesta and the Venetian Cantos) stand out, calling attention to their own significance. Though the Renaissance is the central concern of the poem from Canto 5 to Canto 30, material from a bewildering variety of other times and places is presented in these cantos.

One could call this a problem in historical syntax, and Pound's solution is indebted to his earlier replacement in his poetry of syntactic links by juxtaposition or parataxis. He simply cuts from one time to another, usually—though not always—between cantos. But juxtaposition does not solve the problem so much as recast it: if one canto is about Odysseus and another about Confucius, what is holding together what looks like a bundle of independent poems? The premise of the haiku from which Pound took the method is that the juxtapositions themselves hold the poem together. The relationship they establish is the meaning of the poem. Fenollosa had argued that something quite similar was operative in the Chinese ideogram's essentially paratactic mode of creating meaning. If *The Cantos* are to be more than a group of independent poems, the poem's juxtapositions must also create coherence by establishing relations between and among the material Pound presents.

But there is a crucial difference between the subject matter of haiku and the Early Cantos. To return to the familiar example of "In a Station of the Metro," it is easy to draw a connection between

"Petals on a wet, black bough" and "The apparition of these faces in the crowd." Two perceptual images are being juxtaposed and a clear relationship is established between them. The materials of the Early Cantos, however, are far more conceptual. Canto 1, for example, which is primarily a translation from Homer ends with "So that:" and Canto 2 begins with the lines, "Hang it all, Robert Browning, / there can be but the one 'Sordello.'" No immediately perceptible relationship exists between these juxtaposed lines or cantos; therefore, the juxtaposition does not in any direct sense create meaning. Ultimately, a reader can posit a reason for this juxtaposition and thus construe a meaning. I would argue that Pound's point is that his investigation into the past through translating old poems as in Canto 1 is parallel to (should be related to) that of Robert Browning in *Sordello*. If there can be only one *Sordello*, Pound will not attempt a second, a direct imitation of Browning's poem *Sordello*, but he is up to something quite similar and he is alerting the reader that *Sordello* remains relevant to Pound's enterprise in *The Cantos*. But I must confess that I do not see that abstract, conceptual link as immediately as I see the perceptual link established by "In a Station of the Metro," nor can I ever be as confident that the meaning I draw out of this juxtaposition is what Pound intends for me to draw.

Leon Surette, in his recent study *A Light from Eleusis*, has called Pound's juxtapositional poetic "the poetry of inference" and by this term he means that it is up to the reader to infer the connection between the juxtaposed particulars.[22] When I first encountered Surette's term, I thought it inappropriate because it was too open. In poems built up by means of juxtapositions, the reader should be able to see an already implicit relation between the juxtaposed materials. Nonetheless, the Early Cantos are inferential in the way Surette describes and this characteristic is one of their problems. The reader has to infer relations, not perceive them; he has to do too much work or rather the wrong kind of work.

In other words, Pound applied his already successful juxtapositional technique, in "In a Station of the Metro," to more conceptual material and in a much larger structure without fully anticipating the problems that those changes would create. The problem is not, however, that too few meaningful relations can be inferred from the Early Cantos. It is that too many can be. Put any two things next to one another and, after puzzling long enough, someone will discover something that brings them together. But after fifty such juxtapositions, one finds oneself in a jungle of relations, without enough of a clue as to which are really significant.

The profusion of connections points to the real problem with the form of *The Cantos*. Those who can read *The Waste Land* or *Ulysses* will not demand a diagram or a road map, nor will they insist on every connection being made explicit. But I think they need (as least I need) a sense that the work they are doing will be rewarded, that the connections they are patiently making will in the end connect up to each other and form a unified structure of meaning. This sense is what the reader of *The Cantos* lacks. No matter how subtle or wide-ranging the unifying theme one posits, there will be material that stands outside and seems irrelevant, unless the unifying theme is so all-embracing that anything can be stuffed into it. If one sees *The Cantos* as a record of Pound's personal struggle in writing his poem, for example, as Wendy Stallard Flory does in her recent *Ezra Pound and The Cantos: A Record of Struggle,* then anything Pound includes is a logical part of the poem. But in that case anything he failed to include might have been included as well: principles of inclusion are not useful unless they are also principles of exclusion.

It could be said that I am simply pointing out that there is a great deal of material in the Early Cantos that does not fit *my* scheme. I am saying that, I must confess, but I am also saying that anything precise enough to be called a scheme will find material that does not fit. The problem, finally, is that Pound's forms or schemes, like the reader's, are not sufficient to explain or connect all of the things he includes in his work. Pound later said to Donald Hall that the problem he encountered was "to find a form that wouldn't exclude something merely because it didn't fit." [23] But that statement indicates perilously close to no form at all. The image of the vortex and the theory of the repeat in history are the forms with which he initially hoped to organize his material and provide his poem with a certain form or coherence. But just as whatever form the reader finds is insufficient to organize the complexity of the

Early Cantos, Pound's forms proved insufficient to organize the complexity of history. It is not simply a matter of there being more to history than repetitions and vortices. More importantly, these forms did not enable Pound to answer certain questions that began to trouble him in the 1920s.

The contrast between Malatesta's Rimini and Titian's Venice implicitly asks the question, what happened? What caused the decline in cultural energies revealed in Cantos 24–26? This question grows in force during the 1920s as Pound's hopes for a new renaissance comparable to the Italian Renaissance begin to fade. In 1924 he moved from Paris to Rapallo; in 1927 he began to publish a magazine, *The Exile,* the title of which sounds as if he knew then that he would never willingly come back out of exile. In that same year came Lewis's fierce attack on Pound and Joyce in *Time and Western Man;* the previous year Pound had privately but decisively rejected Joyce's new work which was to become *Finnegans Wake.*[24] The Great English Vortex of 1914, in other words, was dispersing quickly in the late 1920s, and Pound did not see many signs of vital new groups to replace it.[25] This turn in Pound's perception of contemporary history may account for the presentation of Venice's cultural decline in Cantos 24–26; it certainly gives that presentation urgency, making an explanation of why Venice declined pertinent and useful knowledge.

The question is really about historical sequence and therefore cannot be answered by the method of the Early Cantos. The juxtapositional poetic of the Early Cantos cuts from high point in history to high point; it does not recreate a historical sequence, only the most significant moments of any sequence. This method, developed by Pound according to Imagist and Vorticist canons initially as a method of writing brief lyrics, can present certain historical moments with great clarity. But because it necessarily annihilates temporal or historical sequence, it cannot answer questions about historical sequence, about a specific historical development.[26]

In short, two of the most important aspects of the method of the Early Cantos, taken over from Vorticism and from Pound's shorter poems of the Vorticist period, did not prove to be completely adequate to the task of articulating as vast a poetic structure as *The Cantos.* First, the juxtapositional technique of haiku can connect things but cannot be explicit about what the connection might be. Because of the conceptual nature of Pound's materials, the reader of *The Cantos* often wants more information about the meaning of Pound's juxtapositions than can be provided simply by the fact of juxtaposition. Second, the "repeat in history" or ideogrammatic loop, though adequate to the kind of historiography Pound wanted at the onset, was not a suitable method for attacking the questions that began to interest Pound.

Pound began *The Cantos,* in other words, thinking that both cultural history and his poem would have a certain Vorticist order and therefore that the shape of history would help shape his poem. But, towards the end of the 1920s, he began to see both dissolving in chaos: the great cultural epoch of his youth was disintegrating as the Renaissance had and his poem was not developing the degree of internal coherence it ought. I assign this perception to Pound as well as to myself because around Canto 30 and 1930 he began to recast *The Cantos* in ways that attempt to solve these formal problems. This recasting involved a turn away from the comparatively open Vorticist notion of form with which he began, though the extent of the turn has been obscured by Pound himself who, as Ronald Bush has observed, "spoke as if his method had never changed."[27] He felt that he had to speak in this way, I suspect, asserting continuity even in areas where little continuity existed, in order to defend the coherence of his poem.

Nowhere is the interplay between the (real) schism and (apparent) continuity in Pound's aesthetic thinking revealed more clearly than in the promulgation of the "ideogrammic method." Ronald Bush has shown, arguing against those who would see the ideogrammic method as the basis of all of *The Cantos,* that Pound began to use the term *ideogram* programmatically only in 1927.[28] His first precise formulation of the ideogrammic method, in the 1934 *ABC of Reading,* remains the clearest:

> But when the Chinaman wanted to make a picture of something more complicated, or of a general idea, how did he go about it?
>
> He is to define red. How can he do it in a picture that isn't painted in red paint?
>
> He puts (or his ancestor put) together the abbreviated pictures of

ROSE	CHERRY
IRON RUST	FLAMINGO

> That, you see, is very much the kind of thing a biologist does (in a
> very much more complicated way) when he gets together a few hun-
> dred or thousand slides, and picks out what is necessary for his gen-
> eral statement.[29]

This definition of the ideogrammic method also employs the
method, as it establishes the truth of a general statement by means
of a concrete example. Unhappily, Pound's example is incorrect,
as he must have realized when he began to study Chinese seriously
in the 1930s. There is no such character. He found this example in
Fenollosa's papers, but Fenollosa meant it as an example of the
way Chinese works, not as an explanation of an actual ideogram.[30]

However, the fact that this misunderstood example comes from
Fenollosa has helped to perpetuate another misunderstanding. For,
as Herbert Schneidau has pointed out, we need to distinguish
sharply between Pound's original enthusiasm for Fenollosa's
theories about the ideogram and his later ideogrammic method.[31]
The ideogrammic method should not be identified with the juxtapositional method of *Cathay* or the Early Cantos which I have
called the ideogrammatic loop. Instead, it originates in a dramatic
shift in Pound's thinking that takes place around 1930. At that
point Pound drastically reinterprets what Fenollosa had to say
about the Chinese ideogram and comes up with the ideogrammic
method.

What is new in Pound's thinking is his stress on the general statement. Fenollosa's original point had been that by placing concrete
images in juxtaposition the Chinese ideogram creates a vivid, concrete, and richly poetic effect. Pound attempted to attain something similar in his own work, in poems like "In a Station of the
Metro." But this method is an eschewal of generalization, not a
way to generalize. "In a Station of the Metro" does not define
some abstract law; rather, it creates a relation that has quite precise
limits. But that poetic of juxtaposition, as I have argued, had not
worked as well in *The Cantos,* partly because Pound began to be
interested in defining generalities of a kind that were beyond the

poem's scope. The ideogrammic method should be seen, I think, as an attempt to solve the problem created by Pound's juxtapositional poetic in the Early Cantos. It enables Pound to continue to work from particulars; yet his way of handling those particulars changes in the Middle Cantos. Particulars are now included in the poem because they help define a general law or abstract entity that Pound wants to present.

The ideogrammic method goes a long way towards solving the formal problem of the diagram or "road map." In the Middle Cantos, the reader has a much greater sense of being led through these details for a purpose. An ideogram is being articulated; each canto is a fragment that helps to define a law in the way that rose or iron rust helps to define red. This method is a marked shift away from Pound's earlier aesthetic of implications, a marked shift, in other words, away from the Vorticist and Orientalist aesthetic that Pound developed around 1914. The extent of that shift was masked by the appearance of continuity in that he was still talking about ideograms and citing Fenollosa as support for his method. Nonetheless, we should recognize that his concern with aligning particulars so as to define a general law is new, and this new concern develops out of a sense that the Early Cantos in their eschewal of generalization had produced confusion. To set *The Cantos* the task of defining an ideogram was to give the poem a form or order that readers could be expected to grasp and be guided by.

By the time of *Guide to Kulchur* (1938), Pound had begun to relate this method of definition to Confucius and his concern with *ching ming,* or the rectification of names.[32] Confucius, not Fenollosa, is the proper Oriental source for—or analogue to—Pound's concern in the 1930s with the ordering of particulars and precise definition. *Guide to Kulchur* begins with a "Digest of the Analects," and the second passage from Confucius that Pound quotes is about *ching ming,* the characters for which Pound also includes:

> Tseu-Lou asked: If the Prince of Mei appointed you head of the government, to what wd. you first set your mind?
>
> KUNG: To call people and things by their names, that is by the correct denominations, to see that the terminology was exact.

正名

"You mean that is the first?" Said Tseu-leu. "Aren't you dodging the question? What's the use of that?"

KUNG: You are a blank. An intelligent man hesitates to talk of what he don't understand, he feels embarrassment.

If the terminology be not exact, if it fit not the thing, the governmental instructions will not be explicit, if the instructions aren't clear and the names don't fit, you can not conduct business properly.

If business is not properly run the rites and music will not be honoured, if the rites and music be not honoured, penalties and punishments will not achieve their intended effects, if penalties and punishments do not produce equity and justice, the people won't know where to put their feet or what to lay hold of or to whom they shd. stretch out their hands.

That is why an intelligent man cares for his terminology and gives instructions that fit. When his orders are clear and explicit they can be put into effect. An intelligent man is neither inconsiderate of others nor futile in his commanding.[33]

The utility (that Confucian virtue) of Confucius for our discussion is that he enables us to link the ideogrammic method Pound is employing with the content of the ideogram Pound is demarcating in the Middle Cantos. The change in the content of the Middle Cantos is consonant with Pound's changing methods. The poem becomes Confucian both in what it says and in how it says it. The ideogram, so Pound would say in the 1930s, is the definition of a kind of order; particulars are arrayed so as to demonstrate a general truth or law. The ideogram Pound is trying to construct in the Middle Cantos is a definition or clarification of what constitutes civilized order. *The Cantos* begin to function as Pound's rectification of names, the clarification of terms necessary for order to obtain. The Chinese characters *ching ming,* the first characters to be incorporated in the poem, end *The Fifth Decad of Cantos* (Cantos 42–51) as if to imply that the foregoing has been just such a rectification.[34]

Pound's concern with clarifying what constitute the forces of order and disorder is not an entirely new departure, for the Rimini and Venetian Cantos had been concerned with defining constructive and destructive forces. Canto 31, moreover, begins with the words Sigismundo had inscribed on his wife Isotta's tomb before it shifts to its main subject, Thomas Jefferson. This juxtaposition aligns Jefferson with Malatesta, and a fundamental movement in the next forty cantos is to make several more alignments of this kind, to establish an ideogram of the just ruler by going into detail about several of them.

Cantos 31–34 are concerned with Jefferson and the Adamses, 37 with Martin Van Buren, and 41 with Mussolini. Cantos 42–44 and 50 in *The Fifth Decad of Cantos* focus on the Monte dei Paschi Bank of Siena, the only good bank in history according to Pound, and the reforms instituted in Tuscany in the eighteenth century by Pietro Leopoldo.[35] This material is interspersed with material on the forces of disorder that constitute the other side of the ideogram. Pound now thinks he knows the reason why Venice declined, why all cultural centers have declined, which is the corruption caused by usury and usurious banks. Therefore, contrasting with the cantos on just figures like Jefferson are attacks on bad banking practices. These attacks receive their generalized statement in Canto 45, the famous Usura Canto.

There is some material in Cantos 31–51, most obviously the translation of Cavalcanti's *canzone, Donna mi prega,* in Canto 36 and the Seven Lakes Canto, Canto 49, that does not in any obvious way help construct the ideograms of good and evil, order and disorder. Yet the relative paucity of such material shows the extent to which Pound's ideogrammic method has firmed up the structure of *The Cantos.* Cantos 52–71 exhibit an even firmer structure, as everything in these cantos advances the ideogrammic definition of order and disorder. These cantos are comprised of two sections of ten cantos each. The first, Cantos 52–61, is a survey of Chinese history up to the eighteenth century, and the second, Cantos 62–71, is an extended portrait of John Adams. The connection between the two and between this group of twenty cantos and the previous twenty-one is that we are again being shown great rulers in action. Pound presents 4,500 years of Chinese history (in compressed form) as a continuous struggle on the part of a line of Confucian Great Emperors to create order out of chaos.[36] John Adams is such a great ruler in an American context whom we see creating order out of chaos in the aftermath of the American Revolution. Adams, unbeknown to himself, is in Pound's view an exemplar of Confucian statecraft. In case the symmetry between the Chinese History Cantos and the Adams Cantos and the fact that the chron-

icle of Chinese history breaks off in the year of Adams's birth do
not establish this relation, Pound includes the characters *ching ming*
in the Adams Cantos at several points when Adams is manifesting
the Confucian spirit.[37]

Pound's thinking in the Middle Cantos is thus as paradigmatic or
antisequential as ever: Adams for him *is* a Confucian Great Emperor, not simply like one. And the style of the Middle Cantos re-
tains the elliptical, compressed juxtapositional style of his earlier
work. Detail is set against detail in a way that forces the reader to
grasp the implied relation. Moreover, as in the Early Cantos, these
details are being arrayed to make a comment on the present. Yet
the comment the poem is aiming to make reveals the distance
Pound has traveled from the detached vision of Vorticism. The
ideogram the poem builds for forty cantos is the definition of a
Great Emperor and Pound's method, returning as always to the
present, is designed to make us grasp that the Great Emperor of
our time, our equivalent to John Adams and the composite Chinese
Emperor who emerges from the Chinese History Cantos, is Benito
Mussolini, the only contemporary political figure to be mentioned
with any respect in the Middle Cantos (in Cantos 41 and 52). As
Pound concludes in his eccentric work of political analysis, *Jefferson and / or Mussolini* (1935):

> Towards which I assert again my own firm belief that the Duce will
> stand not with despots and the lovers of power but with the lovers of
> ORDER
> τὸ καλόν[38]

Thus, the thrust of the Middle Cantos is to show us that we
should align the Chinese Great Emperors, Thomas Jefferson, John
Adams, and Benito Mussolini as Great Emperors or lovers of order.
Jefferson and / or Mussolini was dedicated—as its title indicates—to
establishing one part of this alignment: "The heritage of Jefferson,
Quincy Adams, old John Adams, Jackson, Van Buren is HERE, NOW
in the Italian peninsula at the beginning of fascist second decennio,
not in Massachusetts or Delaware."[39] Implicit in the arrangement
of these cantos is the additional perception that the essential
impulse behind Jefferson, Adams, and Mussolini is one with the

political thought of Confucius. In Pound's view, each figure shares a respect for culture, a respect for order, an attitude of pragmatism or opportunism, a benevolent concern for the good of the people, and above all a concern for being useful and getting things done. Pound sees his own poem as being useful in the same spirit. The use he imagines for his poem is that we as readers will grasp that these same ideas are again going into action as the poem is being written. Mussolini is the one doing that work.

Ironically, however, to demonstrate this essentially antisequential view of history, Pound has been forced to make his epic more and more sequential. The Middle Cantos cut from era to era far less often, and the number of places they treat is markedly fewer (Confucian China, revolutionary America, Tuscany, and contemporary Europe). The cantos on Jefferson (31–34) and Pietro Leopoldo (42–44) are perhaps no more sequential than the earlier sections on Malatesta and Venice, but, later, the Chinese History Cantos tell 4,500 years in unbroken sequence and the Adams Cantos, while not exactly chronological, present the same subject at length. The Early Cantos had broken up sequences in search of a paradigm with which to order history but, that paradigm once found, the poem returns to sequence.

Yet Pound does his best to disguise this fact. The presentation of material in these cantos is as ideogrammic as ever:

> HOAI of SUNG was nearly ruined by taozers
> HIEN of TANG died seeking elixir
> and in '97 they made a law code
>   a bear walked into Pekin unnoticed
> though they strafed the watch for allowing it
> and there were 53 million folk in the Empire
> at tribute average of five measures
>   of, say, 100 lbs each
> "OU TI of LÉANG, HOEÏ-TSONG of SUNG
> were more than all other Emperors
>   Laoist and foéist, and came both to an evil end.
> To hell with the pyramid
>   YAO and SHUN lived without any such monument
> TCHEOU KONG and Kungfutseu certainly wd/ not have
>   ordered one
>   nor will it lengthen YR MAJESTY'S days

It will shorten the lives of YR subjects
they will, any of 'em, die under new taxes."

(57:313)

This representative passage reveals how compressed and elliptical Pound's presentation of Chinese history is. Detail is placed next to detail, and the arrangement of these details in a historical sequence is only evident from the dates that are periodically to be found in the margin. No syntactic accommodation is made to sequentiality; even words that unobtrusively indicate temporal relations ("when" or "then" or "next") are rarely found in these cantos. For what is important in Pound's eyes are the eternal principles being revealed, not the historical sequence that establishes those principles.[40] Thus, though Pound's method is covertly sequential, his thinking in the Middle Cantos is more antisequential than ever.

This contradiction indicates that Pound had not completely solved the problems concerning the poem's method when he recast *The Cantos* around Canto 30. In fact, the problem here stems directly from that recasting. We have already examined the two major problems in the method of the Early Cantos and the way Pound solved them. First, the juxtapositional method did not connect the web Pound was arranging in a sufficiently forceful manner. Hence Pound introduced the ideogrammic method, enabling him to arrange his particulars so as to define generalities. This method helped to provide *The Cantos* with an argument while maintaining the poem's non-narrative style. But the second problem, which was that the method of juxtaposition did not allow Pound to ask the questions about social and political action that had begun to concern him, was solved by making *The Cantos* more and more sequential. These two solutions developed by Pound in the Middle Cantos which significantly transform the direction and method of *The Cantos* are thus ideologically compatible but formally incompatible. Both advance the Confucian "totalitarian synthesis" Pound wishes to delineate, but one does so by annihilating sequence, the other by articulating it.

The tangle of cross-purposes explains why the Middle Cantos, though much more orderly than the Early Cantos, are so much less interesting and successful. They narrate quite a coherent story but one can grasp that only if one has read Pound's source material, de Mailla's *Histoire Générale de la Chine* or *The Works of John Adams.*[41] These cantos are a product of Pound's archaeological poetic run amok: one is forced, not simply invited, to go beyond the poem to the material Pound is quarrying. For the most part Pound is merely transcribing material from his sources, but he incorporates it in his poem in a way that makes little sense to an uninformed reader (and, as unfortunately, holds little interest for an informed one). The ideogrammic method eliminates most of the connecting links even though the material is historical chronicle that depends upon those links for coherence.

This deeply paradoxical situation, I would like to suggest, should look quite familiar, because Pound in the Middle Cantos has unwittingly put himself in the situation Lewis was in when he wrote *Enemy of the Stars.* The material Pound was working with was historical narrative, but his commitment to a non-narrative poetic method prevented him from accepting the temporal, historical nature of that material. Like *Enemy of the Stars,* the Middle Cantos are a deliberately and perversely unintelligible narrative and are unintelligible for the same reason. Pound withholds from the reader the kind of connectives necessary to make the material intelligible.

In other words, even after seventy-one cantos of his epic had been written, Pound had not quite figured out how to write it. He had begun with certain Vorticist notions about form and method that had not proven adequate to the task of organizing a long complex poem. His solutions to the problems created by those inadequacies helped to recast the poem as a Confucian or totalitarian epic singing of the Great Emperor who would bring and had brought order out of chaos. But what we have seen from our analysis of the Early and Middle Cantos is that Pound had not yet brought order out of his chaos.

Moreover, it is difficult to imagine Pound doing so within the ambit of his poem. For the ordering principles he would like to outline are in his vision eternally valid, not subject to time. Yet it is in time that they are to be revealed and shown to be valid. Therefore, Pound's poem can have a coherent form, can express these principles of order, only if they find expression in history itself, as only then will they be shown to be valid. He thus cannot give his poem a finished shape contrary to that found in history, for to do so would be to aestheticize his vision of history, to deny it its descriptive force. He thus cannot impose a form on his poem; it must find its form in the form of history. In short, Mussolini must bring order out of chaos for Pound to bring order out of his chaos. Pound has linked the destiny of his epic to the destiny of his implicit epic hero. His epic poem is literally being written *in medias res.* [42]

The view of the Middle Cantos I have presented goes a long way towards explaining what a disaster World War II was for *The Cantos* as well as for Pound himself. Pound had staked the coherence of his poem on his political vision, but this vision failed him utterly. Mussolini did not emerge as a worthy analogue to John Adams and the great Confucian rulers: instead, his regime was exposed as a tawdry and incompetent farce. The regime the poem had been obliquely celebrating for forty cantos collapsed ignominiously. Pound's poem, therefore, lay in ruins, like the Fascist state it sought to celebrate.

The Cantos at this point become in a sense both unfinished and unfinishable. The poem cannot end with a vision of Mussolini as this century's Great Emperor; Pound's paradigm can have no modern embodiment; history cannot provide Pound's poem with a coherent form. Yet this collapse of the poem's structure leads not to failure but to its greatest success. Pound cannot continue according to the design of the Middle Cantos; he must either abandon his poem or make a fresh start. Cantos 72 and 73, written in Italian during the war, have been left out of the collected editions of the poem, and the gap their absence creates is one indication of the compulsory fresh start found in Cantos 74–84, *The Pisan Cantos.* Writing in the American detention camp near Pisa he had been taken to when the Allied advance reached Rapallo, under indictment for treason and with no imaginable prospect other than incarceration or execution, aware that his beloved Italy and much of the rest of Europe were in ruins, and equally aware that his political vision and his poem were in a similar state of ruin, Pound could not continue to write the Confucian epic in praise of Mussolini that he had never quite figured out how to write. Instead, in the wonderful and terrible *Pisan Cantos,* miraculously and triumphantly, he abandons his Confucian principles of design, and in so doing, he manages to solve, or rather dissolve, the formal problems that had plagued the first seventy-one cantos. The first Pisan Canto, Canto 74, is where this breakthrough occurs; and in order to show this, I should like to discuss it, the longest single canto, in some detail.

The unforgettable opening of *The Pisan Cantos* presents the terrible situation in which the poet finds himself without direct mention either of Pound or his situation. Perhaps Pound was moved to begin these cantos when he heard of the gruesome death of Mussolini. It is, in any case, his starting point:

> THE enormous tragedy of the dream in the peasant's bent shoulders
> Manes! Manes was tanned and stuffed,
> Thus Ben and la Clara *a Milano*
> > by the heels at Milano
> That maggots shd / eat the dead bullock
> DIGONOS, Δίγονος, but twice crucified
> > where in history will you find it?
>
> > > > > (74:425)

Yet one more dream has ended in tragedy. One more savior has come to a bitter end. Like Manes, or Mani, the founder of Manichaeism, and Christ, unmentioned but ineluctably present in the word "crucified," Mussolini has been killed by those he sought to save—according to Pound—but in a manner that exceeds even the cruelty of their deaths. Dionysus, another dying god, is distinguished by the epithet *digonos,* or twice-born, but Mussolini deserves the epithet "twice crucified": after he was killed, his corpse was hung up in a piazza in Milan like meat, like a bullock, and was disfigured and fired into.

That Pound begins this way indicates both how high his own hopes for Mussolini's government had been and the desperation and peril of his own plight in the wake of its collapse. He is in a prison camp, as we slowly learn, and, it is safe to infer from the references to death cells (74:427) and the hanging of a prisoner named Till (74:430), in some fear for his own life. Pound begins

by writing about various extreme forms of death as a way of won-
dering, perhaps, if one of these is to be his own fate. This extremity of circumstance leads Pound to an apocalyptic perspective:

> yet say this to the Possum: a bang, not a whimper
>   with a bang not with a whimper
>
> (74:425)

These lines (which directly follow the passage on Mussolini's
"crucifixion") echo and seem intent on outdoing the apocalyptic
pessimism of T. S. Eliot's *The Hollow Men*. Pound is saying to his
old friend the Possum (Eliot) that Eliot was wrong about the way
the world ends. And Pound is speaking from personal experience:
his world, after all, has just ended with a bang.

However, this eschatological tone reverses suddenly as the sentence continues:

> To build the city of Dioce whose terraces are the colour of stars.
>
> (74:425)

This is a puzzling juxtaposition. Has something constructive begun to come out of this death and destruction, as the syntax somewhat illogically implies? Or is "to build" an injunction that serves
as an index, if any were needed, of the loss involved in the destruc-
tiveness of war? Whether or not one can locate the rising motion
of constructiveness historically, outside the poem, one can locate
it here in the poem. Having nothing to build on or with, with
everything in ruins, Pound nevertheless begins in his poem to build
at least the theme of the city of Dioce, an alternative to death and
destruction in a world that seems to contain no such alternative.

The theme of the building of the city keeps reappearing in Canto
74 and throughout *The Pisan Cantos*. Its next appearance, as Guy
Davenport has pointed out, is a reference to an African legend
related by Frobenius:[43]

> 4 times was the city rebuilded, Hooo Fasa
>   Gassir, Hooo Fasa   dell' Italia tradita
> now in the mind indestructible, Gassir, Hoooo Fasa
>
> (74:430)

But it is Pound's additional phrase, "dell' Italia tradita," that explains Pound's interest. "Betrayed Italy" is in 1945 full of cities recently destroyed or damaged by bombing. As a later canto notes,

> and the Osservanza is broken
> and the best de la Robbia busted to flinders . . .
> and the front of the Tempio, Rimini.
>
> (80:497)

Pound would like and is trying to assert that the city is indestructible even if destroyed because it lives on in the mind. This is a natural if paradoxical response to the destruction of cities: how different is the Christian use of Jerusalem? Here it lies behind Pound's reference to destroyed cities as if they still existed:

> I surrender neither the empire nor the temples
>   plural
> nor the constitution nor yet the city of Dioce
>
> (74:434)

> I believe in the resurrection of Italy quia impossibile est
>   4 times to the song of Gassir
>   now in the mind indestructible.
>
> (74:442)

To build the city at a time when cities are only being destroyed is something that must take place in the mind, which is the only place the city of Dioce now exists.

But Pound's concern with cities "in the mind" does not mean, as some commentors have argued, that he is turning away from his public concerns to a private and ultimately solipsistic world.[44] Pound is as concrete and as constructive as a man in his situation can be. His ideal city in the mind is no more than the collection of fragments of real destroyed cities that he can hold onto in his mind. The only city he can construct is an ideal one, but he builds this ideal city out of references to specific concrete cities, Ecbatan (the city of Dioce), Wagadu (the city of the legend of Gassir's lute), Siena, and Rimini.

The importance of the theme of rebuilding a city in the mind out of fragments of the real is that it suggests to Pound a way to

come to terms with fragmentation. Cities are not the only things
"busted to flinders" for Pound in 1945:

> Le Paradis n'est pas artificiel
> but spezzato apparently
> it exists only in fragments unexpected excellent sausage,
> the smell of mint, for example,
> Ladro the night cat
> (74:438)

Pound here restates his commitment to the ideal, the paradisal,
and his conviction that, *pace* Baudelaire, it is real, not artificial.
But it is *spezzato,* broken into pieces or fragmented, like Europe
in 1945, like the Fascist state, and like this poem.[45] The ideal or
paradise, then, is as fragmented as the real, or rather it *is* the fragments of the real that Pound can hold in his mind. It exists only in
fragmented particulars, in excellent sausage and the smell of mint.

This passage should show how far Pound has moved from the
ideogrammic method of the Middle Cantos. Canto 74 does restate
this method in Aristotelian terminology:

> as says Aristotle
> philosophy is not for young men
> their *Katholou* can not be sufficiently derived from
> their *hekasta*
> their generalities cannot be born from a sufficient phalanx
> of particulars
> (74:441)

The generalities of the Middle Cantos are born from a phalanx of
particulars; concrete images of good and bad banks and rulers are
built up by means of details that readily lend themselves to generalization and obviously have been selected and presented with
that in mind. But, I would ask, what generalities can be born from
particulars like the excellence of sausage and the smell of mint? In
Pisa paradise exists in fragments, and these fragments are neither
obviously nor directly part of any larger definition, any abstract
entity.

This observation needs precise stating, for an obvious retort would be that paradise is a universal and therefore Pound is still defining universals through particulars. But I think there is a change in *The Cantos* in this respect which first manifests itself in the first Pisan Canto, Canto 74. Pound shows a new willingness to stay with the fragment or detail, truly to respect its concreteness, rather than to align it with other details for the purpose of defining a generality. The universal, in fact, is now utilized to enable the particular: to say that paradise exists in excellent sausage establishes the excellence of the sausage more than it describes paradise. Pound always maintained that the abstract only existed in the concrete; what is new here is that the concrete has been released from the service of the abstract.

The Pisan Cantos, therefore, do not persevere in the ordering and definition of universals so prominent in the Middle Cantos. This shift has broad implications. Pound's formal imperative to order particulars was linked to his Confucian politics of order; in Canto 74, Pound comes to accept a new measure of disorder. He comes to accept that the city and paradise and many other ideals he tried to realize exist only in fragments and perhaps will always exist only in fragments. Pound is warning the reader here that this poem, too, may exist only in fragments. To read these cantos adequately we as readers need in turn to accept Pound's difficult acceptance of fragmentation, which is at the heart of the Pisan sequence. How does one construct something upon which to rejoice when all one has is excellent sausage and the smell of mint?

Pound's new acceptance of fragmentation causes a change in the material included in the poem as well as a change in what he does with that material. He now includes things that resist generalization and abstraction instead of including only those details that help to define generalities. Details from nature, like the smell of mint and Ladro the night cat, enter the poem in a new way. Consider how the opening of Canto 74, that collocation of the thematic departures of *The Pisan Cantos,* continues after the line on the city of Dioce quoted above:

> The suave eyes, quiet, not scornful,
>   rain also is of the process.
> What you depart from is not the way

and olive tree blown white in the wind
washed in the Kiang and Han
what whiteness will you add to this whiteness,
                        what candor?

(74:425)

This passage is itself something of a collocation; the "way" and the "process" will concern us later. What I wish to point out here is the manner in which a detail from nature that Pound can see in Pisa, how an olive tree looks in the wind, finds a place between a definition of process and a quotation from Mencius.[46]

Canto 74 is not, of course, the first time nature has been treated in *The Cantos*. Pound praised the Monte dei Paschi Bank of Siena in Cantos 42 and 43 for basing its banking practices on the abundance of nature. Cantos 2, 4, 47, and 49 contain passages of natural description and Canto 49, the Seven Lakes Canto, feels very much like a Pisan Canto. But these descriptions are transcriptions of Oriental or Greek sources, or, set in Oriental or classical contexts, serve some narrative or descriptive intent. Canto 74 is the first time that the poem includes natural details perceived by the poet directly, not mediated through some setting or voice other than the poet's own. *The Pisan Cantos* are full of moments of perception of processes and actions in nature that Pound sees in his camp. This turn to nature as subject matter is, I think, a correlative of the acceptance of fragmentation and stems from the same political context that necessitated this acceptance. Pound personally always retained the sensitivity towards nature that *The Cantos* now display. (A good demonstration of this is Yeats's anecdote in *A Vision* about Pound feeding cats in Rapallo.)[47] But *The Cantos* were so relentlessly "the tale of the tribe," Pound's vision of man's achievement and potential, that until now there was no room for mere cats or olive trees. There is room now, with Pound in the Pisan Detention Camp.

In the context of Chinese culture, the correlation I am asserting between a turn to nature and political defeat is easily explicable, and consequently that context is useful for understanding the turn *The Cantos* take at this point. The connections between Pound's political ideals and Confucianism should be quite clear by now.

Confucianism, the traditional political philosophy of China, is oriented towards civilization, not nature; order, not fragmentation; politics, not art. But it does not stand alone as a philosophy but in a dynamic relationship of opposition and complementariness with Taoism. Confucianism is obviously the philosophy of the Middle Cantos; but the philosophy of *The Pisan Cantos,* I would insist, is Taoism.

Levenson and Schurmann, in their *China: An Interpretive History,* tell us that "there is an old saw in China which says that men tend to be Confucianists in office, Taoists when out of office."[48] Pound's cast of mind in the Middle Cantos was very much that of a man in office, intent upon influencing the course of events. In the Pisan Detention Camp, Pound is clearly out of office and in a position to see the futility of his actions in office. Taoism is a philosophy for a man out of office because it argues that the things one can do in office are trivial and limited. Chuang Tzu tells of the man who approached a Taoist sage with the question "Please, may I ask you how to rule the world?" The sage responded, "Get away from me, you peasant! What kind of a dreary question is that?" When the dreary peasant persisted, the sage answered: "Let your mind wander in simplicity, blend your spirit with the vastness, follow along with things the way they are, and make no room for personal views—then the world will be governed."[49]

The Taoist view is that the disorder of the world is one with the desire to order it. Accept that the world is much bigger than you are and that you can do little to alleviate its disorder, its evil, its ugliness, and only then will you see its order, its good, its beauty. A central concept in Taoism, from which it takes its name, is the Tao, translated as the way or the process; the Tao, put simply, is the order or form the world has that one can see only after the acceptance of or resignation to disorder and fragmentation. The Tao is everywhere, if only one can accept it. It can be seen most easily in nature, and the way or process of nature is an important image of the Tao. Pound's innate Taoism reveals itself most readily in the attitude he takes towards natural process in *The Pisan Cantos.*[50]

This note is struck early on in Canto 74. A phrase from the passage quoted above, "rain also is of the process" (74:425), is echoed

at the bottom of that page, "the wind also is of the process." The
process that includes the rain and the wind but is larger than either
is the Tao, the character for which appears later in *The Pisan
Cantos* (78:482). Pound continues, "What you depart from is not
the way," and this statement is utterly Taoist in its assumption
that one can never depart from the way, because the way is the
world's norm from which no one departs. *The Pisan Cantos*, thus,
are Taoist in their political quietism, in their turn to nature, and in
their sense that the abandonment of the attempt to order is the
finding of some sort of adequate order in the way or process. Taoism is a term, therefore, that conveniently describes and defines
those elements which are novel in *The Pisan Cantos*. A concise and
accurate way to describe the change from the Middle Cantos to *The
Pisan Cantos* is as a shift from a Confucian poem to a Taoist one.

The only problem is that Pound never had a good thing to say
about Taoism. As the quotation from Canto 57 has already shown,
the Chinese History Cantos call Taoists "taozers" and convey the
impression, not surprisingly or altogether inaccurately, that these
taozers were to be associated with every movement of disintegra-
tion in Chinese history. Pound labeled everything he took from
Chinese culture Confucian, from the admittedly Confucian *Ta Hsio*
to the *Odes* to the nature of the ideogram.[51] He even includes the
character *tao* in his Confucian terminology that heads his translation of the *Ta Hsio*, *The Great Digest*, translating it as process.
Therefore, when Pound uses the word *process* in *The Pisan Cantos*,
he is indeed thinking of the character *tao*.[52]

Pound divides Chinese culture into a good Confucian part and
a bad Taoist part, an action both typical of Pound and highly
Confucian. He divides everything from banks to philosophies summarily into black and white categories, often, as in this case, in
ignorance of the links between his black and his white. The truth
of the matter here is rather Taoist: there has been so much intermingling of Taoist and Confucian ideas that Pound's simplistic
divisions would have been impossible a thousand years ago. Confucian texts contain Taoist ideas; Taoist texts quote Confucius. In
fact this intermingling became something of a game, at least for
the Taoists: the *Chuang Tzu* represents Confucius as running off
to Taoist sages for advice and ridiculing his disciples for their

Confucian ideas. Thus despite Pound's attacks on "taozers," Taoist ideas were absorbed by Pound, both through nominally Confucian texts containing Taoist ideas and through aspects of Chinese culture that Pound inaccurately labeled Confucian. That Taoist ideas found their way into Confucian texts is an image of what I claim happened in *The Cantos*. This intermingling in Pound's Chinese sources furthermore shows that a change like the one in *The Cantos* from Confucianism to Taoism is not inexplicable.

Two Confucian texts, the *Ta Hsio* or *The Great Digest* and the *Chung Yung* or *The Unwobbling Pivot* (these are Pound's translations of the titles; James Legge's are *The Great Learning* and *The Doctrine of the Mean*), are central to Pound's Confucianism and reveal the complexity of that Confucianism. Pound translated the *Ta Hsio* from a French translation in 1928. During World War II, he translated both works from Chinese into Italian, the *Ta Hsio* in 1941 and the *Chung Yung* in 1944–45. Then, in the Pisan Detention Camp, in the same notebooks in which he was writing *The Pisan Cantos,* he translated them both again, this time from Chinese into English.

His Italian title for the *Chung Yung* was *Ciung iung: L'asse che non vacilla* (the axis that does not vacillate), which makes it sound like authoritarian propaganda. Actually it is the *Ta Hsio* whose concern is the Confucian theory of the state. Pound's provocative title is the strongest link between the *Chung Yung* and his involvement with fascism, strong enough for the Allies who burned the Italian edition in 1945. The axis of the *Chung Yung* links heaven and earth, not Rome, Berlin, and Tokyo. Its politics are quietist, not authoritarian and, as Hugh Kenner has pointed out, it is "dense with Taoism";[53] an index is that the line discussed above, "What you depart from is not the way" (74:425), comes from the *Chung Yung.*[54]

The character *chung,* 中, is one of the Chinese characters with special significance for Pound. It appears once in the Adams Cantos (70:413), three times in *The Pisan Cantos* (76:454; 77:464; 84: 540), and many times in the Late Cantos. The great neo-Confucian Chu Hsi in his preface to the *Chung Yung,* included in Pound's version and customarily included in editions of the *Chung Yung,* explains the meaning of *chung* and *yung* in these terms:

> The word *chung* signifies what is bent neither to one side nor to the
> other. The word *yung* signifies unchanging. What exists plumb in the
> middle is the just process [the tao] of the universe and that which
> never wavers or wobbles is the calm principle operant in its mode of
> action.[55]

The pivot, thus, though unwobbling is dynamic: it is the process
of the universe, the principle of ordered change. The superior man
or sage, according to the *Chung Yung,* finds the pivot or mean and
holds onto it unmoved by the turmoil of the world. Implicit in
this "doctrine of the mean," therefore, is the dynamic quietism
also implicit in the Tao. The world is in flux, but the wise man
seeks not to control that flux, but to accept it. That acceptance
leads to an understanding of the process or form that the flux takes.

The fact that Pound translates this work while writing *The Pisan
Cantos* is significant because these ideas are directly addressed to
Pound's condition. They are a counsel of patience and acceptance,
and *The Pisan Cantos* show Pound heeding that counsel. Like the
"superior man," Pound is searching for the pivot from which he
can see that the Tao is calmly operative in the world, ordering
what seems to be chaos and disorder. The relevance to the situation
of the poem as well as the poet—or to the poet's aesthetic as well
as ethical dilemma—should be obvious. Pound would like to find
the pivot from which he can see that the Tao is ordering his poem
as well as the world. In Chinese aesthetics, just as in Pound's life,
these two orders are closely linked. The character in Chinese for
writing, *wen,* also means configuration. Playing on this polysemy,
the Chinese literary theorist Liu Hsieh (d. ca. 523) wrote that "the
reason why the *Words* [or words in general] can arouse the world
is that they are the *wen* [configuration / writing] of the Tao."[56]
But this is a two-way street, as Liu Hsieh pointed out: "Hence, we
know that the Tao, through the sages, perpetuates [or bestows,
ch'ui] *wen* [literature], and the sages, by means of *wen* [literature]
manifest the Tao."[57] The order of language, in short, manifests the
order of the cosmos; however, in turn, the order of the cosmos
helps to order language.

This Taoist conception of language's relation to the world is not
an entirely new departure in Pound's aesthetics. It closely resembles

Fenollosa's notions about the ideogram. Moreover, the aesthetic implications of the ideogram, as Fenollosa presents them, are close to the philosophical implications of the ideograms *tao* and *chung*. In each case, the universe is dynamic, in a state of flux, and the role of language is to encode or represent that flux. Language does not impose order on the flux as much as it shows that the flux is ordered, ordered according to certain dynamic patterns or configurations. Pound, in focusing on certain key ideograms, is also still following Fenollosa in seeing the ideogram as the basis of Oriental poetry and a viable basis for a modern poetic structure.

Thus Pound's turn to the Taoism latent in the *Chung Yung* is really a return to the sources of his first interest in the Orient, Oriental poetry and painting and the aesthetic Fenollosa based on those and on the Chinese ideogram. This side of Chinese culture has always been predominately Taoist, as Ernest Fenollosa clearly understood. In Fenollosa's opinion, Taoism and Buddhism, not Confucianism, have always been "the core of Chinese imaginative life."[58]

Pound's early Oriental interests also align themselves with Taoism, not Confucianism, in their orientation towards moments of insight. The ideogram, according to Fenollosa, like the Oriental ink painting and haiku, is born in a moment of ordering, which can be described as a brief glimpse of the Tao that inheres both in man and the cosmos. It should be remembered that Pound described his two-line poem, "In a Station of the Metro," as "hokku-like," and in this description he is certainly correct. Pound's best imagist poems express an intense moment of perception similar to those expressed in haiku and those which, according to Fenollosa, lie behind the ideogram itself. *The Pisan Cantos* contain one such haiku-like moment after another, as can be seen in the lines I have already quoted. The haiku is usually a form of nature poetry, and the haiku-like moments of *The Pisan Cantos* are generally those moments in which Pound is recording details of nature. Thus, in a number of senses, Pound's Taoist poetics are to be identified with the poetics of "In a Station of the Metro."

But a poetics of haiku-length fragments works best for poems of haiku length. Can one organize an epic-length poem around such moments of insight? Can Taoism ever organize anything? Pound in

1914, we should remember, thought he had found a model for the
use of this poetic as the basis for a long poem in the Japanese Nō
drama. But the seventy-one cantos that followed owed little of
their formal organization to anything found in the Nō. Nonetheless, in Pisa, the Nō returns to Pound's awareness for the first time
in thirty years.[59]

Details from the Nō plays are sprinkled through *The Pisan Cantos*.
The detail that recurs most often is about the moon nymph in the
play *Hagoromo* who lived up to her part of a bargain with a fisher-
man.[60] This seems to be for Pound a luminous detail demonstrating
that figures in Oriental literature show greater honor than those in
Greek literature:

> and the nymph of the Hagoromo came to me,
> >   as a corona of angels
> one day were clouds banked on Taishan
>
> >   (74:430)
>
> Greek rascality against Hagoromo
> >   Kumasaka vs / vulgarity
> >   no sooner out of Troas
> than the damn fools attacked Ismarus of the Cicones
>
> >   (79:485)
>
> >   "With us there is no deceit"
> >   said the moon nymph immacolata
> >   Give back my cloak, *hagoromo*
>
> >   (80:500)

I find no particular pattern to Pound's use of the moon nymph or
any other of the details from the Nō plays. Perhaps part of Pound's
point is contained in the fact that these details form no pattern.
He cannot have forgotten his plans to organize *The Cantos* on the
formal model of the Nō. But the formal aspect of the plays now
seems less important than certain details, how, for instance, a
nymph lived up to a bargain. This detail in turn serves to show
once more that it is individual details, not grand forms, that now
concern Pound.

However, the presence of these remembered details from the Nō
drama do form part of one pattern: these cantos are full of reminiscences of the period of approximately 1912–17, Pound's early

years in London when *The Cantos* were first taking shape. From
Pound's perspective in Pisa, these years seem to have a special importance; this fact begins to make sense when we view the poetic
of *The Pisan Cantos,* as I have suggested, as a return to that developed at the time of Pound's first immersion in Oriental material.
But, of course, Pound's immersion in Vorticism dates from the
same period, and we have already seen how he continually equated
Vorticism with the Oriental poetry and painting that fascinated
him. Applying Pound's use of cultural homologies to what we have
seen of *The Pisan Cantos* helps us to see that the elements in *The
Pisan Cantos* that reveal them to be Taoist also reveal them to be
Vorticist. Vorticism and Taoism could be parallel, perhaps, only in
a cosmos organized by Ezra Pound, but, if Pound was, as I have
claimed, of the Taoists' party without knowing it, he was consciously and explicitly a Vorticist, and his Vorticist period occupies
the years 1914 to 1917, precisely the years that stand out in
Pound's memory in Pisa. The close parallel between Pound's
Taoism and his Vorticism enables us to see that the turn in Canto
74 towards Taoism should also be understood as a return to the
Vorticist aesthetic that Pound was elaborating around 1914.

The ideogram *chung* closely resembles the image of the vortex.
There is, of course, a visual resemblance between the way the vortex was represented in *Blast,* 🔺 and *chung,* 中. Both have a line
passing through the middle of a circle and both attempt to represent a point of stability in the midst of motion and flux. The vortex is also an unwobbling pivot, *l'asse che non vacilla,* and implicit
in Vorticism are assumptions close to those in the *Chung Yung.*
The Vorticist occupies the still point of the turning world in exactly
the same way that the sage holds onto the pivot, as we can see by
juxtaposing the following passages:

> The master man finds the center and does not waver.[61]

> Happiness, rage, grief, delight. To be unmoved by these emotions is
> to stand in the axis, in the center; being moved by these passions
> each in due degree constitutes being in harmony.[62]

> The meaning of the Vortex and Vorticism as propounded by Lewis
> was simplicity itself. "You think at once of a whirlpool," he ex-
> plained. "At the heart of the whirlpool is a great silent place where

all the energy is concentrated, and there at the point of concentration is the Vorticist.[63]

> At the still point of the turning world. Neither flesh nor fleshless;
> Neither from nor towards; at the still point, there the dance is,
> But neither arrest nor movement.[64]

The artist in both views is permanently out of office, but is not
in flight from the world. His subject matter is that chaotic world
which he cannot escape. But he strives for the still center to gain
the necessary stance of detachment. Like Vorticism, Taoism is a
doctrine of detachment. From a Taoist perspective, the history of
The Cantos until Pisa is one of a progressive loss of the necessary
detachment of the sage or "master man." After World War I, as
Pound's interest in political action grew, and his Confucian orientation towards trying to order the chaos of the world began to take
shape, he lost hold of the still point of the vortex. No longer seeing
any order in the chaos of the world, he proceeded to give the chaos
orders. He tried almost single-handedly to call the twentieth century to order. His attempt failed, as all such attempts must, and in
Pisa Pound is back at the still point, in the unwobbling pivot. He is
surrounded by the exploding chaos, fragments of a world that is
blowing up. But no longer with a viable position to push, utterly
without the capacity to give orders, he is forced back into the
detached acceptance of the Taoist or the Vorticist. Fragments are
all he has, all he now sees existing, and this situation, too, he must
and does accept. He can no longer will these fragments into order,
and this recognition is a source of despair for someone so committed for so long to order.

Canto 74 begins in a posture of despair, but quickly it begins to
reverse, and it ends in a moment of celebration and triumph:

> Serenely in the crystal jet
>   as the bright ball that the fountain tosses
> (Verlaine) as diamond clearness
>   How soft the wind under Taishan
>   where the sea is remembered
>   out of hell, the pit
>   out of the dust and glare evil
>   Zephyrus / Apeliota

        This liquid is certainly a
              property of the mind
        nec accidens est   but an element
                    in the mind's make-up
        est agens and functions   dust to a fountain pan otherwise
              Hast 'ou seen the rose in the steel dust
                          (or swansdown ever?)
        so light is the urging, so ordered the dark petals of iron
        we who have passed over Lethe.

                                                      (74:449)

For the twenty-five pages of Canto 74, Pound has set out in a
bewildering if dazzling array fragment after fragment, detail after
detail, of every conceivable kind and in many languages, without
plan or form to order them. But the canto ends in a triumph that
is the pivot of the entire poem. Pound now sees that these fragments are part of a whole, the form of which is now apparent to
him. He compares this form to "the rose in the steel dust," the rose
pattern formed when a field of iron filings is touched by a magnet's
field of force. This is a form of a kind we have met before, a fleet-
ing form that accepts its own provisionality and impermanence,
yet asserts itself nonetheless as a form. The rose in the steel dust
takes its place with the vortex, the ideogram, and specific ideograms such as *tao* and *chung* in the family of dynamic and diagrammatic forms in Pound's work, and in fact Pound used this
image in his prose as early as 1913 and again in 1915 in an essay
on Vorticism.[65]

Yet it differs from those other forms because of its own temporality. The magnet orders the filings *after* they have lain in disorder, and this temporality is completely appropriate in this
context. The iron filings, the steel dust, are the fragments that for
twenty-five pages of Canto 74 Pound has set out without plan or
form, now formed by the poet's moment of insight. It is this
moment of insight which enables or reveals the poet's passage over
the river Lethe, which in Dante's *Commedia* is the entry into Paradise. Paradise has already been glimpsed in fragments, in the smell
of mint and in excellent sausage, but by the end of Canto 74 the
form of those fragments of paradise has been seen by the poet
who turns to the reader and asks: "Hast'ou seen the rose in the

steel dust?'' Hast thou seen the form that inheres in the fragments
I have shored?

It is in the nature of things that different readers will have
different answers to this question. Pound's analogy is inexact
because his magnetic moment of insight cannot actually transform
the shape of his fragments already included in the pages of his
poem. It can at most transform the way they are seen, as it has
already transformed Pound's way of seeing. It is this transformation which enables Pound henceforth to regard the issue of form
in *The Cantos* as solved, or rather dissolved. His mistake had been
to try to find a form for his poem, a form into which he could fit
whatever he wanted to include in the poem. His new approach is
simply to include what he wants, freely moving from particular to
particular by means of haiku-like juxtapositions, in the hope and
expectation that when finished the coherence of the materials will
give the poem form, Taoist or Vorticist form, if not Confucian
order.

The mystery is that it works. In keeping with the Taoist refusal
to give orders, Pound recognizes the impossibility of ordering the
moment of insight of the reader. It is not a rhetorical question
when Pound asks, "Hast'ou seen the rose in the steel dust?" Yet,
for this reader at least, the bewildering variety of *The Pisan Cantos*
does cohere. I do see a rose in the steel dust: though the urging is
so light, the petals are quite ordered.

The sense of order comes primarily, I think, from the fact that
Pound has finally accepted that his poem must unfold in time.
Pound's attack on narrative, like Lewis's, had been inspired by
his desire to make literature be equivalent to painting in its atem-
porality. But Pound realizes at this point, just as Lewis did in his
major novels, that this attack has a fatal flaw in that it leaves the
work of literature without any principle of sequence. Pound's
solution is also to fall back on Vorticism's dynamic or spatio-
temporal conception of form, but his embrace of temporality is
far more thorough than Lewis's. Time now helps to form the work
of art, instead of it being the other way around: the poet sets out
detail after detail until that moment of insight comes to organize
those details. This truce with temporality provides the poem with
the non-narrative principle of sequence it needed all along.

It is in accordance with this acceptance of temporality that *The Pisan Cantos* are the first cantos that explicitly indicate and treat the moment in which they are written. I have argued that the present had always been an important concern in *The Cantos,* but now it is delineated in detail. Pound abandons the indirect approach to the present that he had employed thus far. In these cantos, the passing of the seasons is noted, current conversations are incorporated, and details Pound can see in the camp are included. There is a simple explanation: the context in which these cantos were written is a determinant one. In the Pisan Detention Camp, the present presses on Pound with a special force.

But this treatment of the present also has a broader effect on the poem. From Canto 74 on, the poem makes no attempt to disguise the active presence of the poet working with his materials. It is far less finished in the sense that Pound lets us see him making connections and drawing conclusions rather than presenting us with his finished connections and conclusions. This increased provisionality is another expression of what has already been pointed out, that Pound is no longer proceeding according to a map or plan. He is thinking and working things out as he proceeds, and consequently his thinking and his poem are both more open and less schematic than they had been earlier. This openness brings us closer to the workings of Pound's mind and it is this felt closeness which solves— or, again, dissolves—the problem of sequence. The order of the poem is the order of Pound's thoughts just as the form of the poem is the form of those thoughts.

This, as a look at the Late Cantos may indicate, seems at first glance to be close to no order at all. But, in practice, having at least this minimal explanation of any abrupt transition is enormously helpful to the baffled reader. Moreover, as Canto 74 shows, Pound, like the reader, is waiting for the coherence of his material to be revealed. This lack of rigidity aligns reader and writer yet more closely and, if the reader shares Pound's vision of the rose in the steel dust at the end of Canto 74, the reader will be willing after that to trust the poet, to follow him on his journey, waiting with him for those moments of insight. Finally, with that acceptance, the reader must also accept that it is the reader's role to order the petals as much as it is Pound's. It is "we who have passed over Lethe," as Pound informs us, and the community asserted by Pound at his moment of illumination includes those readers who are responsive to it.

Yet Pound's belated acceptance that his poem must unfold in time, in a sequence, does not mean that he has returned to a traditional time-logic in which the order of the text stands in a mimetic relationship to the flow of time outside the text. It is arguable, in fact, that *The Pisan Cantos,* far from accepting time, annihilate it more thoroughly than before. The temporal montage involved in these cantos is more audacious than anything found in the Early or Middle Cantos. Instead of juxtaposing times in neighboring cantos or sections of cantos, *The Pisan Cantos* do so in neighboring lines. Pound's approach to history is still antisequential or paradigmatic, even if he has accepted the necessity of sequence in literature.

Moreover, despite the increased role played by temporality in *The Pisan Cantos,* they are also in an important sense more pictorial than the earlier cantos. It had been an old aim of Vorticism to produce literature that would be visual as well as verbal, and this aim had inspired the typography of *Blast.* Pound had experimented with the visual appearance of his poem throughout the Early and Middle Cantos, but *The Pisan Cantos* are, I think, the first section of *The Cantos* in which the typographic arrangement of the poem is an essential contributor to the poem's meaning and impact. Anyone who writes on *The Pisan Cantos* discovers this instantly, for when one arranges passages from these cantos in a typed manuscript, immense care must be taken to try to imitate Pound's arrangement on the page. Otherwise, it is a different poem with a very different impact that one is discussing.

The greater number of ideograms is a major reason, as their visual appearance is the only thing that strikes most of us about them. Nor is this fact a flaw or a problem. The late Cantos, particularly *Rock-Drill,* Cantos 85–95, with their plethora of Chinese characters, are beautiful and fascinating to look at, even (or especially) if we do not know the meaning of a single Chinese character. Clearly, one of the functions of the Chinese in *The Cantos* is to give the poem a rewarding visual appearance. Moreover, the non-Chinese part of *The Pisan Cantos* and *The Cantos* after

Pisa is also arranged to appeal to the eye. These cantos are far more fluidly arranged on the page than the earlier cantos, giving them a more open and interesting visual appearance.

In a number of different ways, therefore, Canto 74, the first Pisan Canto, marks both a dramatic turn and an important breakthrough. Moving away from the plan of a Confucian epic celebrating order but not abandoning the interest in Oriental culture that encouraged that plan, Pound turns towards Taoism in what is really a return to his initial interest in Oriental culture. It is also a return to Vorticism, particularly to its detachment and dynamic sense of form. Pound reverts to his aesthetic ideas of 1914 because he can now fulfill them. He solves the problems of form and sequence that troubled the first 71 cantos by dissolving them, or resolving to ignore them. Pound no longer attempts to order his material; instead, he proceeds confident that it is ordered. This confidence is justified by *The Pisan Cantos;* starting with *The Pisan Cantos* the poem achieves a new fluidity in style and method that is both the apogee of literary Vorticism and the reason for the greater brilliance and success of the later parts of *The Cantos.*

That is, of course, my rose in the steel dust, the order I find in the fragments Pound has shored. No more than Pound can I order the reader's insight. Moreover, my own sense of the poem's order is impeded by the development of the poem after *The Pisan Cantos.* Pound is unable or unwilling to sustain the Taoist attitude of Pisa and, although he continues to use the style achieved in the breakthrough of *The Pisan Cantos,* he returns in the next two sections, *Rock-Drill* and *Thrones,* Cantos 85–109, to his Confucian concerns. For he had no more abandoned the positions and attitudes of the Middle Cantos while writing *The Pisan Cantos* than he had abandoned his sensitivity to nature while writing the Middle Cantos. Instead, those concerns had been subordinated for the moment to the dominant direction of the poem. *Rock-Drill,* even though its title comes from perhaps the most important Vorticist work of art, shows Pound once more moving away from the detachment of Vorticism and returning again to the promotion of his views on order.

This return creates the potential for the same kind of contradiction between aims and methods that crippled the Middle Cantos.

A poetic of detail is once more being put in the service of a philosophy of total order and coherence. However, although these cantos do not maintain the high level of achievement of *The Pisan Cantos,* neither do they work as self-contradictorily and self-defeatingly as the Middle Cantos. Pound is no longer trying to make his poem ordered in a way that would express his vision of a desirable political order. He recognizes that he will not see that order realized in his lifetime; in a sense the poem's fragmentation is expressive of that recognition. Nonetheless, he still hopes that his fragmented, disordered poem will ultimately advance the cause of order. Michael André Bernstein has acutely described the basis of that hope:

> After Pisa, Pound realized his epic could never be "finished" through the celebration of an existing just society. However, rather than abandon history entirely, he was intermittently still able to think *The Cantos* might serve as a sourcebook for future generations who would once more have a chance to inaugurate a decent political order. . . . It is not that language has been divorced from politics; rather, the temporal horizon of its social efficacy has been radically deflected. Instead of being directed at the present audience, *The Cantos'* public discourse is now addressed primarily to the future.[66]

Yet the return to a utilitarian or instrumental conception of the work of art sits uneasily with other parts of these same cantos that soar into extended lyric flights outside of history. At times in the Late Cantos, Pound is a prophet who will, he hopes, be justified by history, and at other times, like Stephen Dedalus, he regards history as a nightmare from which he is trying to awake.

By the wonderful yet terrible *Drafts and Fragments,* Cantos 110–117, the mood of nightmare dominates. By this time, the history he wishes to awake from is in large part the history of his own poem. Pound abandons his poem in *Drafts and Fragments* as he abandoned its scheme in *The Pisan Cantos,* and one should not gloss over the despair inherent in those acts:

> I have brought the great ball of crystal;
> > who can lift it?
> Can you enter the great acorn of light?

> But the beauty is not the madness
> Tho' my errors and wrecks lie about me.
> And I am not a demigod,
> I cannot make it cohere.
>
> (116:795-96)

No one, as any Taoist will remind any Confucian, can make it cohere. It is too much to ask, and it leads to errors, wrecks, and madness, exactly where Pound's attempts to order the world led. But beauty exists nonetheless, and Pound, as in Canto 74, moves beyond despair to a difficult but marvelous final affirmation:

> i.e. it coheres all right
>   even if my notes do not cohere.
> Many errors,
>   a little rightness,
> to excuse his hell
>   and my paradiso.
> And as to why they go wrong,
>   thinking of rightness
> And as to who will copy this palimpsest?
>   al poco giorno
>   ed al gran cerchio d'ombra
> But to affirm the gold thread in the pattern
>   (Torcello)
> al Vicolo d'oro
>   (Tigullio)
> To confess wrong without losing rightness:
> Charity I have had sometimes,
>   I cannot make it flow thru.
> A little light, like a rushlight
>   to lead back to splendour.
>
> (116:797)

Pound's degree of self-knowledge in this passage is remarkable. He sees both errors and rightness in his poem, but he hopes that, despite the errors, in "this palimpsest," in this poem, as in the works of Dante, there is a vortex, an unwobbling pivot, a rose in the steel dust, or, as he puts it here, a "gold thread in the pattern," to be seen by whoever will copy and seek to understand it. But it is not quite *in* the poem that the gold thread will be found, as "it" coheres even though Pound's notes, these 117 cantos, do not. Pound here posits something beyond the material art work that coheres. The reader is invited to grasp that something, which I think is the Tao, the root principle of coherence itself.

At this point the alignment of Vorticism and Taoism breaks down, as Pound's aesthetic thinking moves beyond the limits of anything usefully labeled Vorticism. In going beyond the material art work, Pound at the very end of his poem moves beyond the materialist aesthetic developed in Vorticism, adopting instead a mystical and unequivocally Taoist conception of the work of art. His evolution is in certain respects parallel to Lewis's in *The Human Age,* but Pound as always marks out his own distinctive path, both in the Oriental basis of his mysticism and in his thoroughly affective aesthetic. His mysticism and his aesthetics, moreover, are firmly connected, for a central principle of Chinese aesthetics is that in art "objective symmetry is not desired, for in its very completeness it keeps the observer out. But asymmetry leads man into the natural scene depicted, for *his mind* completes the formal design."[67] The reader, like the poet, cannot make it cohere, but one finds that it does cohere. In this way the reader completes what the poet could not complete. Splendor there undoubtedly is, and with charity one sees the rightness and one enters the great acorn of light.

Notes

Prologue: Towards the Condition of Painting

1. Walter Pater, *The Renaissance: Studies in Art and Poetry* (New York: Macmillan, 1905), p. 140.

2. The quotation is given without a source by Keith Bosley in his introduction to Mallarmé, *The Poems*, trans. Keith Bosley (Harmondsworth: Penguin Books, 1977), p. 13.

3. Clement Greenberg, "Modernist Painting," *Art and Literature* 4 (Spring 1965), 194.

4. Pater, *The Renaissance*, p. 136.

5. Pater, *The Renaissance*, p. 139.

6. Pater, *The Renaissance*, p. 140.

7. Charles Baudelaire, "L'Oeuvre et la vie de Delacroix," *Oeuvres complètes* (Paris: Gallimard, 1961), pp. 1116-17; I take my translation from Charles Baudelaire, *The Mirror of Art: Critical Studies,* trans. and ed. Jonathan Mayne (London: Phaidon Press, 1955), p. 306. It was Michael Fried who pointed out to me that Pater was echoing Baudelaire.

8. Baudelaire, *The Mirror of Art*, pp. 104-5.

9. Much the same point has been made by Wendy Steiner, who, in *The Colors of Rhetoric: Problems in the Relation between Modern Literature and Painting* (Chicago: University of Chicago Press, 1982), has argued that "the relation between literature, painting, and art theory forms the very core, I believe, of the artistic activity of our day" (p. 218). Though our emphases are similar, she argues not for the primacy of painting as I do but for the primacy of the "interartistic comparison," which leads her to see phenomena such as concrete poetry as central.

10. Harold Bloom, *Wallace Stevens: The Poems of Our Climate* (Ithaca, N.Y.: Cornell University Press, 1977), pp. 120-21.

11. Several critics in a number of studies of Cubism and literature obviously disagree with me here. They include Gerard Kamber, *Max Jacob and the Poetics of Cubism* (Baltimore: Johns Hopkins University Press, 1971); Elly Jaffe-Freem, *Alain Robbe-Grillet et la peinture cubiste* (Amsterdam: J.M. Meulenhoff, 1966); Bram Dijkstra, *Cubism, Stieglitz, and the Early Poetry of William Carlos Williams: The Hieroglyphics of a New Speech* (Princeton: Princeton University Press, 1969); and Wendy Steiner, *Exact Resemblance to Exact Resemblance: The Literary Portraiture of Gertrude Stein* (New Haven: Yale University Press, 1978). However, Steiner, at least, is aware of the problems inherent in drawing analogies between art and literature:

It is ironic that Stein's portraiture broke down precisely when it took the "Rosetta Stone" analogy too seriously, when it tried to make a translation of cubist technique and psychological theory into a medium that was fundamentally different from paint and canvas, and from "raw perception." Rather than serving as a key to cubism, Stein's writing illustrates the very real barriers between painting and literature. (p. 160)

One: Vorticism among the Isms

1. William C. Wees, *Vorticism and the English Avant-Garde* (Toronto: University of Toronto Press, 1972), especially pp. 9–72, is extremely good on the English context of Vorticism in the 1910–14 period.

2. For Pound's letter, see *Pound / Joyce: The Letters of Ezra Pound to James Joyce with Pound's Essays on Joyce,* ed. Forrest Read (New York: New Directions, 1967), p. 26; the advertisement in *The Egoist* was reproduced by Hugh Kenner in *The Pound Era: The Age of Ezra Pound, T. S. Eliot, James Joyce and Wyndham Lewis* (London: Faber & Faber, 1975), p. 237.

3. Pound's claim of finding the word *Vortex* comes from a letter of 1916 to John Quinn, included in *The Letters of Ezra Pound, 1907–1941,* ed. D. D. Paige (New York: Harcourt, Brace & Co., 1950), p. 74. Lewis corroborates this claim in his 1937 autobiography, *Blasting and Bombardiering* (London: Calder & Boyars, 1967), p. 252.

4. W. J. T. Mitchell, *Blake's Composite Art: A Study of the Illuminated Poetry* (Princeton: Princeton University Press, 1978).

5. *Ezra Pound and Music,* ed. Murray Schafer (New York: New Directions, 1977), p. 253. The article did not have this opening quotation when it was originally published in *The Criterion* 2 (1924), 321–31, but appeared with this quotation in *Antheil and the Treatise on Harmony* (Paris: Three Mountain Press, 1924).

6. Douglas Goldring, *South Lodge* (London: Constable & Co., 1943), p. 65.

7. Ezra Pound, "Affirmations II Vorticism," *The New Age* 16, no. 11 (14 January 1915), 277.

8. Ronald Bush (in *The Genesis of Ezra Pound's Cantos* [Princeton: Princeton University Press, 1976], pp. 24–41) has argued that Pound's reliance upon Whistler and Pater shows the retrograde nature of his aesthetic thinking in this period, his need for the modernization Lewis and others would force upon him. I would put it rather differently: Pound quotes both Whistler and Pater in "Vortex Pound" because he saw that their Greenbergian stress on purity was indeed part of the "ancestry," as he calls it in "Vortex Pound," of the Vorticist aesthetic. But Bush's sense of Pound's aesthetic thinking as a little passé would certainly have been Lewis's sense as well, as we shall see later.

9. Caroline Tisdall and Angello Bozzolla (in their *Futurism* [London:

Thames & Hudson, 1977], p. 8) say that Marinetti was called this but they give no source.

10. W. C. Wees has a detailed treatment of the impact of Futurism on England, *Vorticism and the English Avant-Garde,* pp. 87–118.

11. Eight hundred thousand copies, according to Luigi Scrivo, *Sintesi del futurismo: storia e documenti* (Roma: Bulzoni, 1968), p. 15. Scrivo reprints both this manifesto and Marinetti's subsequent "Futurist Discourse to the Venetians," pp. 15-16. All other Futurist manifestoes mentioned are available in English translation in *Futurist Manifestos,* ed. Umbro Apollonio, trans. Robert Brain, R. W. Flint, J. C. Higgett, Caroline Tisdall (New York: Viking Press, 1975).

12. Tisdall and Bozzolla, *Futurism,* p. 9.

13. Apollonio, *Futurist Manifestos,* p. 21.

14. One version of this story is in R. W. Flint's Introduction to *Marinetti: Selected Writings,* ed. R. W. Flint, trans. R. W. Flint and Arthur A. Coppotelli (New York: Farrar, Straus & Giroux, 1972), pp. 22-23.

15. Vladimir Markov, *Russian Futurism: A History* (London: Macgibbon & Kee, 1969), p. 150; for Marinetti's entire visit, see pp. 147-63.

16. See *Apollinaire on Art: Essays and Reviews, 1902-1918,* ed. Leroy C. Breunig, trans. Susan Sulieman (New York: Viking Press, 1972), pp. 503-6 for Breunig's account of the affair. It is relevant to note, though I doubt that Lewis was directly alluding to this affair, that the climax of Lewis's first novel *Tarr* is a bungled duel between two equally touchy artists.

17. See Wees, *Vorticism and the English Avant-Garde,* pp. 110-13 and Richard Cork, *Vorticism and Abstract Art in the First Machine Age* (Berkeley and Los Angeles: University of California Press, 1976), pp. 229-34 for the Vorticist response to the "Vital English Art" manifesto.

18. The reference here is to the Futurist painter Giacomo Balla's "Futurist Manifesto of Men's Clothing" of 1913 (reprinted in Apollonio, *Futurist Manifestos,* pp. 132-34).

19. Wees, *Vorticism and the English Avant-Garde,* p. 192.

20. This manifesto has been widely reprinted and is easily available in Francis Steegmuller, *Apollinaire: Poet among the Painters* (New York: Farrar, Straus & Co., 1963), pp. 64-65, or in Richard Cork, *Vorticism and Abstract Art,* p. 249. Cork reprints the Italian translation that appeared in *Lacerba* 1, no. 18 (15 September 1913), 202-3.

21. Wees, *Vorticism and the English Avant-Garde,* pp. 167-72, 217-27.

22. Of the 11 signers of the manifestoes in *Blast* #1, 7 were painters (L. Atkinson, J. Dismorr, C. Hamilton, W. Roberts, H. Saunders, E. Wadsworth, and Wyndham Lewis—revealingly the only signer whose full name was printed), 2 were poets (R. Aldington and E. Pound), 1 was a photographer (Arbuthnot), and 1 was a sculptor (Gaudier-Brzeska).

Two: The Aesthetic of Vorticism

1. André Malraux, *Museum without Walls,* trans. Stuart Gilbert, Bollingen Series 24 (New York: Pantheon Books, 1949). p. 76.

2. Lewis was obviously thoroughly familiar with the work of both movements by the time *Blast* was published in July 1914. His acquaintance with Futurist painting needs little documentation: major Futurist exhibitions were mounted in London in March 1912 and again in April and May 1914. Most of the major Futurist paintings were in one or another of these shows. How he obtained his extensive knowledge of Cubist painting is less clear. Roger Fry's Second Post-Impressionist Exhibition at the Grafton Galleries (5 October to 31 December 1912) contained a number of Cubist paintings by Picasso. However, Lewis's 1912 illustrations of *Timon of Athens* (see fig. 1 for the most striking of these, *Alcibiades*), which show Lewis having already assimilated the aspects of Cubism which were to be adopted by the Vorticists, were also in that exhibition. So we need to assume a number of trips by Lewis to Paris between 1908 and 1914, even though Jeffrey Meyers's "Chronology" (in *The Enemy: A Biography of Wyndham Lewis* [London: Routledge & Kegan Paul, 1980], pp. 333–34) shows Lewis in Dieppe in 1911 and 1913 and in Dunkerque in 1912 but never in Paris in these years. However, *The Letters of Wyndham Lewis,* ed. W. K. Rose (Norfolk, Conn.: New Directions, 1963) contains a draft of a letter (# 45, p. 46) written in Paris which is dated 1913 by Rose. We also know that Lewis had access to Gertrude Stein's collection (though we do not know when), as *The Autobiography of Alice B. Toklas* (New York: Harcourt, Brace & Co., 1933), p. 150, mentions that Lewis used to come to the Stein house and "measure pictures." Hence we can assume he knew what he was criticizing.

3. The distinction I am making between Analytical and Synthetic Cubism is a conventional one; the dividing line is customarily seen to be the discovery of collage and papier collé early in 1912. But see John Golding, *Cubism: A History and an Analysis, 1907–1914* (New York: Harper & Row, 1968), pp. 114–17, for a challenge to this distinction.

4. It has generally been recognized that the style of Vorticism is indebted to both Cubism and Futurism. I quote Cork's summary of the indebtedness below in note 24 to this chapter; Daniel W. Taylor (in his Ph.D. dissertation, "The Great London Vortex: Art as Patterned Energy," Emory University, 1974) puts it this way: "Very broadly, Vorticism can be seen as a fusing of the Cubist formal vocabulary with Futurist energy, resulting in an art which is significantly different from both" (p. 36).

5. Umbro Apollonio, ed., *Futurismo* (Milan: Mazzotta, 1970), p. 90. This is the same volume translated as *Futurist Manifestos,* trans. Robert Brain, R. W. Flint, J. C. Higgett, Caroline Tisdall (New York: Viking Press, 1975), but when I cite the Italian, as I do here, it is because the English translation is inaccurate.

6. Umberto Boccioni, "Fondamento plastico della scultura e pittura futuriste," *Lacerba* 1, n. 6 (15 marzo 1913), 52. All previously untranslated material will be cited first in Italian and then (parenthetically) in my translation.

7. Boccioni, *Estetica e arte futuriste* (Milano: il Balcone, 1946), p. 22. This is a reprint minus illustrations and manifestoes of his 1914 *Pittura scultura futuriste.*

8. Apollonio, *Futurismo,* p. 51.

9. "Les Peintres futuristes italiens," reprinted and translated in *Apollinaire on Art,* ed. Leroy C. Breunig, trans. Susan Sulieman (New York: Viking Press, 1972), pp. 200–205.

10. Apollonio, *Futurist Manifestos,* p. 46.

11. Boccioni, *Estetica e arte futuriste,* p. 131.

12. I am quoting here from Jean Laude (*La Peinture française [1905–1914] et l'art nègre,* 2 vols. [Paris: Editions Klincksieck, 1968], p. 265), who may be paraphrasing Cézanne's words, not quoting them, as he gives no source.

13. Clive Bell, *Art* (1914; rpt., New York: Capricorn Books, 1958), p. 139.

14. Lewis always agreed with their estimate of the centrality of Cézanne; long after Vorticism, Cézanne continued to be for Lewis the most important modern painter: see *Wyndham Lewis on Art: Collected Writings, 1913–1956,* ed. Walter Michel and C. J. Fox (New York: Funk & Wagnalls, 1969), passim.

15. The statement comes from a 1913 letter to G. L. Dickinson, quoted in Virginia Woolf, *Roger Fry: A Biography* (New York: Harcourt, Brace & Co., 1940), p. 183.

16. Later in this chapter we will be concerned both with the issue of representation and that of the influence of African art on modern art.

17. The quotation appears in John Golding's *Cubism: A History and an Analysis, 1907–1914,* p. 88.

18. "Reply to the Questionnaire: 'Chez les Cubistes,'" in Daniel-Henry Kahnweiler, *Juan Gris: His Life and Work,* trans. Douglas Cooper, rev. ed. (New York: Abrams, 1969), pp. 201–2.

19. Breunig, *Apollinaire on Art,* p. 198.

20. Clement Greenberg, in an interesting parallel, has argued that Kant is, in a sense, the first modernist. See his "Modernist Painting," *Art and Literature* 4 (Spring 1965), 193–201.

21. This article is reprinted and translated in the excellent collection of material on Cubism edited by Edward F. Fry, *Cubism* (New York: McGraw-Hill, n.d.), p. 74.

22. Fry, *Cubism,* p. 130.

23. Arthur Schopenhauer, *The World as Will and Idea,* trans. R. B. Haldane and J. Kemp, 4 vols., 4th ed. (London: Kegan Paul, 1896), 1, 217–41.

24. Richard Cork's summary of the Vorticist position is apposite:

This, then, was the slice of pictorial territory Lewis saw the rebels exploring: an area of synthesis, essentially, that would temper Futurist melodramatics with Cubist sobriety, Italian movement with French monumentality. Despising Futurism for its unconditional love of machinery, and Cubism for avoiding the theme altogether in favour of the old studio repertoire of portraits and still life, he aimed for a half-way house situated neatly between the two, tapping the strengths of both and leaving their weaknesses severely alone.

(Cork, *Vorticism and Abstract Art* [Berkeley and Los Angeles: University of California Press, 1976], p. 246).

25. I have not been concerned in this study with the origin of the term *vortex*, beyond noting that Pound was the Vorticist who came up with the term. For discussions of the disputed origin of the term, see Cork, *Vorticism and Abstract Art*, pp. 254–56; Ian F. A. Bell, *Critic as Scientist: The Modernist Poetics of Ezra Pound* (London: Methuen, 1981), pp. 12–16, 145–47; and Timothy Materer, *Vortex: Pound, Eliot, and Lewis* (Ithaca, N.Y.: Cornell University Press, 1979), pp. 15–18.

26. The passage from Douglas Goldring quoted in chapter 1 shows that the Vorticist wants to occupy the vortex's still point. Pound criticism has been especially sensitive to Vorticism's reconciliation of form and flux; see both Herbert Schneidau, *Ezra Pound: The Image and the Real* (Baton Rouge: Louisiana State University Press, 1969), pp. 147–54, and Daniel W. Taylor, "The Great London Vortex: Art as Patterned Energy," Ph.D. diss., Emory University, 1974.

27. Cork, *Vorticism and Abstract Art*, p. 392.

28. In an interesting parallel, the Dutch painter Van Doesberg's breakthrough into abstraction came in his 1917–18 *Rhythm of a Russian Dance*.

29. These combat drawings precede the war. See Walter Michel, *Wyndham Lewis: Paintings and Drawings* (Berkeley and Los Angeles: University of California Press, 1971), plates 6, 12, 20, 22, 25 for examples.

30. I am drawing upon Cork's discussion of these works, *Vorticism and Abstract Art*, pp. 341–49.

31. By 1915, at least, Lewis knew of Picabia's work, though from his brief description of it (*WLOA* 64) I cannot tell which work of Picabia's he is describing.

32. Cork, *Vorticism and Abstract Art*, passim.

33. Lewis made the same point at greater length in the article "Automobilism," *The New Weekly* 2, no. 1 (20 June 1914), 13 and much later in *Blasting and Bombardiering* (London: Calder & Boyars, 1967), p. 34.

34. Lewis was not the only person to make this point. Giovanni Papini, an editor of *Lacerba*, noted that in a country like America "Futurism would be ridiculous" ("Il significato del futurismo," *Lacerba* 1, n. 3 [1 febbraio 1913], 25).

35. Reyner Banham, *Theory and Design in the First Machine Age* (London: Architectural Press, 1967), p. 102. I assume Banham's term "the first machine age" is the source of Richard Cork's title.

36. For Marinetti's term, see Renato Poggioli, *The Theory of the Avant-Garde,* trans. Gerald Fitzgerald (Cambridge: Harvard University Press, 1968), p. 218; and Apollonio, *Futurist Manifestos,* p. 181.

37. For the speeding automobile remark, see Apollonio, *Futurist Manifestos,* p. 21; and for Carrà's characteristically inane remark, Apollonio, *Futurist Manifestos,* p. 203.

38. Cork, *Vorticism and Abstract Art,* p. 346.

39. Cork, *Vorticism and Abstract Art,* p. 482.

40. Timothy Materer, *Vortex: Pound, Eliot, and Lewis* (Ithaca, N.Y.: Cornell University Press, 1979), p. 86.

41. Miriam Hansen, "T. E. Hulme, Mercenary of Modernism, or Fragments of Avantgarde Sensibility in pre-World War I Britain," *ELH* 47 (1980), 374.

42. T. E. Hulme, *Speculations: Essay on Humanism and the Philosophy of Art,* ed. Herbert Read (London: Routledge & Kegan Paul, 1924), p. 104.

43. T. E. Hulme, *Speculations,* p. 105.

44. Epstein was never explicit about why he recast *Rock Drill,* saying only that because he grew less interested in machinery, he got rid of the drill. (See *Epstein: An Autobiography,* 2d. ed. [New York: E. P. Dutton, 1955], p. 56.)

45. Probably the best work to show this principle is Lewis's *A Battery Shelled* (1919), a war painting of the period just after Vorticism, now in the Imperial War Museum (reproduced in Walter Michel, *Wyndham Lewis: Paintings and Drawings,* plate VII, p. 89), in which the officers directing the battery are rendered far less abstractly than the men doing manual labor in the background.

46. My distinction between modernism and programmatic modernism is parallel to one Clement Greenberg has made between the avant-garde and avant-gardism, the program of being avant-garde.

47. Wees is quite informative on the contemporary response to Vorticism (*Vorticism and the English Avant-Garde,* pp. 193-97).

48. Boccioni, *Estetica e arte futuriste,* p. 72.

49. Boccioni, *Estetica e arte futuriste,* p. 87.

50. Apollonio, *Futurist Manifestos,* p. 28.

51. Apollonio, *Futurist Manifestos,* p. 48.

52. Boccioni, "Il dinamismo futurista e la pittura francese," *Lacerba* 1, n. 15 (1 agosto 1913), 171.

53. Boccioni, "Fondamento plastico della scultura e pittura futuriste," *Lacerba* 1, no. 6 (15 marzo 1913), 52.

54. Henri Bergson, *An Introduction to Metaphysics,* trans. T. E. Hulme (New York: Putnam, 1912), p. 1.

pp. 243-50. For his theory of satire see *Men Without Art* (London: Cassell & Co., 1934).

88. Materer, *Vortex: Pound, Eliot, and Lewis,* pp. 193-97.

89. T. S. Eliot, *The Complete Poems and Plays, 1909-1950* (New York: Harcourt, Brace & World, 1971), p. 142.

90. Leon Trotsky, *Literature and Revolution,* trans. Rose Strunsky (New York: International Publishers, 1925), p. 139. Trotsky's entire discussion of Futurism is valuable.

91. Cork, *Vorticism and Abstract Art,* p. xxiii.

92. Wees, *Vorticism and the English Avant-Garde,* p. 151. His list of exceptions is on p. 154.

93. Materer, *Vortex: Pound, Eliot, and Lewis,* p. 87.

94. Anthony d'Offay, *Abstract Art in England, 1913-1915* (catalogue of an exhibition held at the d'Offay Couper Gallery, London, 11 November–5 December 1969), p. 8.

95. d'Offay, *Abstract Art in England, 1913-1915,* p. 5. The other critics who have written on this issue also form part of this consensus; see William Charles Lipke, "A History and Analysis of Vorticism," (Ph.D. diss., University of Wisconsin, 1966), pp. 85-122 and Daniel W. Taylor, "The Great London Vortex," pp. 24-28, 106-8.

96. d'Offay, *Abstract Art in England,* p. 6.

97. Cork, *Vorticism and Abstract Art,* p. 532.

98. Cork, *Vorticism and Abstract Art,* p. 540.

99. Epstein, tellingly, was rather embarrassed later by his avant-garde work and by his association with Vorticism: see *Epstein: An Autobiography,* 2d ed., pp. 56-59.

100. Wees (between pp. 164 and 165) and Cork (p. 555) both reproduce the one example of his later work clearly of interest to students of Vorticism, his 1961-62 painting, *The Vorticists at the Restaurant de la Tour Eiffel: Spring 1915,* which shows Lewis, Pound, and others drinking and admiring a copy of *Blast.*

101. Obviously a discussion of this work lies outside the scope of this study: for Lewis's development, see Walter Michel's study, *Wyndham Lewis: Paintings and Drawings;* for Bomberg, see William Lipke, *David Bomberg: A Critical Study of His Life and Work* (London: Evelyn, Adams & Mackay, 1967).

102. See Lewis's reviews of Ayrton and Bacon in *WLOA,* pp. 393-94 and *The Demon of Progress in the Arts* (London: Metheun & Co., 1956), passim.

103. The works in the exhibition are reproduced in his catalogue, *Abstract Art in England, 1913-1915.*

104. It suffices to quote Maurice Denis's oft-quoted dictum of 1890: "It should be remembered that a picture—before being a warhorse, a nude or

an anecdote of some sort—is essentially a flat surface covered with colors assembled in a certain order."

105. Meyer Schapiro, "The Nature of Abstract Art," in *Modern Art, 19th and 20th Centuries: Selected Papers* (New York: George Braziller, 1978), p. 185.

106. Wassily Kandinsky, "Reminiscences," in *Modern Artists on Art,* ed. Robert L. Herbert (Englewood Cliffs, N.J.: Prentice-Hall, 1964), p. 32.

107. Mondrian, "Plastic Art and Pure Plastic Art," in *Modern Artists,* ed. Herbert, p. 126.

108. Apollinaire's advocacy of pure painting can be found in a number of places, though his most famous discussion is in *The Cubist Painters: Aesthetic Meditations,* trans. Lionel Abel (New York: George Wittenborn, 1949), pp. 12–13.

109. Alfred Barr, *Cubism and Abstract Art* (New York: Museum of Modern Art, 1936), p. 13.

110. For Hilla Rebay, see the introductions to the *Second Enlarged Catalogue,* the *Third Enlarged Catalogue,* and the *Fourth Catalogue of the Solomon R. Guggenheim Collection of Non-Objective Paintings* (1937–1939); Jerome Ashmore, "Some Differences between Abstract and Non-Objective Painting," *The Journal of Aesthetics and Art Criticism* 13 (1955), 486–95.

111. Harold Osborne, *Abstraction and Artifice in Twentieth-Century Art* (Oxford: Clarendon Press, 1979), pp. 25–27.

112. See Rose-Carol Washton Long, "Kandinsky and Abstraction: The Role of the Hidden Image," *Artforum* 10, no. 10 (1972), 42–49.

113. It is relevant in this context to note that the titles of Mondrian's paintings in this period were divided between abstract titles like *Composition* and representational ones like *Pier and Ocean.*

114. Edward Wadsworth, "Inner Necessity," *Blast* #1, 119–25.

115. Pound, *Gaudier-Brzeska,* p. 44; Pound does not give the year but it must be 1913.

116. The question of which works of Kandinsky came to London is important because Lewis was in Munich, according to Meyers' "Chronology" (in his *The Enemy: A Biography of Wyndham Lewis*), in 1906, but not after.

117. For this anecdote, see Will Grohmann, *Wassily Kandinsky: Life and Work* (New York: Abrams, 1958), p. 128. Kandinsky's account, however, cannot be accepted as an account of the oil shown in London. A *Study for Improvisation #30* exists and that could be the work into which the cannons made their way unconsciously; but the *Improvisation #30* itself is too closely based on that study, in which the cannons can clearly be seen, for their presence not to be deliberate.

118. T. E. Hulme, *Further Speculations,* p. 131.

119. Gaudier-Brzeska's letter is printed in H. S. Ede, *Savage Messiah*

(London: Heinemann, 1931), pp. 91–92. It is a letter to Sophie Brzeska of 3 June 1911.

120. For a good discussion of Pound's use of mathematical analogies, see Bell, *Critic as Scientist,* pp. 5–42.

121. John Berger, *The Moment of Cubism and Other Essays* (New York: Pantheon Books, 1969), p. 20.

122. Hugh Kenner, *The Pound Era* (London: Faber & Faber, 1975), pp. 145–72, passim.

123. According to the recent biography of Roger Fry (Frances Spaulding, *Roger Fry: Art and Life* [Berkeley and Los Angeles: University of California Press, 1980], p. 170), the Second Grafton Group Exhibition (primarily an exhibition of the work of Fry and his friends) in January 1914 contained photographs of Picasso's recent constructions. These photographs may be all that Lewis had seen of these works, as his discussion of them is a little vague.

124. Clement Greenberg, "Collage," in *Art and Culture: Critical Essays* (Boston: Beacon Press, 1961), p. 77.

125. Osborne, *Abstraction and Artifice in Twentieth-Century Art,* passim.

126. My discussion of primitivism draws upon three general studies of the subject: Robert Goldwater, *Primitivism in Modern Art,* rev. ed. (New York: Vintage, 1966); Jean Laude, *La Peinture française (1905–1914) et "l'art nègre": Contribution à l'étude des sources du fauvisme et du cubisme,* 2 vols. (Paris: Editions Klincksieck, 1968); and André Malraux, *The Psychology of Art,* trans. Stuart Gilbert, 3 vols., Bollingen Series 24 (New York: Pantheon Books, 1949).

127. Picasso denied that he knew of African art when he painted *Les Demoiselles,* but his denial has not proved persuasive. See Laude's discussion, *La Peinture française,* pp. 243–68.

128. Cork, *Vorticism and Abstract Art,* pp. 454–65.

129. Epstein's *First Marble Doves,* which according to Cork is lost (p. xii), is in the collection of the Hirshhorn Museum and Sculpture Garden, Smithsonian Institution, Washington, D.C.

130. Roger Cole, *Burning to Speak: The Life and Art of Henri Gaudier-Brzeska* (Oxford: Phaidon, 1978), p. 103, refers to "some speculation as to its authenticity" in his discussion of the *Portrait of Ezra Pound* without going into details. He considers the piece, now in the Yale University Art Gallery, authentic; it looks a great deal like the *Hieratic Head,* but to my knowledge is never mentioned by Pound himself. Cole reproduces both pieces.

131. Cork, *Vorticism and Abstract Art,* p. 182.

132. Lewis, "Early London Environment" (1948), reprinted in *T. S. Eliot: A Collection of Critical Essays,* ed. Hugh Kenner (Englewood Cliffs, N.J.: Prentice-Hall, 1962), p. 31.

133. There is one important forerunner of Epstein's use of titles as a

bridge between the modern and the primitive, Gauguin's *Where Do We Come From? What Are We? Where Are We Going?* However, Gauguin's approach to the primitive is always empathic; Epstein's is empathic only when there is a detached or alienated figure to empathize with.

134. Cork, *Vorticism and Abstract Art,* p. 463.

135. Hugh Kenner has told me that Michael Ayrton told him that Epstein was deeply troubled by the conflict between his work and his culture's traditional prohibition of graven images.

136. Cork, *Vorticism and Abstract Art,* p. 481.

137. Cork, *Vorticism and Abstract Art,* p. 482.

Three: Vortex and Ideogram

1. *Tarr* began its serialization in *The Egoist* on 1 April 1916.

2. Wyndham Lewis, *Time and Western Man* (London: Chatto & Windus, 1927), pp. 39–40.

3. I am correcting the *Blast* text here from Ezra Pound, *Collected Shorter Poems* (London: Faber & Faber, 1968), p. 167.

4. Hugh Kenner, *The Pound Era* (London: Faber & Faber, 1975), p. 243.

5. Richard Aldington, "Blast," *The Egoist* (15 July 1914), 273. This review of *Blast #1* is generally perceptive.

6. W. C. Wees, *Vorticism and the English Avant-Garde* (Toronto: University of Toronto Press, 1972), p. 205; Richard Cork, *Vorticism and Abstract Art in the First Machine Age,* 2 vols. (Berkeley and Los Angeles: University of California Press, 1976), pp. 292, 293.

7. Pound, *Collected Shorter Poems,* p. 131.

8. Ezra Pound, "Affirmations II Vorticism," in *The New Age* 16, no. 11 (14 January 1915), 277.

9. The essential documents of Imagism have been collected in *Imagist Poetry,* ed. Peter Jones (Harmondsworth: Penguin Books, 1972). The best study of the movement, at least from Pound's perspective, is Herbert Schneidau, *Ezra Pound: The Image and the Real* (Baton Rouge: Louisiana State University Press, 1969); Schneidau's study is as good an understanding of Pound's aesthetic as one could arrive at, given the choice of Imagism—not Vorticism—as one's focus. Hugh Kenner's treatment of Imagism in *The Pound Era* (pp. 173–91) is perceptive if a little irreverent.

10. F. S. Flint, "Imagism," *Poetry* 1 (March 1913), 199; reprinted in *Imagist Poetry,* ed. Peter Jones, pp. 129–30.

11. Ezra Pound, "A Few Don'ts by an Imagiste," *Poetry* 1 (March 1913), 200; reprinted in *Literary Essays of Ezra Pound,* ed. T. S. Eliot (New York: New Directions, 1970), p. 4.

12. This passage is quoted from *The New Republic* of 22 May 1915

by Noel Stock in *The Life of Ezra Pound* (Harmondsworth: Penguin Books, 1974), p. 225.

13. A.C.H. [Alice Corbin Henderson], "Imagism, Secular and Esoteric," *Poetry* 11 (March 1918), 340.

14. Skipwith Cannell, "Nocturnes," *Imagist Poetry*, p. 59.

15. Peter Jones recounts the anecdote in his introduction to *Imagist Poetry*, p. 36.

16. Sergei Eisenstein's principle of montage is virtually the same principle, and is also influenced by Oriental art. See his essays "The Unexpected" and "The Cinematographic Principle and the Ideogram," in his *Film Form* and *The Film Sense*, ed. and trans. Jay Leyda (New York: Meridian Books, 1957), pp. 18–27, 28–44.

17. Wallace Stevens, *Opus Posthumous*, ed. Samuel French Morse (New York: Knopf, 1972), p. 161.

18. Schneidau, *Ezra Pound: The Image and the Real*, p. 45.

19. Pound, *Collected Shorter Poems*, p. 119.

20. *The Cantos* were begun in 1915 but "Pound had been planning an epic poem of one kind or other ever since his undergraduate days at Hamilton." I quote Ronald Bush, *The Genesis of Ezra Pound's Cantos* (Princeton: Princeton University Press, 1976), p. 22, the best study of this subject. Pound himself claimed once that he "began the *Cantos* about 1904, I suppose." ("Ezra Pound: An Interview," *Paris Review* 28 [1962], p. 23).

21. Pound puts Picasso on the good side here, whereas Lewis puts him on the bad side, so Pound is modifying Lewis's polemic in light of his own perceptions, but the distinction he draws is Lewis's.

22. Ezra Pound, *ABC of Reading* (1934; rpt., New York: New Directions, 1960), p. 52.

23. Pound himself quotes Yeats's comment in a 1934 letter. (*The Letters of Ezra Pound, 1907–1941*, ed. D.D. Paige [New York: Harcourt, Brace & Co., 1950], p. 257).

24. Pound himself told this anecdote, in his obituary of Ford reprinted in *Pound/Ford: The Story of a Literary Friendship*, ed. Brita Lindberg-Seyersted (New York: New Directions, 1982), p. 172. It should be said that Ford's pressure on Pound to be modern came before and may in part explain his association with the Vorticists: it was Ford who most often used the term *modern* as an honorific.

25. Lewis, *Time and Western Man*, p. 39.

26. This praise comes from a letter to Harriet Monroe of 30 September 1914. (*The Letters of Ezra Pound, 1907–1941*, p. 40).

27. Pound's translation is reprinted in *The Translations of Ezra Pound* (London: Faber & Faber, 1970), p. 121.

28. For Pound's admiration, see his *Gaudier-Brzeska: A Memoir* (New York: New Directions, 1970), pp. 48, 95–102, and passim.

29. Hugh Kenner, *The Pound Era*, p. 202.

30. Pound stated the theme in a 1931 letter, *The Letters of Ezra Pound, 1907-1941,* p. 231.

31. The best discussion of the relation of Pound's poem to the original is in J. P. Sullivan, *Ezra Pound and Sextus Propertius: A Study in Creative Translation* (Austin: University of Texas Press, 1964). But for a contrasting perspective, see Donald Davie, *Ezra Pound* (New York: Viking Press, 1976), pp. 54-61.

32. Pound's reflection appears in a letter of 1932, *The Letters of Ezra Pound, 1907-1941,* p. 239.

33. I am using what has become the standard form for referring to *The Cantos:* Cantos 1-30 are Early, 31-71 are Middle, 74-84 are *The Pisan Cantos,* 85-117 are Late. Of course, these subdivide: Cantos 52-61 are the Chinese History Cantos and 62-71 are the Adams Cantos.

34. I thought that I had coined the term *presentism,* but I find that Lewis uses it in a diametrically opposed sense: in *WLOA* (212), he describes (and criticizes) Futurism's Bergsonian stress on the moment as presentist.

35. *The Collected Poems of W. B. Yeats* (New York: Macmillan, 1953), p. 210. Yeats's lines, in a reflection of the process he is writing about, echo lines by Virgil and Shelley.

36. Hugh Kenner, *The Pound Era,* p. 202.

37. Petrarch's definition comes from a letter to Boccaccio, *Rerum familiarum libri* 23:19. I cite the translation of Morris Bishop, ed. and trans., *Letters from Petrarch* (Bloomington: University of Indiana Press, 1966), pp. 198-99.

38. On Petrarchan imitation, see Thomas M. Greene, *The Light in Troy: Imitation and Discovery in Renaissance Poetry* (New Haven: Yale University Press, 1976), particularly pp. 81-103; for a wider discussion of imitation in the Renaissance, see the rest of Greene's book and Nancy Struever, *The Language of History in the Renaissance* (Princeton: Princeton University Press, 1970), pp. 154ff.

39. Petrarch is at his most extreme in poem 70 of his *Canzoniere;* for Manet, see Michael Fried, "Manet's Sources: Aspects of His Art, 1859-1865," *Artforum* 7, no. 7 (March 1969), 28-82.

40. Obviously, I have not ventured here to give a complete history of imitation: Renaissance literature and French modernist painting are two obvious and pertinent places in which to see notions of imitation at work; they are not the only places in which such notions can be seen.

41. His contempt for Petrarch emerges most clearly in a comparison between Guido Cavalcanti and Petrarch that he drew a number of times:

> the gulf between Petrarch's capacity and Guido's is the great gulf, not of degree, but of kind. In Guido the "figure," the strong metamorphic or "picturesque" expression is there with purpose to convey or to interpret a definite meaning. In Petrarch it is ornament, the prettiest ornament he could find, but not an irreplaceable ornament,

or one that he couldn't have used just about as well somewhere else. In fact he very often does use it, and them, somewhere, and nearly everywhere, else, all over the place. ("Cavalcanti," *Literary Essays,* pp. 153–54)

42. These examples are Kenner's; see *The Pound Era,* pp. 76–78.

43. The two best examples are furnished by Sextus Propertius and by the Tempio Malatestiana built by Sigismundo Malatesta in Rimini; J. P. Sullivan, who has written the most thorough study of Pound's relation to Propertius (*Ezra Pound and Sextus Propertius: A Study in Creative Translation* [1964]), went on to work on Propertius himself, work resulting in his *Propertius: A Critical Introduction* (Cambridge: Cambridge University Press, 1976); Adrian Stokes's work on quattrocento sculpture and the Tempio in particular, which led to his well-known—if a little heterodox—works, *The Quattro Cento* (London: Faber & Faber, 1932) and *Stones of Rimini* (London: Faber & Faber, 1934), was directly inspired by Pound.

44. On Pound's Orientalism, see *The Pound Era,* pp. 192–231, 445–69; Wai-Lim Yip, *Ezra Pound's Cathay* (Princeton: Princeton University Press, 1969) for the definitive discussion of *Cathay's* relation to the Chinese originals; and Earl Miner, *The Japanese Tradition in British and American Literature* (Princeton: Princeton University Press, 1958), pp. 108–55, for a thorough discussion of Pound's use of Japanese literature.

45. Pound himself tells this story in *Gaudier-Brzeska,* p. 29.

46. Pound tells this story in *Gaudier-Brzeska,* p. 46 and in the *ABC of Reading* p. 21.

47. Pound refers on a number of occasions to Vorticism while discussing the Orient or vice versa; for some examples of this, see *Gaudier-Brzeska,* p. 126, and *Selected Prose, 1909–1965,* ed. William Cookson (New York: New Directions, 1973), p. 81.

48. Hugh Kenner's discussion, in *The Pound Era,* pp. 223–31, is excellent. James J. Y. Liu, in *The Art of Chinese Poetry* (Chicago: University of Chicago Press, 1962), p. 3, summarizes the situation as follows:

While one can understand [Fenollosa's] enthusiasm for a language that he imagined to be free from the tendencies towards jejune logicality of modern English, and while one is flattered by his attribution of superior poetic qualities to one's mother tongue, one has to admit that his conclusions are often incorrect, largely due to his refusal to recognize the phonetic element of Chinese characters.

49. Ernest Fenollosa, *The Chinese Written Character as a Medium for Poetry,* ed. Ezra Pound (1918; rpt., San Francisco: City Lights, 1969), pp. 9–10.

50. Schneidau, *Ezra Pound: The Image and the Real,* pp. 56–73. Ronald Bush goes further and calls the "ideogrammic method" a "red herring." See his *The Genesis of Ezra Pound's Cantos,* pp. 10–16.

51. It is significant that before he received the Fenollosa manuscripts Pound had translated some Chinese poems from H. A. Giles's *History of Chinese Literature*, "After Ch'u Yuan," "Liu Ch'e," "Fan-Piece, for her Imperial Lord," and "Ts'ai Chi'h," *Collected Shorter Poems*, pp. 118-19.

52. Relevant here is Santayana's 1940 reaction to Fenollosa's *Essay*, as reported by Noel Stock in *The Life of Ezra Pound* (pp. 476-77): "he wished there had been more about the Chinese signs and 'less romantic metaphysics.'"

53. Earl Miner is very good on the strengths and weaknesses of Pound's work on the Nō, *The Japanese Tradition*, p. 137.

54. Though it must also be pointed out that he was less interested in the Nō. In a 1917 letter to John Quinn (*The Letters of Ezra Pound*, p. 102), we find this comment:

> China is fundamental, Japan is not. Japan is a special interest, like Provence, or 12-13th Century Italy (apart from Dante). I don't mean to say there aren't interesting things in Fenollosa's Japanese stuff (or fine things, like the end of Kagekiyo, which is, I think, "Homeric"). But China is solid. One can't go back of the "Exile's Letter," or the "Song of the Bowmen," or the "North Gate."

This is a fascinating passage, as it reveals Pound's own awareness of the eccentricity (in a literal sense) of some of his interests. We do not have to endorse Pound's view of the relative importance of Chinese and Japanese art to see that what he says is true of the relative importance of his work on Chinese and Japanese material in his *oeuvre*.

55. Hugh Kenner has made these points in his introduction to *The Translations of Ezra Pound*, p. 13.

56. Two books have been written on this subject, Akhtar Qamber's *Yeats and the Noh* (New York: Weatherhill, 1974) and Richard Taylor's *The Drama of W. B. Yeats: Irish Myth and the Japanese Nō* (New Haven: Yale University Press, 1976).

Four: Lewis's *Enemy of the Stars*

1. Wyndham Lewis, *Rude Assignment* (London: Hutchinson & Co., 1950), pp. 128-29.

2. Obviously, this is not an adequate characterization of mimesis, though an adequate summary of Lewis's characterization of it.

3. Hugh Kenner, in an excellent brief discussion of "Vorticist Prose" (pp. 14-17), makes this pertinent comment: "Lewis didn't succeed in making his new prose *move* rather than accumulate, until, in the 1930's, he had struck his truce with Time." (*Wyndham Lewis* [Norfolk, Conn.: New Directions, 1954], p. 15).

4. Kenner again has a relevant point, that in *Enemy of the Stars* when "nothing is happening, however, the effect is memorable." (*Wyndham Lewis*, p. 15).

5. Richard Aldington, "Blast," *The Egoist* 1, no. 14 (15 July 1914), 272.

6. Omar S. Pound and Philip Glover reproduce a page of the rewritten *Blast* version in their *Wyndham Lewis: A Descriptive Bibliography* (Folkestone: Dawson & Sons, 1978), pp. 32-33.

7. These thematic complexities are really beside my point here, but to the 1932 version of the play, Lewis appended an abstruse 1925 essay on metaphysics, "The Physics of the Not-Self," (also reprinted in the recent *Collected Poems and Plays*), and some of the ideas in this essay are operative in the revised version of the play as well.

8. The relative paucity of conjugated verbs and complete sentences in "The Game of Chess" make it resemble *Enemy of the Stars* in its syntax as well as in its program, though *Enemy of the Stars* is both prior and more adventurous.

9. I am conflating two separate claims in this sentence: I quote from *Time and Western Man* (London: Chatto & Windus, 1927), p. 110; Lewis referred specifically to "Circe" in a blurb for the 1932 version of *Enemy of the Stars* reprinted in *Collected Poems and Plays,* ed. Alan Munton (Manchester: Carcanet Press, 1979), pp. 221-22.

10. See David Hayman, ed., *A First-draft version of Finnegans Wake* (Austin: University of Texas Press, 1963).

11. Besides Lewis's account in *Rude Assignment,* pp. 128-29, see Timothy Materer, *Wyndham Lewis the Novelist* (Detroit: Wayne State University Press, 1976).

12. See in particular Michael Begnal's half of *Narrator and Character in Finnegans Wake* (Lewisburg, Pa.: Bucknell University Press, 1975).

13. Joseph Frank, "Spatial Form in Modern Literature" (1945), reprinted in *The Widening Gyre* (New Brunswick, N.J.: Rutgers, 1963), pp. 3-62; "Spatial Form: An Answer to Critics," *Critical Inquiry* 4 (1977), 231-52; "Spatial Form: Some Further Reflections," *Critical Inquiry* 5 (1978), 275-90. See also Frank Kermode, "Reply to Joseph Frank," *Critical Inquiry* 4 (1978), 579-88 and *Spatial Form in Narrative,* ed. Jeffrey R. Smitten and Ann Daghistany (Ithaca, N.Y.: Cornell University Press, 1981).

14. Frank, *The Widening Gyre,* pp. 12-13.

15. Frank, *The Widening Gyre,* p. 59.

16. Frank, *The Widening Gyre,* p. 60.

17. Frank, *The Widening Gyre,* pp. 12-13.

18. James Joyce, *Finnegans Wake* (London: Faber & Faber, 1975), 23:16.

19. Joyce, *Finnegans Wake,* 70:35-36.

20. Frank has warned in advance against anyone trying to connect his notion of spatial forms with diagrams or maps. In his 1978 essay, "Spatial Form: Some Further Reflections," he comments: "Of course, if one persists in thinking that to speak of literature in terms of spatial forms means to wish

to construct maps, charts, diagrams, and blueprints, then its weakness as a critical concept is perfectly obvious" (p. 175). I take it that his primary reference here is to the static diagrams of excessive Formalist critics, but I expect that he would still take issue with the way I modify his concept here.

21. Joyce's comment is quoted without a reference by Richard Ellmann in *Eminent Domain: Yeats among Wilde, Joyce, Eliot and Auden* (New York: Oxford University Press, 1967), p. 51.

22. W. B. Yeats, *A Vision,* 2d ed. (1937; rpt., London: Macmillan, 1962), p. 5.

23. Yeats, *A Vision,* 2d ed., p. 8.

24. Yeats, *A Vision,* 2d ed., p. 25.

25. Frank, "Spatial Form: An Answer to Critics," p. 237.

26. T. S. Eliot, *The Complete Poetry and Plays, 1909-1950* (New York: Harcourt, Brace & World, 1971), p. 118.

27. Eliot, *The Complete Poetry and Plays,* p. 136.

28. Eliot, *The Complete Poetry and Plays,* p. 144.

29. Perkins, however, has never really defined what he means by the term *High Modernist Mode.* See David Perkins, *A History of Modern Poetry: From the 1890s to the High Modernist Mode* (Cambridge: Belknap Press, 1976).

30. Pound, *ABC of Reading,* p. 39.

31. Not uniquely, I should say, remembering Gertrude Stein, though her problem, perhaps, was that the painters she knew were too good.

32. Addressing rather different issues, Michael Fried has anticipated my claim here:

> In fact, I am tempted far beyond my knowledge to suggest that, faced with the need to defeat theatre, it is above all to the condition of painting and sculpture—the condition, that is, of existing in, indeed of secreting or constituting, a continuous and perpetual *present*— that the other contemporary arts, most notably poetry and music, aspire.

("Art and Objecthood," in *Minimal Art: A Critical Anthology,* ed. Gregory Battcock [New York: Dutton, 1968], p. 146). See also Michael Fried, *Morris Louis* (New York: Abrams, n.d.), p. 41.

Five: Wyndham Lewis and the Trial of Man

1. Hugh Kenner, *Wyndham Lewis* (Norfolk, Conn.: New Directions 1954), p. 92.

2. Wyndham Lewis, *Tarr* (1928; rpt., London: Calder & Boyars, 1968), p. 5. The conception of Tarr, if not its composition, dates back to 1910, as the preface to the first *Tarr* informs us.

3. Wyndham Lewis, *Rude Assignment* (London: Hutchinson & Co., 1950), p. 129.

4. Lewis, *Rude Assignment,* p. 129.

5. Wyndham Lewis, *Tarr* (1918; rpt., New York: Jubilee, 1973), p. 67.

6. Lewis, *Tarr* (1928), p. 69.

7. William H. Pritchard, *Wyndham Lewis* (New York: Twayne, 1968), p. 30. See also Robert T. Chapman, *Wyndham Lewis: Fictions and Satires* (New York: Barnes & Noble, 1973), p. 77.

8. Kenner, *Wyndham Lewis,* p. 36. I think Kenner is correct, and the passages I have just quoted support his contention: "wounded insects of cloth" is changed in 1928 to "wounded insects hither and thither," which is clearer but much less interesting. See also Timothy Materer, *Wyndham Lewis the Novelist* (Detroit: Wayne State University Press, 1976), p. 52.

9. Hugh Kenner, *Wyndham Lewis,* p. 15.

10. On occasion, an equal sign follows a colon or stands in lieu of any other punctuation. See *Tarr* (1918), pp. 58, 322.

11. Kenner, *Wyndham Lewis,* p. 30.

12. Lewis, *Tarr* (1918), p. 4.

13. Lewis, *Tarr* (1918), p. 4.

14. Lewis, *Tarr* (1918), p. 6.

15. Lewis, *Tarr* (1918), pp. 150–51.

16. See *The Letters of Wyndham Lewis,* ed. W. K. Rose (Norfolk, Conn.: New Directions, 1963), pp. 74–106.

17. Tom Kinninmont, in *"Tarr:* A Detective Story," *Lewisletter* 7 (October 1977), uses this fact to suggest that Lewis never intended there to be any equal signs in *Tarr* in the first place, and that it was a form of punctuation possibly invented by that notoriously creative editor, Ezra Pound. In my *"Tarr:* More Detective Work," *Enemy News: Newsletter of the Wyndham Lewis Society* 17 (Autumn 1982), 23–24, I show that unpublished correspondence proves that Kinninmont's suggestion is wrong and that the equal sign was clearly intended by Lewis to be in *Tarr.*

18. The passage from Schopenhauer that Lewis quotes can be found in Arthur Schopenhauer, *The World as Will and Idea,* trans. R. B. Haldane and J. Kemp (London, 1896), 1, 239. Lewis seems to have read this translation, as his quotations agree with this text in every detail except that Lewis characteristically replaces semicolons with colons. Lewis's first quotation follows the second in Schopenhauer, with an omitted sentence in between.

19. Though I do not think that Lewis consulted the original German text, at one point its language is closer to Vorticism than that of the translation. What Kemp and Haldane render as "the course of time stops" is actually "art halts the wheel of time" ("das Rad der Zeit halt sie an"). It should be pointed out that Lewis, never to be accused of total consistency, subsequently attacked Schopenhauer from a rather different angle in *Time and Western Man,* pp. 314–27.

20. Hugh Kenner, "The Visual World of Wyndham Lewis," in Walter

Michel, *Wyndham Lewis: Paintings and Drawings* (Berkeley and Los Angeles: University of California Press, 1971), pp. 20–21.

21. Wyndham Lewis, *Time and Western Man* (London: Chatto & Windus, 1927), p. 461.

22. Lewis, *Time and Western Man*, p. xv.

23. Lewis, *Time and Western Man*, p. 138.

24. Lewis, *Time and Western Man*, p. 428.

25. Wyndham Lewis, *Men Without Art* (London: Cassell, 1934), p. 118.

26. Lewis, *Men Without Art*, p. 128.

27. Lewis, *Men Without Art*, pp. 120–21.

28. On the titling of *The Revenge for Love*, see Lewis, *Rude Assignment*, p. 214.

29. Timothy Materer in a chapter on *The Apes of God* entitled "The Great English Vortex" (pp. 83–97 of his *Wyndham Lewis the Novelist* [Detroit: Wayne State University Press, 1976]) has already used the term *vortex* to analyze *The Apes of God*. But his focus is style, not form; the only way in which his analysis anticipates mine is that he notes that Lewis obviously intended Pierpoint to be the detached observer at the still point of the vortex.

30. Wyndham Lewis, *Self Condemned*, New Canadian Library No. 112 (Toronto: McClelland & Stewart, 1974), p. 407.

31. The alternative ending is briefly described in W. K. Rose, *Wyndham Lewis at Cornell* (Ithaca, N.Y.: Cornell University Library, 1961), p. 16.

32. Kenner, *Wyndham Lewis*, p. 153.

33. I think I can use the plural here: every writer on Lewis I have read who has indicated which of Lewis's novels he thinks is the finest has chosen one of these four works (in order of popularity): *The Revenge for Love, Self Condemned, The Human Age,* and *The Apes of God*.

34. Lewis, *Tarr* (1918), p. 316.

35. Lewis, *Tarr* (1918), p. 317.

36. Lewis, *Men Without Art*, p. 116.

37. See Fredric Jameson, *Fables of Aggression: Wyndham Lewis, the Modernist as Fascist* (Berkeley and Los Angeles: University of California Press, 1979); and Geoffrey Wagner, *Wyndham Lewis: A Portrait of the Artist as an Enemy* (New Haven: Yale University Press, 1957).

38. Wyndham Lewis, "The Code of a Herdsman," *The Little Review* 4, no. 3 (July 1917), p. 4.

39. Wyndham Lewis, *The Wild Body* (London: Chatto & Windus, 1927), p. 5.

40. "The Meaning of the Wild Body" (in *The Wild Body*, pp. 243–50) contains Lewis's exposition of this dichotomy and its implications for art, in particular for comedy.

41. See in particular "Part VII—Thersites and Apemantus," in *The Lion and the Fox* (1927; rpt., London: Methuen & Co., 1966), pp. 231–62.

42. Lewis, *Time and Western Man,* p. 135.

43. The only contemporary who possessed this detachment, according to Lewis, was the French intellectual Julien Benda, whose *La Trahison des clercs* also emphasizes the need for detachment. What Benda stresses, in an anticipation of Lewis's position in later works such as *America and Cosmic Man* (1948), is the need to break down nationalism. Timothy Materer, in *Vortex: Pound, Eliot, and Lewis,* pp. 184-94, has an excellent discussion of Benda's relevance to the modernists.

44. Kenner, *Wyndham Lewis,* p. xv.

45. Lewis, *Time and Western Man,* p. 41.

46. Wyndham Lewis, *The Childermass* (1928; rpt., London: John Calder, 1965), p. 290.

47. Kenner, *Wyndham Lewis,* p. 106.

48. Wyndham Lewis, *The Apes of God* (1930; rpt., London: Nash & Grayson, 1932), pp. 271-72.

49. Kenner, *Wyndham Lewis,* p. 107.

50. Lewis, *Time and Western Man,* p. 89.

51. Lewis, *Men Without Art,* p. 289.

52. Swift tells us in the Preface to *The Battle of the Books:* "Satire is a sort of glass wherein beholders do generally discover everybody's face but their own." His satiric description of the effect of satire certainly describes the effect of Lewis's satire.

53. Lewis, *Blasting and Bombardiering* (1937; rpt., London: Calder & Boyars, 1967), p. 259.

54. Lewis, *Time and Western Man,* p. 193.

55. This essay was reprinted in 1932 as a commentary on *Enemy of the Stars* and is therefore available in the recent *Collected Poems and Plays,* ed. Alan Munton (Manchester: Carcanet Press, 1979), pp. 193-204.

56. *The Letters of W. B. Yeats,* ed. Allan Wade (New York: Macmillan, 1955), p. 762.

57. Wyndham Lewis, *The Human Age* (London: Methuen & Co., 1955), p. 345. (This volume contains only Books Two and Three, *Monstre Gai* and *Malign Fiesta.*)

58. Rose, ed., *The Letters of Wyndham Lewis,* p. xxii.

59. Tobias Smollett, *Humphry Clinker,* ed. Lewis M. Knapp (London: Oxford University Press, 1972), p. 347.

60. According to Padraic Colum; see Mary and Padraic Colum, *Our Friend James Joyce* (Gloucester, Mass.: Peter Smith, 1968), p. 95.

61. Lewis, *The Human Age,* p. 566. D. G. Bridson informs us that the revision took place on the galley proofs; see his "*The Human Age* in Retrospect," in *Wyndham Lewis: A Revaluation,* ed. Jeffrey Meyers (Montreal: McGill-Queen's University Press, 1980), p. 240.

62. Lewis, *The Human Age,* p. 566.

63. If the reference to Pullman's Jesuit education, Irish birth, and

fame as the greatest writer of his epoch do not suffice, D. G. Bridson has written that Lewis told him that Pullman "was a portrayal of James Joyce." (D. G. Bridson, *"The Human Age* in Retrospect," in *Wyndham Lewis: A Revaluation,* p. 242).

64. Lewis, *The Human Age,* p. 262.

65. Lewis, *The Human Age,* pp. 263, 266.

66. Hugh Kenner, *"The Trial of Man,"* an appendix to Wyndham Lewis, *Malign Fiesta* (London: John Calder, 1966), p. 238.

67. Lewis, *The Human Age,* p. 377.

68. Lewis, *The Human Age,* pp. 372–73.

69. T. S. Eliot's acute remark about Pound's Hell in *The Cantos* is pertinent here: "it is a Hell for the *other people,* the people we read about in the newspapers, not for oneself and one's friends." (T. S. Eliot, *After Strange Gods: A Primer of Modern Heresy* [New York: Harcourt, Brace & Co., 1934], p. 47). Until this point, Lewis's Hell had also been for the other people.

70. Lewis, *The Human Age,* p. 528.

71. Lewis, *Malign Fiesta,* p. 218. This edition of *Malign Fiesta* prints as an appendix the extant fragment of *The Trial of Man.*

72. The difference is shown by the rest of this scene, through Sammael's frenzied reaction to God's suspected presence when Sammael does recover consciousness, *Malign Fiesta,* pp. 218–21.

73. *The Letters of Wyndham Lewis,* p. 546.

74. T. S. Eliot, *The Complete Poems and Plays, 1909–1950* (New York: Harcourt, Brace & World, 1971), p. 142.

75. *The Letters of Wyndham Lewis,* p. 546.

76. Testimony to his closeness, beyond Lewis's late letters to Eliot printed by W. K. Rose, is found in Eliot's two late essays on Lewis, both published in *The Hudson Review:* "A Note on *Monstre Gai,"* 6, no. 4 (Winter 1955), 522–26 and the obituary "Wyndham Lewis," 10, no. 2 (Summer 1957), 167–70.

77. Lewis, *The Human Age,* p. 511.

78. Fredric Jameson has pointed out Lewis's inability to keep the two separate in *Fables of Aggression,* p. 167.

79. See, among other places, *The Human Age,* pp. 263, 345, 463–65.

Six: *The Cantos* in the Context of Vorticism

1. Michael F. Harper, "Truth and Calliope: Ezra Pound's Malatesta," *PMLA* 96 (1981), 102.

2. Leon Surette, *A Light from Eleusis: A Study of Ezra Pound's Cantos* (Oxford: Clarendon Press, 1979), p. vii.

3. See Hugh Kenner, *The Poetry of Ezra Pound* (Norfolk, Conn.: New Directions, 1951), pp. 254–55, 314–16, passim.

4. See in particular his discussion of the subject-rhyme in *The Pound Era* (London: Faber & Faber, 1975), pp. 423–27.

5. I have argued this point elsewhere, in "Dante's Hell and Pound's *Paradiso: tutto spezzato,*" *Paideuma* 9 (1980), 501–4.

6. Daniel D. Pearlman, *The Barb of Time: On the Unity of Ezra Pound's Cantos* (New York: Oxford University Press, 1969), pp. 8–9.

7. Each has written a book largely on *The Cantos:* Ronald Bush, *The Genesis of Ezra Pound's Cantos* (Princeton: Princeton University Press, 1976); Leon Surette, *A Light from Eleusis;* Wendy Stallard Flory, *Ezra Pound and The Cantos: A Record of Struggle* (New Haven: Yale University Press, 1980); Michael André Bernstein, *The Tale of the Tribe: Ezra Pound and the Modern Verse Epic* (Princeton: Princeton University Press, 1980). My linking of these critics should not be taken as saying that they are in fundamental agreement on *The Cantos* beyond the question of major form.

8. See Joseph N. Riddel, "Pound and the Decentered Image," *The Georgia Review* 29, no. 3 (Fall 1975), 565–91. Michael Harper's recent article, "Truth and Calliope," is in my opinion a devastating attack on Riddel's approach.

9. The indebtedness of Charles Olson and the tradition of American "postmodernist" poetry that stems from his work to the "open form" of *The Cantos* has been widely discussed. A new journal, *Sagetrieb,* "devoted to poets in the Pound-Williams Tradition," has recently commenced publication; Olson, Creeley, Levertov, and Zukovsky are specifically mentioned as some of the poets the journal has in mind. Michael André Bernstein's study, *The Tale of the Tribe,* treats Williams and Olson in addition to Pound; and Sherman Paul's *Olson's Push: Origin, Black Mountain and Recent American Poetry* (Baton Rouge: Louisiana State University Press, 1978) has a long discussion (pp. 1–29) of Olson's indebtedness to Pound.

10. Bush, however, thinks that this shift "has perhaps been given too much emphasis." See *The Genesis of Ezra Pound's Cantos,* p. 255.

11. *The Letters of Ezra Pound, 1907–1941,* ed. D. D. Paige (New York: Harcourt Brace & Co., 1950), p. 210.

12. Surette makes this point in *A Light from Eleusis,* p. 15.

13. *The Letters of Ezra Pound,* p. 210. The third and final theme is the "'magic moment' or moment of metamorphosis, bust through from quotidien into 'divine or permanent world.'"

14. The quotation comes from a letter of 10 August 1922 to John Quinn, printed in an appendix to Pearlman, *The Barb of Time,* p. 302. Michael Harper's recent article, "Truth and Calliope," is the best study of the Malatesta Cantos.

15. *Literary Essays of Ezra Pound,* ed. T. S. Eliot (New York: New Directions, 1968), p. 220.

16. Hugh Kenner has already argued (in *The Pound Era,* p. 420) that "Venice is perhaps the central preoccupation of the sequence."

17. Kenner, *The Pound Era,* p. 360.

18. *The Letters of Ezra Pound,* p. 28.

19. Pound's point sparks an instant rebuttal, what about New York? It is significant that Pound never thought of New York as a center of any fundamental importance. Note his assumption that W. C. Williams in New Jersey is doomed to extreme isolation.

20. This view of the Renaissance is, of course, a traditional, nineteenth-century one, absorbed by Pound via Burckhardt and Symonds, as Michael André Bernstein has pointed out in *The Tale of the Tribe,* p. 42.

21. Kenner, *The Pound Era,* p. 376.

22. Surette, *A Light from Eleusis,* pp. 23-26.

23. "Ezra Pound: An Interview," *Paris Review* 28 (1962), 23.

24. See *Pound / Joyce: The Letters of Ezra Pound to James Joyce with Pound's Essays on Joyce,* ed. Forrest Read (New York: New Directions, 1967), p. 228.

25. I am not forgetting Pound's support of the Objectivists, Cummings, Basil Bunting, and others, but I would argue that these poets did not, in Pound's opinion, reverse what he saw as a general cultural decline.

26. In rather different ways, both Michael Harper and Michael André Bernstein have convincingly argued that we must take Pound's historiographical intentions far more seriously then they have been taken: see Michael Harper, "Truth and Calliope" and Bernstein's "A Poem Including History," pp. 29-74 of his *The Tale of the Tribe.* Nonetheless, their arguments should not be taken as proving (or in Bernstein's case, as even arguing) that Pound's historiographical intentions found successful embodiment in *The Cantos* at every stage.

27. Bush, *The Genesis of Ezra Pound's Cantos,* p. 3.

28. Bush, *The Genesis of Ezra Pound's Cantos,* pp. 10-12.

29. Pound, *ABC of Reading* (1934; rpt., New York: New Directions, 1960), pp. 21-22.

30. See Kenner, *The Pound Era,* p. 158.

31. See Herbert N. Schneidau, *Ezra Pound: The Image and the Real* (Baton Rouge: Louisiana State University Press, 1969), pp. 58-73.

32. The term is more properly *chêng ming,* in the Wade-Giles system of romanization, but I have found it simpler to keep to Pound's usage throughout.

33. Ezra Pound, *Guide to Kulchur* (1938; rpt., New York: New Directions, 1970), pp. 16-17. Pound is translating from the *Analects,* book 13, chapter 3. For a more extended classical Chinese treatment of the Confucian concern with rectifying names, see *Basic Writings of Hsün Tzu,* trans. Burton Watson (New York: Columbia University Press, 1967), pp. 137-56.

34. The character at the end of Canto 34 was added much later.

35. "Two kinds of banks have existed: The MONTE DEI PASCHI and the devils." From *Social Credit: An Impact* (1935) and included in Ezra

Pound, *Selected Prose: 1909-1965,* ed. William Cookson (New York: New Directions, 1975), p. 270.

36. Pound makes the claim, both in *Jefferson and / or Mussolini* (1935; rpt., New York: Liveright, 1970), p. 113, and *Guide to Kulchur* (p. 32), that Confucians have been at the root of every movement towards order in Chinese history.

37. In the Adams Cantos, *ching ming* appear together twice (66:382, 68:400) and *ching* appears alone twice (63:352, 67:387). Only two other characters appear in the Adams Cantos, the character for tea (62:341; in a reference to the British tax on tea that led to the Boston Tea Party) and *chung* (70:413) which will concern us later. In *The Pound Era* (pp. 432-34), Hugh Kenner established the relation between Adams and China which I am drawing on here.

38. Pound, *Jefferson and / or Mussolini,* p. 128.

39. Pound, *Jefferson and / or Mussolini,* p. 12.

40. A comment Pound made about Chinese in his later translation of the *Ta Hsio* is pertinent: "As to the frequent lack of tense indications, the ideogramic mind assumes that what has been, is and will be." This is quoted from Confucius, *The Unwobbling Pivot, The Great Digest, The Analects,* trans. Ezra Pound (New York: New Directions, 1969), p. 53.

41. The relevant source material for the Adams Cantos has been gathered together by Frederick Sanders in *John Adams Speaking: Pound's Sources for the Adams Cantos* (Orono: University of Maine Press, 1975).

42. Michael André Bernstein has an excellent discussion of these tensions in *The Tale of the Tribe,* pp. 115-19.

43. See Guy Davenport, "Pound and Frobenius," in *Motive and Method in The Cantos of Ezra Pound,* ed. Lewis Leary, English Institute Essays, 1953 (New York: Columbia University Press, 1954), pp. 52-57. For the theme of the city in *The Cantos,* see also Guy Davenport, "Persephone's Ezra," in *New Approaches to Ezra Pound,* ed. Eva Hesse (Berkeley and Los Angeles: University of California Press, 1969), pp. 145-77.

44. William Chace, for example, in *The Political Identities of Ezra Pound and T. S. Eliot* (Stanford: Stanford University Press, 1975), p. 105, closes his discussion of Pound by characterizing the world of *The Pisan Cantos* as "a world at once lyrical, decomposed, and solipsistic."

45. *Spezzato* here is a reference to the *Inferno,* 21, 108; for a fuller discussion of the implications of the reference, see my "Dante's Hell and Pound's *Paradiso: tutto spezzato.*"

46. The last two lines come from Mencius, book 3, part 1, chapter 4, 13. In a note heading his translation of the *Analects,* Pound tells us, "After Confucius' death, when there was talk of regrouping, Tsang declined, saying, 'Washed in the Keang and Han, bleached in the autumn sun's-slope, what whiteness can one add to that whiteness, what candour?" (Mencius III, 1; IV,

13.)" Confucius, trans. Pound, p. 194. The context of the quotation is relevant in view of the death of Mussolini.

47. William Butler Yeats, *A Vision* (1937; rpt., London: Macmillan, 1962), pp. 5-6.

48. J. R. Levenson and Franz Schurmann, *China: An Interpretive History* (Berkeley and Los Angeles: University of California Press, 1969), p. 110. The passage comes from a discussion of the relationship between Taoism and Confucianism on which I depend in my treatment of the matter here. See also Burton Watson's introduction to *The Complete Works of Chuang Tzu,* trans. Burton Watson (New York: Columbia University Press, 1968), pp. 10-12.

49. *The Complete Works of Chuang Tzu,* pp. 93-94.

50. Hugh Kenner (in *The Pound Era,* pp. 455-57) has already discussed Pound's innate Taoism; I push this further than he does and perhaps further than he would as I see a shift towards Taoism, not simply an amalgamation of Taoism and Confucianism. Massimo Bacigalupo in *The Forméd Trace: The Later Poetry of Ezra Pound* (New York: Columbia University Press, 1980) refers on several occasions to the "suspiciously Taoist" nature of Pound's Confucianism but does not go into detail. Anthony Woodward (in *Ezra Pound and The Pisan Cantos* [London: Routledge & Kegan Paul, 1980], p. 48) makes the similar general point which he also does not support in detail that "the true Pound—the poet of Canto 49—was a Taoist in spirit, notwithstanding his rudeness about Taoism in the 'China' Cantos."

51. The *Shih Ching* are usually referred to in English as the *Book of Odes* or simply as the *Odes;* Pound called his translation *The Confucian Odes.* In his essay, "Immediate Need of Confucius" (1937), Pound linked the ideogram itself with Confucianism; see *Selected Prose 1909-1965,* p. 78.

52. Confucius, trans. Pound, p. 22. Hugh Kenner wonders in *The Pound Era* (p. 458) when Pound discovered that the *tao* of Taoism was his "process." One piece of evidence is that the character does not reappear in *The Cantos* after Canto 78.

53. Hugh Kenner, *The Pound Era,* p. 456.

54. Confucius, trans. Pound, p. 101. Here *tao* is rendered as process, not as way.

55. Confucius, trans. Pound, p. 97.

56. I cite the translation of James J. Y. Liu, *Chinese Theories of Literature* (Chicago: University of Chicago Press, 1975), p. 24. His discussion of Liu Hsieh and the entire chapter from which this comes, "Metaphysical Theories," pp. 16-72, is of great interest. It is his point that Liu Hsieh is playing on the polysemy of *wen* and the material inside brackets is his attempt to draw out the various meanings of *wen* that seem appropriate.

57. Liu, *Chinese Theories of Literature,* p. 24.

58. Ernest Fenollosa, *Epochs of Chinese and Japanese Art,* 2d

rev. ed. (London: Heinemann, 1913), 2, 142. The best confirmation of this claim that I have found is unintentional: James F. Cahill, attempting to prove the opposite in his "Confucian Elements in the Theory of Painting," in *The Confucian Persuasion*, ed. Arthur F. Wright (Stanford: Stanford University Press, 1960), pp. 115-40, uses *tao* so often and in general sounds so Taoist that his essay begins to sound like one of the slyly subversive anecdotes about Confucius in *Chuang Tzu*. James J. Y. Liu makes the pertinent point (on p. 31) that "it is no exaggeration to say that the *Chuang Tzu* has influenced Chinese artistic sensibility more profoundly than any other single book."

59. On only one occasion in the intervening thirty years do we know that Pound was thinking about his Nō translations. In a 1927 letter to Glenn Hughes (*The Letters of Ezra Pound,* pp. 213-15), Pound indicated that he was interested in having a Japanese who knew enough about No drama revise and correct his Fenollosa translations. Nothing came of this, however.

60. Pound translated this play; it is in *The Translations of Ezra Pound* (London: Faber & Faber, 1970), pp. 308-14.

61. Confucius, trans. Pound, p. 103.

62. Confucius, trans. Pound, p. 101.

63. Douglas Goldring, *South Lodge* (London: Constable, 1943), p. 65.

64. T. S. Eliot, "Burnt Norton," *The Complete Poems and Plays, 1909-1950* (New York: Harcourt, Brace & World, 1971), p. 119.

65. Ezra Pound, "Through Alien Eyes I," *The New Age* 12 (16 January 1913), 252; "Affirmations: Vorticism," *The New Age* 16 (14 January 1915), 277. See also *Guide to Kulchur,* p. 152.

66. Bernstein, *The Tale of the Tribe,* p. 154.

67. Levenson and Schurmann, *China: An Interpretive History,* p. 112.

Index

Boldface numbers indicate the important discussions of each topic

The Johns Hopkins University Press
The Literary Vorticism of Ezra Pound and Wyndham Lewis

This book was composed in Aldine Roman text and Helvetica display by A. W. Bennett, Inc., from a design by Chris L. Smith. It was printed on S. D. Warren's 50-lb. Sebago Eggshell Cream Offset paper and bound in Holliston's kingston natural by Bookcrafters.